WHOLESOME COUNTRY COOKING

OTHER BOOKS BY THE AUTHORS:

Old-Fashioned Dutch Oven Cookbook

The Complete Sourdough Cookbook

Food Drying, Pickling and Smoke Curing

WHOLESOME COUNTRY COOKING

by

Don and Myrtle Holm

The CAXTON PRINTERS, Ltd.
Caldwell, Idaho 83605
1985

Library of Congress Cataloging in Publication Data

Holm, Don.
Wholesome country cooking.

Bibliography: p.
Includes index.
1. Cookery, American. I. Holm, Myrtle.
II. Title.
TX715.H747 1984 641.5973 84-22975
ISBN 0-87004-302-1 (pbk.)

Lithographed and bound in the United States of America by
The CAXTON PRINTERS, Ltd.
Caldwell, Idaho 83605
141445

In loving memory of two country gals
who taught us the most . . .
Annie Brown Tate
Minnie Victoria Luke Holm

CONTENTS

PREFACE

WHEN THE CHAUTAUQUA came to town it was an event in Velva, North Dakota, a village of about six hundred souls in those days. The huge circus-type tent was pitched in an open square block of land in the center of town, and for about a week in early summer the tent show offered lectures, musical programs, magic shows, drama, and audience participation programs, including spelling bees and sing-alongs. Folks came into town from miles and miles around, camping out in the park along the shady Mouse River. It was fun, entertainment, and education for everyone from the tots to great-grandmother.

The Chautauqua was founded in 1874 by a Methodist minister and a wealthy manufacturer as a training center for Sunday school teachers. It quickly expanded into a tent show that each summer roamed the backroads of America, spreading the new middle class culture of a burgeoning country. It was a household word in that period of transition from a frontier-rural society to a better-educated, more nationalistic one. The name of the show was taken from the town in southwestern New York State where it originated.

Among the seminars, craft classes, and instructional events was the cookout, wherein local experts could pit their skills against the "fancy dames" from 'way back East who came with the show to teach the locals the ways of the more sophisticated households. Young as we were, we can still remember the local gals whipping up a cake or one of the old country dishes with quick, sure, efficient motions, measuring not with graduated cups or spoons but with a dash of this or a pinch of that or a handful of something else. Nothing was weighed, nothing was measured, but it all came out perfectly in the final test — the eating.

This, of course, was the result of years of constant practice and development of a sense of "right," which is what the art of cooking is all about.

Until the end of the nineteenth century almost all recipes were concocted without exact measurements. The cookbooks of that era called for, instead of a level tablespoon, "butter the size of a small egg." Flour and sugar were measured by "handfuls" or by "teacup," and so on. All recipes were handed down from one generation to another by oral rather than written means, and always something was lost or added in the translation. For this reason, the old cookbooks of a century or more ago are unreliable.

In this book, all recipes were tested and/or analyzed to provide proportions as close to the original as possible. Naturally there are always variations due to different grades and qualities of ingredients, local climatic conditions, water supply, and other variable factors. Some products, like flour, have been refined by modern methods, and this greatly affects the texture and taste, as well as cooking times. Whenever possible we point this out in recipes. In almost all cases it is possible to obtain the old-fashioned ingredients, such as stone-ground or high-gluten flour, from specialty stores and health food shops. We strongly recommend this, especially for baking.

All this leaves quite a lot of room for experimentation on the part of the reader — who should not hestitate to do so. In some instances substitutions are quite in order. For example, most of the old farm recipes called for lard, or the rendered fat of hogs. This was so common in our childhood that the ubiquitous lard pail was used for many other purposes, such as lunch buckets to take to school. Modern cooking oils or shortenings can usually be used in about the same proportions.

One should be careful, too, about the old cookbooks. Until the turn of the century almost nothing was known about bacteria and the connection between disease and sanitation. Food was usually heated in an open kettle, packed into jars, or let stand without refrigeration for long periods. (This is one reason why sour milk was used in so many recipes and dishes.) Most canning was done by the hot-bath or open-kettle method. No one knows how many people "took sick" and died, probably from botulism.

In our households the water-bath method was used for all canning; a pressure cooker was unheard of. Each autumn, hundreds of jars of fruits, vegetables, fish, and meat were "put up." Sometimes a jar would "go bad" and would be thrown out without opening (the smartest thing that could have been done!). No one in our households ever got sick from eating canned food, but this was probably due just as much to luck as to expertise.

Modern research proves that all low-acid foods such as vegetables, fish, meat, and poultry *must be* processed in a pressure cooker to be safe. Only such processing can destroy the *Clostridium botulinum* bacteria. The open-kettle method was unsafe even for high-acid foods. Fruits and vegetables must be processed in a boiling water bath to destroy organisms that cause spoilage. Only jams and jellies are safe when preserved by the open-kettle method. More on this subject will be found in the section on food processing.

Some ingredients have changed since grandma's time, usually for the better. An example is vinegar, once a large item in the food budget because of all the pickling that was done. The acidity of vinegar available in stores has been standardized and formulated to provide a specific level of acidity to prevent spoilage.

The reader will note that most of the recipes in this book are not complete meals but only "dishes" that provided one or more of the "choices" that were set on the family table. However, with today's emphasis on calorie counting, along with the more sedentary life we lead, many of these dishes can make a whole meal.

The recipes are roughly grouped into four sections, representing the seasons of the year, which is the way we best remember life in those days and the times associated with various dishes and recipes. In some cases it may seem that recipes are duplicated, but a closer reading will show these are merely variations.

Sharp-eyed readers will also notice that some recipes are marked with an asterisk (*). This identifies those old recipes found in Myrtle's long-lost, teen-age notebook, in which she recorded those she learned from her mother, the neighboring farm ladies, and from church groups. All the other recipes originate from sources lost in the dim past but handed down in one form or another and collected over the past forty years or more by the authors.

We acknowledge a great debt to the old grange and rural church groups who contributed so many authentic recipes to our collection. We hope this book will help preserve many of them intact.

Finally, the format of this cookbook was designed for browsing — not only for instruction and suggestions for more wholesome kitchen fare but also for casual reading, hopefully for entertainment, and not a little nostalgia and vicarious pleasure. It is perfectly okay to jump around from here to there like a grasshopper in a hot stubble field, pick out those parts that interest you at the moment, and suit the words to your whim.

The idea is to have fun and good cooking at the same time. The proof of this will be in the eating.

D.H. & M.T.

INTRODUCTION

A GOOD MANY years ago, when I was single and freewheeling, in a moment of nostalgia I got to thinking about all the good wholesome country cooking of my childhood days back on the prairies of North Dakota. A staff writer at the time on *The Oregonian*, the Pacific Northwest's biggest newspaper, I sat down at the typewriter during a break in the routine and dashed off a little essay for the "op ed" page.

It was about the girls in the home ec class in Velva High School back in the thirties, the years of the Great Depression, and the delectable dishes they turned out as part of their class assignments.

Maybe it would be simpler just to repeat it here, rather than try to describe it:

Gourmet Blues: Feed Me Again On The Lone Prairie

The most vivid memory I have of my old high school back in Velva, North Dakota, is of the wonderful smells that used to drift into study hall from the home ec department two mornings a week.

On these mornings, the mouth-watering fragrance of Danish delights, exotic curries, and stews and tender prairie meats tantalized us boys. We could only groan with hunger, spitball practice forgotten.

In our minds we could picture the trays of fresh berliner kranze or krum kage, or perhaps even the Mennonite girls's favorite — nutfilled snowballs.

How we envied the home ec girls who got to eat their lessons.

Two mornings a week the home ec teacher, who had a couple of degrees from some high-fallutin' Eastern university, instructed our North Dakota farm girls in the culinary arts — which made about as much sense as a gym coach telling Lou Gehrig how to hit a homer.

These girls had the best teachers in the world: their mothers and grandmothers, who brought to the lonely prairies the Old Country kitchen skills along with all those wonderful Scandinavian and German dishes with the umlauted names, (which sounded like something you rode, wore, or ran from, rather than ate).

After a couple of generations of blending with the tart and rare prairie-produced victuals, the result was a gastronomical phemomenon.

These girls began learning kitchen skills about the time they could see over the top of the big woodburning range with its built-in hot water reservoir. By the time they were 14, they could put together a meal for a hungry harvest crew as easy as tossing a shock of wheat into a bundle wagon.

They could make sandbakeser (Swedish sand tarts) or finska kakor (Finnish butter strips with nuts), before they could even pronounce the names.

Lumberjackophiles have made much of the western logging camp cooking. But this greasy garbage was quite a comedown for a lad who started in the North Dakota harvest fields at 13 and was spoiled by the tender loving cooking of those milk-skinned farm gals.

On a harvest crew we slept in the haymow, got up before daylight, fed and watered the horses, and then went out into the fields to work a couple of hours before breakfast.

When we came in and washed up for breakfast, the girls had waiting for us, roast pork and rib steaks, scalloped potatoes, scalloped corn, hot homemade sourdough bread with melted dairy butter and fresh-packed wild berry chokecherry jelly, sourdough flapjacks with thick real maple syrup; ham, bacon, and homemade pork sausage with big brown farm eggs; corn bread and hot muffins, and big pewter pitchers of raw milk cooled in the root cellar.

And this was only breakfast.

During the long, dark winters the monotony was broken by frequent church suppers (the Lutheran women always tried to outdo the Methodists and the Methodists the Catholics and the Catholics the Nazarenes and so on).

Even after 25 years, I can still remember the lutefisk suppers in December, the sauerbrauten cooked North Dakota style, romme grot or flode grot (a cream mush with butter and sugar), lebkucken (the Christmas honey cake.)

Then there was lefse, a thin, unleavened bread, flat and pliable and baked on top of a wood stove like a pancake; fattigsman bakelse (or something like that), a crisp cookie with powdered sugar; a blood sausage, cooked in milk; a salt fish shipped in from the Great Lakes or New England in wooden firkins during the winter and transformed into dinner delights; and the Spanish rice and breast of prairie chicken my mother specialized in; rhubarb sauce and pie, wild plum preserves, gooseberry and lingonberry jelly, and juicy cactus berries picked late in the summer; fresh-ground horseradish with vinegar and homemade catsup.

It wasn't only the variety and bounty of North Dakota prairie cooking, but the artistry with which it was prepared.

I don't know what gentle alchemy was handed down to these girls over the generations; but whatever it was, the blend of prairie and Old Country ways inspired the kind of cooking that will never be forgotten in this new world of packaged cake mixes, fast-food chains, TV dinners, and dietary food supplements.

I didn't win a Pulitzer Prize with it, but the mail and telephone calls from homesick refugees from the Midwest plains and prairies swamped me for weeks afterwards. It also introduced me to one of those North Dakota farm gals, who subsequently became my bride.

I was born and raised in Velva, North Dakota, at the southern or bottom of the loop made by the Mouse or Souris River, which comes down from Canada into the north central part of the state and then turns around and runs back again almost to its source. Myrtle was born and raised at Portal, a little border town on the Soo Line and not far from the Mouse River, a major port of entry in those days.

Like all farm gals she learned to cook as soon as she could walk. During her high school years she kept a notebook of her favorite recipes. After she left home for college, and later marriage and a career, the hand-written cookbook disappeared. More than forty years later, when we returned to Portal for her mother's funeral and subsequently the administration of the family heirlooms, her old notebook turned up among Annie Tate's papers. Now yellowed and much frayed from decades of use around the farm by family and neighbor women, much of it was still legible — and all of it was priceless.

We brought the old cookbook home with us. Into this

latest in our series of cookbooks of old-time and traditional recipes, we have incorporated some of the best of her girlhood — and thoroughly farm-tested — creations. They are not the kind you would find in the White House or the Escoffier or Mornay cookbooks, but they are the kind you would find in the kitchens of rural America in the days when life was simpler and, in cooking anyway, more wholesome.

In those days the farm or home kitchen was the center of the household's daily life and routine, and the center of the kitchen was the huge, often ornate, cast-iron wood or kerosene range, with its expansive griddlelike surface for pots and pans, its water reservoir in back, its warming compartments above, and generous oven below.

We like to think of this collection of gems as the Wholesome Country dishes that survive a life-style that, for good or not so good, is part of our heritage.

In those days life was geared to sharply defined seasons — even in regions where climatic conditions blended the months together — and each had its special activities and anomalies, linked to the land and the phenomenon of weather. Because we believe this will change little, even in the twenty-first century, we have arranged this book in four divisions representing Springtime, Summertime, Autumn, and Wintertime.

We thought it would be more natural this way.

Don Holm
Cape George, State of Washington
1984

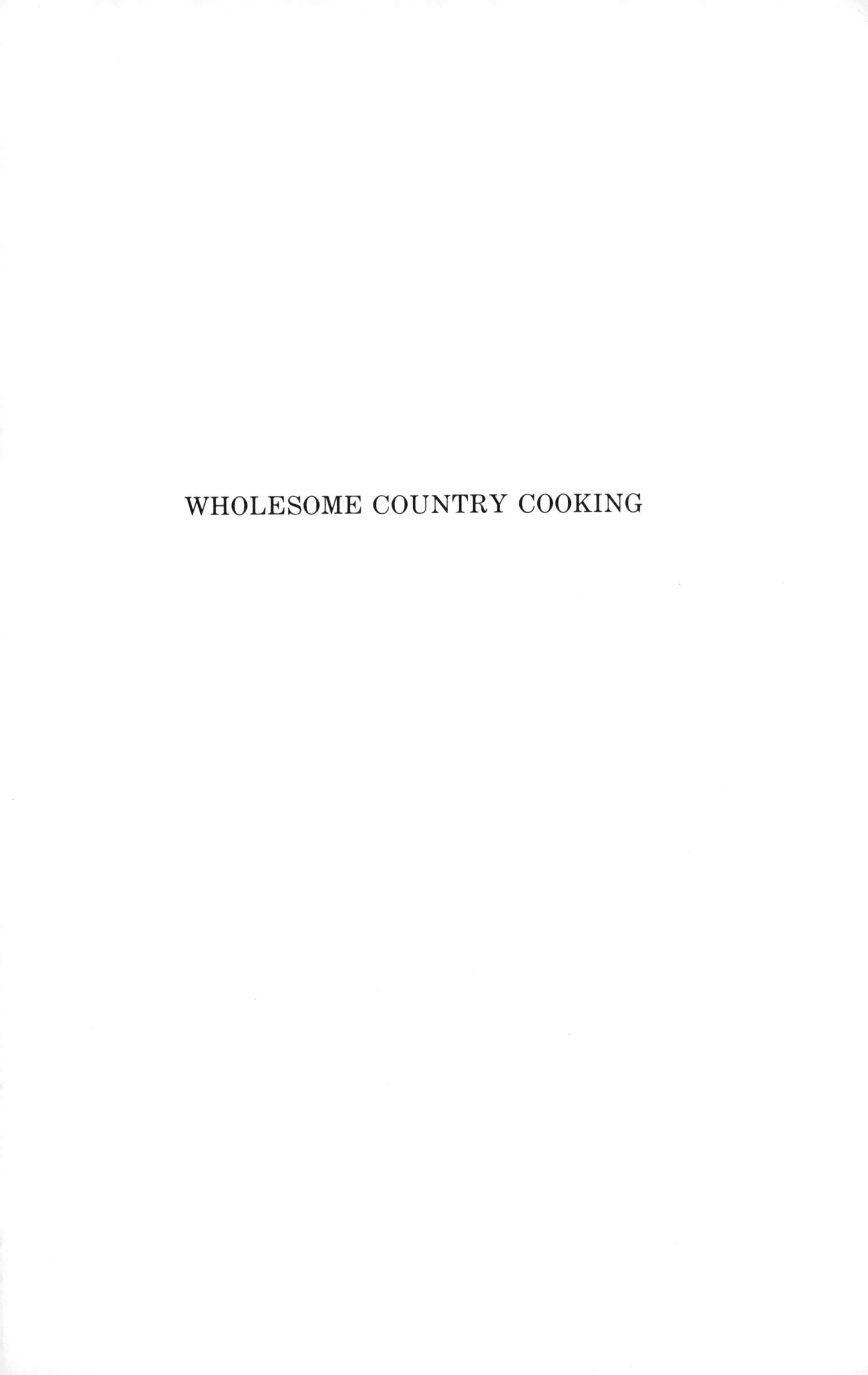

WHOLESOME COUNTRY COOKING

Part One

Springtime

. . . for whatsoever a man soweth,
that shall he also reap.

Galatians 6:7 New Testament

IN THE SPRING, the poet said, a young man's fancy turns to thoughts of love.

Spring is when all of nature turns to the reproduction and renewal of the land and all the living things in it, on it, and over it.

The cold, brittle grip of winter relaxes under a bright, warm sun and the softening of the earth. Life that has lain dormant all winter begins to germinate, as if at the touch of a Supreme Wand.

Melting snow leaves piebald hills and lingering drifts in the north-turned coulees. Seeps become trickles, then merry rivulets, then happy creeks tumbling over rocks to join the swelling rivers. The ice breaks up in big chunks which are carried downward in the swift, turbid torrent until they melt or pile up in jams.

The beaver and muskrat emerge from their snug quarters to repair the ravages of winter and to dine on new sapling growth. Spawning pickerel fight upward against the current to the creeks and then to the quieter pools in profligate response to ancient urges.

Endless Vs of ducks, geese, and sandhill cranes make their way northward across the empty sky toward the potholes and marshes of Canada and the Arctic to begin the nesting cycle all over. Robins appear suddenly,

A mountain ranch scene in Montana, with the Continental Divide in the background.

energetically pecking at the new earth for grubs and worms. The meadowlarks' cheery love calls shrill across the old stubble fields; and the moaning notes of the turtledoves haunt the hedgerows. Soon, in the nests in the box elders and hazelbush will appear fragile speckled or pale blue eggs.

Along the fencerows the delicate pink petals of the wild rose open. Chokecherries and wild plums bud out. The tough little crocuses show off their tiny blue flowers, and the queen of the plains, the tiger lily, once again flaunts its gorgeous red orange petals.

The first brave kids plunge nude into the old swimmin' hole — and then spend the next week in bed with "spring fever."

The ancient horse-drawn school bus trades its snow runners for a wagon frame with wheels. It continues to lumber over the six or seven miles on its route morning and evening, the pace quickening to match the kids' joyous sense of impending freedom as they anticipate Easter and then June "let-out" time.

The blacksmith's anvil rings from hammerblows on red-hot plowshares, showering sparks over the goggled-eyed youngsters come by to watch the village smithy work his alchemy over hard metal in preparation for spring seeding.

In the fields the gang plows move slowly and systematically around and around, turning up the rich black loam to make it ready.

Unsettled weather, mixing chinook winds with cycles of cold and warm fronts, sends thunderstorms crashing across the land dumping cloudbursts of rain and hail, to make way only minutes later for bursts of sunshine that turn the landscape into a riot of sparkling prisms of rainbow colors.

Showers of another kind are for brides celebrating

coming nuptials with friends and neighbors — and younger hopefuls. Months later, in December, January, or February, the cries of firstborns will be heard.

The first seed catalogs arrive in the mail, to be pored over in the evening after supper when the chores are done.

Such are the memories of the present authors, whose roots go far back to the bleak land of the Dakotas; but to more or less degree they are the same for anyone born or "grown up" on the farms and in the small towns of North America.

It is a heritage to rejoice in — and preserve.

— 1 —

. . . whatsoever a man soweth . . .

ALONG WITH YOUR daily bread, do you have to settle for just peas and corn every single meal? Of course not. This is the copout of the lazy cook and the indifferent hashhouse. Herein you will encounter a cookbook that begins with procurement of the necessary ingredients: *vegetables*, *fruits*, and *berries*.

When the authors were kids on farms in rural North Dakota, a large garden was part of the household. Everyone planted and maintained a garden plot and usually a small orchard and berry patch. The necessary adjunct to this, in the days before home refrigeration was common, had to be the *root cellar*, where the winter's supply of food was stored. The average garden plot measured from a minimum 25 by 25 feet up to an acre or two, depending on the size of the family and whether or not a surplus was raised for the town market. The garden and orchard provided a major part of the family's food supply. Most of all they provided a source of fresh-picked vegetables, fruits, and berries that was, and still is, impossible to obtain any other way.

One year my family planted two acres in garden stuff, but much of this was in surplus tomatoes, corn, and potatoes for the local fresh market as a cash crop. The average city backyard can provide a family all the fresh vegetables and fruit that can be consumed. We have an elderly friend who plants seeds and sets in every little crook and cranny around the yard, including open spaces in the flower beds and around the sidewalk, and grows enough for her own use. With a little more effort you can raise all the fresh produce you can consume and also, by canning or preserving, "put by" the surplus for the rest of the year. Our root cellar would be crammed with hundreds of jars of vegetables, fruits, jams and jellies, relishes, berries, sauces, and meats. Hanging from the rafters would be bunches of garlic, onions, and other goodies for drying. Some years not a single thing was purchased in town except coffee, tea, sugar, and flour — and there was never a lack of bountiful, wholesome meals, loaded with vitamins and minerals.

All this is not just ruminating about the good old days. It is to remind readers that it is entirely practical — even desirable — to grow and raise the food a healthy family needs, or at least most of it. You don't have to live on a farm, nor do you have to be a horticulturist. You don't even have to like hoeing weeds. All you have to do is like eatin'. Eatin' good, that is.

By combining a small backyard plot and today's food technology and modern plant science, with an incredible variety of fruits, vegetables, and berries available, you can save money and eat better than ever before. You can even raise much of this indoors, in the basement or kitchen or utility room, to supplement the available outdoor space. You can not only harvest a continuing supply of vitamin-saturated seed sprouts like alfalfa and Mung beans for fresh salads, but you can even grow things like oranges, lemons, limes, and bananas in potted arrangements.

There are literally thousands of varieties of old and new exotic plants now available that were not even dreamed of when we were kids. They can be raised almost anywhere at various times of the year, depending on climate and altitude. No matter where you live, you have a wide selection to choose from. Your local nursery or garden store can usually supply seeds and sets suited for your area. I have found that the large mail-order seed

A bountiful collection of homegrown foods that anyone can produce, to some extent.

catalogs are not only dependable but also usually have a wider selection of plants to offer. In fact, the seed catalogs, sent out mostly in the spring, are sources of endless reading, planning, and lip smacking. In addition, the catalogs usually include much information on when, where, and how to plant the various species. They also can provide tools, chemicals, plant food, and other related products for the active gardener.

If you have not been close to a vegetable garden since childhood days, when hoeing the weeds was a hateful chore that kept you from getting an early start for the old swimmin' hole, send for one of these catalogs. You are in for a surprise. You may also get hooked.

Among the growing aids you probably never heard of are indoor seed-starter pots, concentrated fertilizer pellets, portable hothouses, tomato "pens," tiered strawberry rings, and boxes for dwarf fruit trees that produce up to five kinds of apples. You can buy realistic-looking snakes and owls to keep birds at bay, live worms for enriching the soil (and to provide fish bait), certain types of insects that organic gardeners use to control pests the natural way, and even dehydrators for drying food.

You'll say; Where have I been all these years?

Instead of covering your lot with pretty — but useless — things like flowers, trees that dump leaves on your lawn every fall, and shrubs that only provide cover for rodents and other pests, make use of the space to feed yourself and family. Don't plant and raise things in all that precious space that do not earn their keep!

Don't settle for just canned peas and corn.

Vegetable Yield Chart (seedpacket)

Kind	Age to Bear	Typical Yield per Plant
Pole beans	40–80 days	1 bushel
Broccoli	50–80 days	50 pounds
Cabbage	50–70 days	75 pounds
Carrots	60–70 days	1 bushel
Lettuce	40–60 days	35 pounds
Onion sets	50–60 days	1 bushel
Parsnips	105 days	1 bushel
Peas	50–80 days	1 bushel
Potatoes	90–100 days	2 bushels
Pumpkins	40–80 days	45 pounds
Radishes	20–30 days	50 pounds
Sweet corn	60–90 days	50 ears
Tomatoes	50–90 days	3 bushels

As can be seen from the typical yield chart, the time needed to raise your own fresh ingredients takes up only a fraction of the year and produces an enormous amount of food from one or two packets of seed, plant sets, or blossoms. There is, in fact, no more efficient method of producing energy.

The Vegetable Kingdom — Root Crops

• *Potatoes:* If you are a meat-and-potatoes man, like I am, this will be a basic staple of your garden. When I was a kid in North Dakota we raised only two kinds — Early Ohios, for eating before the Fourth, and red russets for baking. Nowadays you have a wide choice of new varieties and hybrids for every purpose. Like the new Butte Russet — for more yield, vitamin C and protein, pearly white flesh, and excellent baking characteristics. The new Crystal from the Red River Valley is another example of a high-yield white potato with a white skin, excellent for shoestrings, baking, or boiling, and very disease resistant.

The little Lady Finger German potato is about an inch in diameter and four or five inches long with a bananalike color and a unique flavor. Good for salads, it can be boiled, baked, or fried. This is a real treat.

The All Blue potato has a bluish colored skin and a bluish tint right through the flesh. It yields well, is excellent for salads, and is a good boiler or baker.

The Bake King is one of the symmetrical, russet-skinned, firm-fleshed potatoes with small shallow eyes and low water content that is superb for baking.

The Explorer is a white potato you can grow from seed instead of sets. It is excellent for boiling, with a white flesh and smooth skin.

The McNeilly is a new development which is *everbearing*. This was one of those happy hybrid accidents that occurred when research horticulturists were experimenting along other lines. This variety continues to set new potatoes all season long. The foliage stays green and makes new potatoes well into September. It has a light reddish skin, light yellowish flesh, and excellent flavor.

There are dozens of other standard varieties suited to every locality, with characteristics of high yield, disease resistance, and multiple use such as baking, boiling, or frying. Some are especially adapted for long storage through the winter. These include White Cobbler (early), Red Pontiac (medium late), Norgold Russet (medium early), Norland (very early), Kennebec (late), and Russet Burbank (late). These are usually planted in seed sets, which are selected chunks of certified and treated seed potatoes. They are usually planted in hills, with one set to a hill.

• *Sweet Potatoes:* What is Thanksgiving, or any other holiday, without this delicious tuber? They can be prepared in many ways, including in a pie such as my sister-in-law, who came from the South, used to make.

Sweet potatoes take about 100 days to grow and have a pleasing foliage. One of the most popular is Centennial, which has a copper skin and deep orange flesh, is well shaped and a good yielder.

Vineless Porto Rico is an original of the red species, has an excellent flavor, and matures early. With small runners, it is ideal for small gardens.

All Gold is another early one, with a yellow gold color inside and out. Excellent flavor.

Nancy Hall is one of the old-fashioned kind that us older gents remember from childhood days. It is sweet and yellow-fleshed and has nice foliage.

New Jewel is an improved Centennial, a little smaller, of excellent quality.

Sweet potatoes are planted in hills with sets, just like Irish potatoes. They are well worth the space in any backyard garden.

• *Onions:* Here is another staple that comes in dozens

of varieties and has endless possibilities. A good example is the world-famous Walla Walla Sweet. This is a large, round, yellow-skinned type of Spanish onion developed for the large irrigated farms around Walla Walla, Washington. It weighs over a pound and has a flavor so sweet and mild you can almost eat it like an apple. A single slice will fill a hamburger sandwich. It is, unfortunately, not a good storage onion, so the best way to utilize it is to start digging when about the size of a golf ball and continue using until the harvest is over.

A good winter storage onion is the White Sweet Spanish. Like the Walla Walla it is large, sweet, and mild. Another good storage onion is the Yellow Sweet Spanish, which is also an early variety. The White Bermuda is a table onion, the sweetest, juicest, and mildest to be eaten raw. The Texas Yellow Grand is another sweet one with a high yield, especially adapted for southern states. Ringmaster is a round type of White Spanish that is excellent for frying rings. The large Red Globe is a popular fine-textured variety with a rich, red skin and is an excellent keeper. The Red Torpedo is a long, narrow onion with a mild and sweet taste that matures early and is excellent for slicing. The Owa is a bottle-shaped tubular type that also has good slicing qualities;, is excellent for sandwiches and salads, and will store all winter.

The early green table onions are popular and can be eaten fresh right out of the ground. The He-Shi-Ko is a stalk-type that never forms bulbs but grows in clumps of pearly white stalks. Just snip the roots away and munch raw or sprinkled with salt.

The White Portugal is a cocktail and pickling-type onion with a mild flavor and fine white texture. It is also used for relishes and garnishes.

Other types include the early Yellow Ebenezer, red

"hamburger" types, White Sweet Slicer, and a number of hybrids especially adapted for dipping in batter and frying.

Onions are usually grown from sets but can be raised from seed.

• *Radishes:* Probably the favorite of backyard gardens is the radish, the first vegetable to be ready for table use and one of the most prolific and easiest to raise. As with other root vegetables, they come in many shapes and sizes.

The Giant White Globe is a white, tender, mild-tasting variety that keeps growing bigger until you use it. The Long White Icicle is another white one that is crisp and white. It only takes 27 days to mature. It is shaped like a carrot, remains solid, and tastes sweet and mild. The sweetest is the Tendersweet Red Prince, a small round red type. The Crimson Giant is about twice as big and grows vigorously with a snowy white flesh. The Champion is a large, solid-flesh variety that takes 28 days. It is often grown in greenhouses. Excellent for salads.

There is a pure white Summer Cross Hybrid that is excellent for slicing. It is highly resistant to hot weather and disease. The roots are two inches in diameter and up to eighteen inches long. The French Breakfast type is scarlet, with a whitish bottom trim, and has a crisp, juicy, mild taste.

Other types include White Mammoth (58 days), Round Black Spanish (60 days), Chinese Rose (50 days), Cherry Belle (22 days), Pax (28 days); Firecracker, German Giant, Sparkler, Silver Dollar, and many more.

Radishes are always grown from seed. A single packet, costing less than a dollar, will give a mighty harvest of good eating, first on the table.

• *Beets:* I have a particular yen for small pickled beets — just can't get enough of them. In fact, I can make a whole meal of 'em. Fortunately, beets are easy to grow, keep well, and come in a wide variety to suit all tastes. They contain more iron than other vegetables, mature early in the season, and are versatile for table use, including salads, hot dishes, and stews. They are planted from seed, and a packet goes a long way.

The Detroit dark red, short-top variety is one of the best all-around beets. It is good for table use, canning, or freezing. The Ruby Queen is another early type, almost perfectly round and solid red. The Early Wonder has a smooth skin and is excellent for table, canning, and pickling. Cylindra is a long, dark red beet, only an inch or two in diameter and up to eight inches long, very tender. Burpee's Golden is an excellent salad variety and also pickles nicely. The tops can be boiled like spinach and are delicious. The Green Top is grown primarily for the tops, which have a fine flavor. The roots are round and deep red.

There is a Dark Red Canner, with a deep color that doesn't fade in cooking or pickling. Its small globe shape makes it prized for pickling. The hybrid Earlisweet is not only the earliest but also the sweetest type. Another good canner is the Badger Baby, only an inch long and bite-sized. Some special-purpose beets are the Long Red Mangel, for livestock feed, and the Giant Western Sugar Beet, a garden novelty.

Pickling is one of the best ways to preserve beets. Special beet pickling mixes can be obtained from garden stores and seed catalogs.

• *Jersualem artichokes:* This is an excellent but often overlooked vegetable that is fine in salads and for baking, boiling, or creaming raw. It is also low in calories and high in fiber content, although not mealy. It is not, incidentally, a native of the Holy Land, nor is it an artichoke. It was first discovered by the Lewis and Clark Expedition in 1804 being used by the Indians along the Missouri River, where it grew wild. Some of the tribes had domesticated it and were growing it in garden plots. It is a relative of the sunflower.

• *Salsify:* Even less known than the Jerusalem artichoke, this is an excellent soup vegetable that is also superb when baked or creamed. It has a tender white flesh, with a sweet flavor like an oyster. In fact, it is sometimes called the "garden oyster." Comes in white or black varieties.

• *Parsnips:* This is a delicious vegetable for hot dishes or stews. Boiled and smothered with butter, well-seasoned, it is one of my favorites. The roots are long and slender, the flesh fine, tender, and covered with white skin. A basic garden vegetable, for sure.

• *Rutabagas:* A large, cabbagelike vegetable with a globe-shaped root. It is a good storage vegetable and cooks up crisp and tender. Another of my favorites. American Purple Top is the most common variety; growing time about 105 days.

• *Turnips:* Even songs have been written about this old favorite, a staple in many backwoods communities. They are prolific and grow fast, from 30 to 60 days being the usual time. It produces a row twenty-five feet long from a single packet of inexpensive seeds. The main crop is usually sowed late for July harvest, but it is well to start some early, too. Turnips keep well in root cellars. The turnip is a favorite of President Reagan, who has it served once a day in the White House.

The Purple Top White Globe is a popular variety. It is tender, sweet, and crisp. Shogoin is another crisp and tender variety, with tops that are delicious as greens. The Tokyo Cross Hybrid is a very early type which is disease resistant. The Milan, Royal Crown, and Just Right are other varieties.

• *Carrots:* This old favorite table vegetable, cooked or raw, is certainly a basic vegetable. It keeps well and is loaded with vitamins, including vitamin A for night vision. It comes in dozens of varieties and hybrids, and in many shapes and sizes.

Most popular probably is the Tender Sweet, a crisp and sweet, long and slender type which matures in 75 days. It is excellent for soups, stews, or after-school snacks, for carrot sticks, for creaming, and all kinds of cooking. It keeps well, has few root hairs, is deep orange in color, and is a natural health food. The Danvers Half Long is a red-cored strain for good storing and canning. The Chantenay is a sweet and tender one that is chunky and heavy. There is the Scarlet Nantes, an early coreless type for freezing and storing in bunches. The Carrot Stick is an improved hybrid, coreless and crisp. Oxhearts are heavy yielders of high quality. The Golden Nugget is a round-ball type for snacks and relish trays. The juiciest is the Gold Pak, a long, thin carrot.

Others include the Glow Ball, Hybrid Spartan, Baby Nantes, and Lady Finger. There is a variety for every use and almost every soil.

— 3 —

The Vegetable Kingdom — Above Ground

• *Corn:* If there is such a thing as a one-plant staff of life, it is most certainly corn — which to the British is any type of cereal, such as wheat, rye, oats, or barley, but which in the New World is the ancient, cultivated, eared stalk plant sometimes known as maize, or Indian corn, or just plain corn. Maize comes from the Spanish *maiz* and the Taino *mahiz* and refers to color, the familiar golden yellow.

The earliest European adventurers to the New World discovered a number of well-advanced native civilizations in which maize or corn was a staple of the diet. It was often highly cultivated and used not only as food but as part of the religious and ceremonial customs. It is a versatile plant, with nutritious qualities not fully appreciated even by experienced gardeners. There is an entire field of horticultural science concerned with corn. As a food for man and beast it is unsurpassed.

To the average person it is familiar mostly as roasting ears, cattle food, and popcorn kernels, but the general term corn or maize covers hundreds of varieties, hybrids, and types.

Mention Gold Jubilee to a gourmet, and his eyes will light up with visions of succulent, juicy, golden ears swimming in butter and seasonings. This treat compels even the most fastidious to abandon his manners and pitch in with wide-open mouth. Not all corn is edible, though, for humans. I recall a fishing trip with a couple of buddies on the Coos River in southwest Oregon. We were returning after dark down the winding river, hungry and wet and cold, when we passed a field of tall corn ready to pick. Doc Buck and Vince Aleksa, the local boys, at once expounded on the quality and superb eating of the corn grown by this riverbank farmer. They became so enthusiastic that we put into shore and indulged in an orgy of ear-picking, until we had nearly filled the boat.

My mouth watered in anticipation all the way home. I couldn't wait to get the water on and boiling. The letdown came when I tried to eat an ear. Pulpy and tasteless. Actually, what we had so cunningly "requisitioned" was field corn, grown primarily for silage to feed a dairy herd.

Most eating-type sweet corns are hybrids nowadays. Golden Jubilee is an old favorite, but there are dozens of others. A new supersweet variety is called Kandy Corn, a fast-growing, high-sugar, golden-kerneled, long-eared delight which also can be obtained in a sweet white style known as Snow Queen. The average growing time for sweet corn is about 80 days, but some can be harvested by July 4. You can have fresh ears for every dinner all summer if you plant several varieties at spaced-out intervals. The best time to eat corn on the cob is within an hour of picking. The longer you wait, the more rapid the chemistry changes sugar to starch. All corn is grown in rows or hills, from seed kernels spaced four to six inches apart.

Iochief has large, deep-gold kernels and is excellent for freezing and canning. Pearls N'Gold has both white and golden kernels on the same cob. It is a good roaster. Early Sunglow is, as it says, an early type and stays edible longer than most. Y-81 is a hybrid with a nutty flavor that can stand a lot of heat and holds its condition for a long time. Silver Queen is tasty and sweet with small tight kernels. B-Queen is a vigorous fast grower with sweet, tender white and yellow kernels, adaptable to any climate. Polar Vee is an extremely early type and fast growing. Elephant Ear is a huge cob with deep tender kernels. Silver Beauty is a white hybrid with large fine kernels and a rich sweet flavor. Candystick II is a slender, large kernel, small cob, tender sweet variety. Earliglow is another first-of-season type with tender, sweet kernels. Golden Cross has a high yield of extra sweet kernels on stalks that grow seven feet high.

The sweetest variety is probably Illini Chief Extra Sweet and the Early Xtra Sweet. There is also a twenty-foot-tall Giant Corn that is bred from old Mexican strains, but you'll need a stepladder to pick the ears, according to the breeder. On the other hand there is a four-inch ear from Midget Sweet corn that grows only thirty inches tall; ideal for young corn-on-the-cob *aficionados* and for small gardens, or for porch and flower-bed tubs.

Old-fashioned types include Country Gentleman, a long-eared, slender white corn, and Golden Bantam, a tall, heavy producer with an early harvest. A hardy black type is Mexican Black, which is creamy white to start but turns blue-black when mature. A very late, very tender white variety is Stowell's Evergreen.

I am very partial to hominy but seldom get it except out of cans. A good variety, and a favorite in the South, is White Hickory King; another is Reid's Yellow Dent. Hominy is made by special processing of the kernels.

Some others include Butterfruit, Florida Staysweet, White Lightning, Seneca Chief, Seneca Sentry, Sunglow, Merit, Butter and Sugar, Seneca Pinto, Trucker's Favorite, and Tastyvee.

• *Popcorn:* Hybrid South American is a top quality type, as are Hybrid White Cloud, Hybrid Best Yellow, Hybrid White Hull, and Calico. There are also Japanese White Hulless, White Cloud, Dynamite, Calico, Black, and even a Strawberry popcorn.

Popcorns are grown like sweet corns but are not

picked until well dried. Store shelled corn in mason jars in a refrigerator, or on the cob in a dry place. You can grow a forty-foot row with only one packet of seed, which costs less than a dollar. Compare this with what you pay for an eight-ounce jar in the store.

Oh, one more thing: No matter what color the kernels are, they all pop white.

• *Tomatoes:* A native of South America, tomatoes were once called "love apples," because they were thought to be poisonous. Nowadays no meal is complete without this vegetable in one form or another, as a garnish or in soup or salad. Most varieties now are hybrids. The largest, like Gurney's Crimson Giant, weigh over a pound. Another, like the Golden Giant, was developed for yellow flesh and mild flavor. The Cold-Set is a hardy early plant that can withstand both heat and cold. The Yellow Husk is the size of a cherry and is bright yellow. Royal Chico is a catsup type. Sugar Red and Sugar Yellow are cherry tomatoes, sweet and juicy and salad favorites. Beefeater is a large, almost seedless, heavy-fruited variety which often weighs up to two pounds. Golden Boy is another yellow hybrid with a mild flavor. Better Boy is a high-yield, disease-resistant type. Early Girl bears early and continues until first frost. Rushmore will take cold springs and hot summers, growing fast and heavy. Gurney Girl was bred for high yield and flavor.

Red Champions are large, smooth, early-bearing types. The Hybrid Sakata Red bears clusters of ball-shaped fruit. Park's Whopper is a large, firm, red favorite. Spring Giant is large and scarlet. Burpee Big Boy is large, round, firm, and scarlet. Bragger is a big beefsteak type. Then there is Sugar Lump, small sweet bite-size; Tiny Tim, a pot plant that can be grown in your window; Burgess Early Salad, of small size to serve whole; Yellow Plum for salads and preserves; Heinz for canning, paste, and cooking; Roma, another paste type; Manalucie, wilt and disease resistant, grows almost anywhere; Climbing Trip-L-Crop, large fruit that climbs up eight-foot vines and bears heavily; Little King, a tough salad type that continues to bear all summer; Bitsy, an ornamental type that also has a high sugar content and tastes good.

Tomatoes are usually started from sets but can also be started indoors with seeds. Some varieties asre adapted for pot-raising and cold frames, others have profuse vines and trailers. Some have thick, strong stocks that do not need propping up. Indeed, tomatoes now come in an infinite variety of size, taste, bearing, color, and eating and preserving qualities. Whole books have been written just about raising tomatoes. Check with your friendly neighborhood nursery or favorite seed catalog. But don't overlook this versatile vegetable.

• *Beans:* The bean is another staple that comes in an infinite variety — for soups, chili, steamed side dishes, canning, pickling, freezing; in green, yellow, purple, burgundy, white, red, black, and multicolor.

Bush varities grow on large spreading plants. They mature all at once and are ideal for freezing and canning. These include Blue Lake, Roma, Slenderette, Avalanche, Commodore, Contender, Tendergreen, Half Runner, Royal Burgundy, Tendercrop, Stringless, Golden Wax, Cherokee, Moongold, Daisy Bush, Kentucky Wonder, Italian, Butterwax, Pencil Pod, and many others.

Pole beans bear later than bush beans but with a heavier yield, and they must be supported with poles, fences, or trellises. Some varieties are Kentucky Wonder, Blue Lake, Romano, Selma Star, Zebra, Purple Pod, Missouri Wonder, and Kentucky Wonder Wax.

Limas include Climbing Baby, Florida Butter Man, Christmas, Henderson's Cangreen, Fordhook, Jackson Wonder, and King of the Garden.

Unusual types include Swedish Brown, Black Turtle, Garbanzo, Viva Pink Chili, Fava (the only bean known in Europe before the New World was discovered), and Disoy Soybean.

Soup beans are Great Northern, popular for baking; Red Bean, for a heavy yield; Dwarf Taylor, excellent for baking or for succotash; Red Kidney, used in many Mexican dishes; Navy, which makes the famous bean soup in the congressional cafeteria; Pinto, for frijoles, tacos, and other Mexican dishes; Soldier, handed down for generations from New England origins.

It might be said, with some justification, that it was the bean, "the musical fruit," that really won the West. In cattle country, for example, beans or frijoles comprised about 75 percent of the chuckwagon cook's repertoire. The pinto, named for the brown spots on it, was the first choice, but the navy and red types were also popular. The bean was cheap, crammed with vitamins and proteins, and "stuck to yer ribs," as the hardworking cowboys said.

Cookie prepared his beans by washing and soaking overnight. In the morning they were drained, covered with cold water, and set in a dutch oven* to simmer slowly over a bed of coals. Chunks of dry salt pork were added for seasoning, but no salt was added until the beans were done. The beans were cooked at least five hours, but if conditions permitted, all day or all night, depending also on the altitude. (When done properly the bean will split open at a touch; if mushy, they have been cooked too long.) Sometimes a can of tomatoes was added when the beans became tender, along with a couple of diced onions, salt, pepper, a dash of cayenne, garlic, and anything else available.

---

*See *Old-Fashioned Dutch Oven Cookbook*, The Caxton Printers, Ltd.

Bean Hole Beans

"Bean hole" beans were prepared the same way, but the pot was filled with water, salt pork added, and the lid put on. A hole was dug and a wood fire built. When this was reduced to coals or embers the pot was placed in the hole on the coals. Ashes and coals were banked around the pot and on the rimmed lid. Then a layer of dirt was sprinkled on top and a second fire built on this. You could start it in the morning, go away and leave it all day, and come back at night and find the beans ready to eat. Laced with molasses they were mouth-waterin'.

Fresh-picked bean pods, canned or frozen, add a great deal to any winter meal, prepared in many ways. One of my favorites is pickled pods. Take long, succulent golden or green wax beans, "put them by" in a pickling solution, and process in mason jars for later enjoyment. I eat them like candy sticks, and, like candy, I can't get enough of them. Pickled beans are superb for camping, fishing trips, and picnics.*

• *Peas:* One of the most prolific and versatile stars of the garden is the pea which, again, comes in infinite varieties, for every season, taste, and gourmet purpose. One of my fondest memories as a kid was eating the tender, juicy, new green peas, pod and all, right off the bush in early summer.

Peas can be canned and frozen as well as eaten fresh out of the garden. Sweet peas and pods for eating include Sugar Snaps, Dwarf White Sugar, Mammoth, Sugar Bon, Sugar Rae, Dwarf Gray, Pea Sugar Snap.

Good soup peas are Blackeyed, Brown Crowder, Purple Hull. Early Alaska is a very early type and is a good

---

*See *Food Drying, Pickling, and Smoke Curing*, Caxton Printers, Ltd., for complete details.

canner and freezer. Perfection is another good canner with dark skin and large pods. and it is also delicious served with a cream sauce and new potatoes. Laxtonian is a jumbo-sized pea, sweet and tender and good for freezing. Some are easy to pick, like the Green Arrow. Frost Bite is a late, frost-resistant type.

If you have not eaten peas right out of the garden, you do not know how good this vegetable really is. Peas should be among the first vegetables to be planted, with several varieties set out at intervals in order to have them fresh all summer long. Select varieties best suited for your climate, garden space, soil, and purpose, such as canning, freezing, or fresh-eating.

Of Cabbages and Kings

• *Cabbage:* Set out in plants. Some hardy types are Jersey Wakefield, Badger Market, Early Flat Dutch, Golden Acre, Red Dutch, and Late Flat Dutch, the best keeper.

There is an early succulent Chinese type called Michihli Jade Pagoda and a salad variety called Chinese Michihli.

A small cabbage is Darkri Hybrid. All Seasons Wisconsin, Early Jersey, Golden Acre, Mammoth Red Rock, Harvester Queen, Savoy Ace, Savor King, Stonehead, Morden Dwarf, and Emerald Cross are the popular varieties.

• *Cauliflower:* Similar to broccoli, this can be started indoors. When set out it matures quickly, some varieties in little over a month. King Hybrid is an early one. So is Snow Crown. Other varieties include Royal Purple, Snowball Self Blanching, and Pioneer.

• *Artichoke:* Seems like a lot of plant for the small edible portion, but these are delicious when cooked and dipped, section by section, into butter, sauce, or mayonnaise. They can be raised from seed or sets. Some types are Globe and Silver Green.

• *Brussels Sprouts:* This is one of my favorites when steamed and swimming in butter. They are easy to raise and early to bear. Hybrid Jade Cross and Long Island are a couple of popular varieties.

• *Eggplant:* Often overlooked, this is a delicious plant baked, panfried, or in casserole. Black Beauty, Beauty Hybrid, Dusky, Black Bell, Ichiban are some popular ones. They are early croppers and prolific. Grow from seeds.

• *Asparagus:* Easy to grow, popular with everyone, and succulent, this is now very expensive to buy at the market but cheap if it comes out of your garden. Can be frozen, canned, or eaten table-fresh. Brock Imperial is large, plump, and tender and a big producer that will continue to produce for years. There is Waltham for high production and uniform size; Mary Washington, for high quality; California 500, and High Yield Roberts. Asparagus needs rich soil and should be planted in rows three feet apart, with plants spaced fifteen inches. Takes a lot of room. (There is no harvest the first year.)

• *Rhubarb:* This perennial need almost no care and comes up each year like a weed. Needless to say, rhubarb is a versatile, deliciously tart plant that can be frozen, canned, eaten fresh, in sauces, pies, and even as icecream topping. The leaves are poisonous, incidentally. No garden is complete without one or two plants. Some good producers are Flare, Valentine, Canada Red, and Victoria.

• *Broccoli:* A fine vegetable, especially with a cheese sauce or cream sauce served steaming hot. Early Spartan is the most common type. Hybrid Green Duke is another, as is Hybrid Premium Crop.

• *Okra:* Not so common, but almost indispensable for good soups and stews, okra is prolific and easy to raise. It comes in many varieties, including Emerald Green Velvet, Dwarf Long Pod Green, Red Okra, and Clemson Spineless.

• *Celery:* Favorite of the dieters, celery is excellent in sticks to munch on and in soups and stews. Giant Pascal and Gold Self Blanching are popular.

• *Kohlrabi:* Not common, but delicious with a cheese sauce or in salads or steamed with melted butter and lemon juice. White Vienna and Hybrid Kohlrabi, Grand Duke, and Purple Vienna are common types.

• *Parsley:* Universally used for garnishing roasts, aspics, souffles, and fast-food sandwiches, it can be used green or dried and is high in potassium content, a necessary mineral for good health and body chemical balance.

• *Peppers:* For pickling, drying, and enhancement of soups, meat loafs, and dozens of other dishes, peppers are among the most versatile garden plants but need a warm growing season and do not tolerate frost. They should be started indoors.

Some standard varieties are King of the North, Cherry Sweet, Big Bertha, Sweet Pepper Mixture, Spartan Garnet. Real hot peppers include Hungarian yellow, Jalapeno, Hot Pepper Mix.

Rare Mexican sizzling hot types are firebrands, like Anahiem TMR, Ancho 101, Red Chili, Pepperoncini, Santa Fe Grange, Fresno Chili, Numex Big Jim, Serrano; Pepper Park's Whopper, Sweet Banana, Gypsy Hybrid, Tequila Sunrise, Aconcagua, Golden Belle, Dutch Treat, Cayenne Long Red Slim, Golden Spike, and Jalapeno, among others.

Greens, Salads, and Such

With the exception of okra, which loves hot weather, leafy vegetables should be planted early in the season, and again in late summer as a fall crop. They like it cool, and as table greens and fixin's for salads, they are really cool. There simply is no comparison between garden-fresh greens and the limpid, tasteless things you buy at the market. Not even considering the cost.

• *Spinach:* Kids are supposed to turn up noses when this fine vegetable is placed before them. That never happened to me. I loved it fresh or cooked, and still do. Hybrid Avon is a vigorous type, maturing in only 44 days. New Zealand is a summerlong variety of fine flavor. Giant Nobel is another early one, with a heavy yield. Bloomsdale Long is a succulent early dark type. Dixie Market is ready in only 38 days. Northland is a 40-day spinach, rich in vitamins C and A.

• *Lettuce:* No meal or snack is complete without this. Lettuce Tom Thumb is a miniature butterhead type, the size of a tennis ball, which can be served whole with dressing and can be grown in a window box. If you're eating out, you'll only find it at places like the Waldorf or the Ritz.

Lettuce should be sown at intervals so you can have it fresh for the entire season. Growing time varies from 30 to 80 days, depending on variety. Looseleaf types are Black Seeded Simpson, Salad Bowl, Red Salad Bowl, Oak Leaf, Prizehead, Ruby, Crispy Sweet, Romaine, Chicken, Grand Rapids, Slo-Bolt, Sweetie, and Oak Leaf. Head lettuce includes Buttercrunch, Great Lakes, Iceberg, Ithaca, Creamy Heart, Continuity, and Caracrolle. Butterheads are Augusta, Dark Green Boston W.S., and Hot Weather.

• *Mustard:* Young plants are used in salads for piquancy, older ones for cooked greens. In any case, they are zesty additions to any meal. Green Wave is one. Dixie Market, Southern Giant, Tendergreen are among the others. Bok Choy is a Chinese mustard.

• *Kale or Borecole:* High in vitamins A and B, this can be eaten raw or boiled and creamed. It is good for steamed dishes, salads, and sandwiches. Easy to raise, matures early. Dwarf Green Curled is one type. Dwarf Blue Curled Vates is another.

• *Collards:* A member of the cabbage family, a great old-time green. Vates is a common type.

• *Endive:* Large, two-foot heads, resists hot weather.

• *Swiss Chard:* Fordhook Giant is an early type that bears all season. Another is Lucullus.

The Vegetable Kingdom — Vine Crops

• *Cucumbers:* I don't know what we would do without this member of the plant kingdom. The expression "cool as a cucumber" is not for nothing. To cool off on a hot summer day, nothing is more refreshing than a cucumber salad. I used to eat them raw, right out of the garden. Now I like to sprinkle a little salt on them.

They can be sown indoors for a month before putting outside. They need fertile, warm soil and plenty of space, but vines can be trellised up a fence. The first ones can be picked in little over a month. The young, early ones make the best pickles. Some varieties are developed especially for this, others for salads. Some are even burpless, such as Park's Burpless Bush, Burpless Tasty Green No. 26, and Euro-American. The Sweet Slice Hybrid is sweet and burpless, too.

Salad types include Park's Whopper, Comanche Hybrid, Patio Pik, Amira, Saladin, Early Surecrop, Gemini, Victory, Spartan Valor, Damascus — all hybrids. Standards include Marketmore, Poinsett 76, and Bush Whopper. Picklers include Pickle-Dilly Hybrid, Liberty Hybrid, Spartan Dawn Hybrid, Peppi Hybrid, Pioneer Hybrid, and Tiny Dill. National Pickling is the earliest kind. Be sure to raise some dill for the pickle mix.

• *Watermelons:* This is one crop that is so valuable you may have to chain a guard dog in the garden to keep out poachers. When I was a kid, "cooning" watermelons was a favorite nighttime sport. The practice is still carried out by kids, but the revisionists among us have cleaned up the word, thinking that it is an ethnic slur. This is especially true of young editors. It is nothing of the kind. It is a contraction of "raccoon," a nocturnal animal with a habit of sneaking around looking for food.

Anyway, today the horticulturalists can provide a wide array of mouthwaterin' types, ranging from the traditional, like the Rattlesnake and Congo, to grapefruit-size delights that have either red meat or golden. They should be planted as soon as the ground is warm, with four seeds to a hill, thinned later to two plants. Northern Sweet matures in 70 days. The Golden Midget is a tiny one that is ripe inside when it is yellow gold outside. Garrisonian is a Rattlesnake type, almost two feet long and ten inches in diameter. Black Diamond is also called Cannonball, from its shape. A seedless type is Gurney's Hybrid Tri-X. Congo is sweet as sugar; so is Sugar baby. For dry country, the Hybrid Dixie Queen is fine. Sugar Bush is great for small plots. King and Queen is a Christmas melon, a good keeper. Yellow Doll has a delicious yellow flesh. Field's Fourth of July is one of the earliest. Florida Giant is a large market type. Finest tasting of all is said to be the Charleston Gray. The Black Diamond or Yellow Belly is a huge, tough-rind type.

Melons are ripe when the bottom changes from greenish white to creamy white and gives a dull thump when rapped. You'll never buy another market melon after you've raised your own.

One reason I like to raise melons is for the rinds, which make the most scrumptious pickles you've ever swooned over.

• *Cantaloupe:* These were called "muskmelon" where I came from, and the term is more appropriate for they have a slightly musky scent, which is one way to tell when they are ripe. They should be left to ripen on the vine. When the stem begins to pull away from the vine and separates easily, the melon should be picked. A packet of 700 seeds will plant 100 hills, enough to supply the whole neighborhood. Melons mature in from 60 to 90 days, depending on variety.

Some types are Saticoy Hybrid, Minnesota Midget, Oval Chaca Hybrid, Short N' Sweet, Bushwhopper Hybrid, Samson Hybrid, Busheloupe, Iroquois, Giant Perfection, Jumbo Hybrid Roadside, Golden Honey, Pride of Wisconsin, Heart of Gold, Hale's Best, Honeyloupe, Hybrid Sweetie, Hybrid Chieftan, Rocky Ford, Honey Rock, Hybrid Earli-Dew, Crenshaw, Banana Melon, Golden Champlain, Gurney's Mammoth, Far North; plus the honeydews like Pineapple Hybrid, Honey Drip Hybrid, Oliver's Peal Cluster, and Tam Dew.

The Choice is yours.

• *Pumpkins:* For the pumpkin eater, another wide selection of devloped hybrids and conventional varieties is available. Pumpkins are easy to grow but do take a long time to mature, like around 100 days, which is why they seem to be ready in late October for the Halloween and jack-o'-lantern trade. They also take up a lot of space, but there are a couple of varieties that are suited for the small garden plot.

Bix Max is a huge one that weighs over 100 pounds. Big Moon is another giant that under some conditions might reach 200 pounds. Show Queen is a squash-pumpkin that has been known to reach more than 300 pounds.

The earliest of all is the Spirit Hybrid bush pumpkin, which matures in 80 days. Connecticut Field makes a fine jack-o'-lantern. Funny Face is another. Little Boo is a novelty, especially good for lanterns and painted faces. Streaker is a delicious seedless that can be roasted or eaten raw and is full of protein. It is small, only six inches or so in diameter. The Striped Cushaw cooks up like a squash. Connecticut Field and Cushaw are ideal for pies.

Take a lot of space, but worth the effort.

• *Squash:* Here again there is a wide selection. Everyone knows how versatile and prolific zucchini squash is. Whole cookbooks have been written about this garden wonder. Squashes some of which mature in only 40 days, include Black, Golden Crookneck, Grey, Black Magic, Aristocrat, Ambassador, Clarita, Dark Green, Park's Green Whopper, Seneca Gourmet, Gourmet Blob, and Vegetable Harrow.

A winter keeper is Golden Delicious — good frozen or canned, too. Bennings Green Tint, Gold Rush Hybrid, Hybrid Scallopini, Hybrid Sundance, Early Butternut, Table Ace Hybrid, Bush Jersey Golden Acorn are some good ones.

Some bush types are Buttercup, Bush Baking, Bush Cucumber, and Bush Pumpkin.

Among the best winter varieties, which ripen late and keep well when stored in a cool, dark place, are Golden Delicious, Ebony, Gold Nugget, Table Queen, Baby Hubbard, Hercules Butternut, Waltham Butternut, Early Butternut, Warted Hubbard, Hungarian Mammoth, Gurney's Jumbo Pink Banana, Buttercup, Delicata, Table Ace, Kindred, and Blue Hubbard.

Two novelties are Vegetable Spaghetti and Scallopini Squash. A real sweet one with a deep orange flesh and rich flavor is the Delicata Sweet Potato Squash. Tahitian winter squash is a new one that will grow 100 pounds of food from one 25-foot vine. It tastes like a melon and stores like a squash.

There are also a number of ornamental gourds that are fine for esthetic reasons if you have the space: Super Warted, Dipper Gourd, Luffa Sponge, Birdhouse Gourd, and so on. These are fun to grow and can be used to decorate trellises or fences and for landscaping sloping banks. They can be used to make birdhouses, pipe bowls, lamps, pitchers, and candleholders, among other things. But you can't eat 'em.

Herbs, Seasonings, and Condiments

In the old days the family plot always had several rows of herbs for adding zest and fragrance to family life. Contrary to popular impression today, you don't have to depend upon expensive bottles and cans offered by the supermarket. You can raise any or all you want at a fraction of the cost of the store-boughten ones, and in quality nothing can equal the fresh garden variety. Here are some ideas:

Sage — A perennial, so easy to raise you should never be without it as seasoning for meat, poultry stuffing, used fresh or dried.

Horehound — A perennial for cakes and candies. We used this as a medicinal candy, good for colds and sore throats.

Oregano — Perennial, for flavoring meat, soups, sauces, Italian dishes. I use it a lot in omelets and on poached eggs.

Summer Savory — An annual, fine for salads, gravies, and vegetables.

Caraway — Biennial. Excellent in seeds for breads, cakes, salads.

Borage — Annual. Tastes like a cucumber and is used for garnishes on salads and in drinks.

Sweet Basil — Also an annual. The leaves are chopped for use in soups, stews, salads, and many kinds of recipes.

Thyme — A perennial, for salad dressing, gravies, soups.

Spearmint — A cool, cool perennial, fine for drinks, jellies, teas.

Chives — Perennial member of the onion family, indispensable for soups and stews, salads.

Lavender — Perennial. Dried for scents, and for garnishes.

Sweet Marjoram — Annual, for meat, stews, sausage, soups, and omelets.

Florence Fennel — Annual. Tastes like licorice. Fine anise flavor for salad, soup, and meat.

Lemon Balm — Annual, for teas, soups, sauces. Has a soothing effect.

Anise — Annual, for candy flavoring, such as licorice.

Rosemary — Annual. A sweetish seasoning for sauces and meats.

Curled Cress An annual that matures in 10 days. Fine for salads, sandwiches, dips.

Hamburg Turnip-Rooted Parsley — Roots are ground up for soup, stews, salads.

There are dozens of others like catnip to please your pet, chicory for a coffee supplement or substitute, coriander for oriental cooking, dandelion for salads and wine, hops for making beer, guayule for making rubber (!), burnet for cold drinks, sweet woodruff for medicinal wine and teas, *Allium fistulosum* for eating like an onion and for salads, angelica as a tonic, jojoba as a medicinal oil, lovage as an aromatic seed for cakes, *Monarda citriodora* for lemon-scented oil to treat wounds, pennyroyal for an aid to digestion, Russian comfrey for treating wounds, sore throats, and other medical problems, safflower for low-cholesterol cooking, sorrel for French cuisine, tansy for an insect repellant, *Thea sinesis* for tea making, and many others.

Raising herbs, in fact, is a fascinating pastime in itself, to say nothing of raising cooking to an art. Herbs are also attractive in the garden, and some of them have a fine fragrance like expensive perfumes. They can be easily raised indoors; special kits for this can be purchased reasonably.

• *Horseradish:* Somehow my life has been tied closely to this pungent, prolific plant. As a kid I harvested our patch (which grew among the rhubarb), ground up the stalk and mixed it with vinegar. I then sold it by the mason jar at the village store. It was in high demand.

Forty years later a school chum from my old hometown, who became one of the world's leading suppliers of mustard and other condiments and spices, sought me out for help in acquiring a couple of dozen sets of a particularly unique and superb commercial variety developed in the high, rich plateau country of Klamath Falls, Oregon. When he tried to buy some himself, the local growers closed all doors to him, wanting to maintain their monoply. Since I had some connections he asked me to help. It took me a month, and I used up all my Brownie points and collected all favors owed me in the process, but I came up with two dozen sets and a few over. He had them hand-delivered and subsequently planted them in his test fields. I managed to keep one bunch, which is now part of my garden.

Fresh-grated homemade horseradish surpasses in flavor and piquancy anything you can buy in a store. It can be used as the "pure quill" or mixed with mustard and other seasonings to suit yourself. It's fun to experiment. New Bohemian is a popular variety, available in roots or heavy crowns. A few cuttings in sandy soil will supply the whole family with zesty seasoning for dips, relishes, and meats.

To prepare, peel the fresh root and chop or grate. Add white vinegar or sour cream for desired consistency and store in small glass jars.

• *Garlic:* Almost essential for pickling, soups, meats, sauces, dips. It stores like an onion or can even be left in the garden all winter. It is very hardy and prolific. Two varieties are California White and Elephant.

Exotics and Novelties

If you have the space, there are a lot of fun things you can raise, indoors or outdoors. These include *sugar beets* and sweet sorgums, already mentioned, as well as *jicama,* the Mexican water chestnut. How about *broom corn,* which the pioneers used for making sweepers? It also can provide bird seed. *Luffa sponge* is a plant that will actually grow usable, flexible sponges. The *banana muskmelon* grows sixteen inches long and is delicious sliced and eaten out of the garden. *Ornamental cotton* is another novelty. *Garden huckleberry* grows like tomatoes and makes super pies, jellies, and jams. Little Minnie is a midget cucumber with a vine only two feet long. *Finger roots* are easy to grow and are excellent for salads, soups, vegetables, or meats; essential for curries and oriental dishes. *Peanuts* are also fun to raise, taking about four months to mature. There are several types, including the tiny Spanish variety, the Virginia, and a new variety that has a pod more than two inches long containing six or more nuts. *Ginseng* root, the medicinal plant, is simple to grow.

There is a new *Winged Bean* that is 100 percent edible — beans, leaves, stems, pods, tendrils, tuberous roots, and flowers. It is prolific and has more protein and fat than yams or taro. Moreover, the flowers are decorative.

Tips for Novice Gardeners

Once a plot is selected, which should be of good soil and well drained, there are four basic elements to growing vegetables successfully:

• *Fertilizing:* This is a necessary element of every good garden. Local nurseries and garden shops can provide all the chemicals and equipment needed for this, but it is hard to beat well-rotted manure. This can usually be obtained free from livestock growers. Manure and fertilizers should be well mixed with the soil. Instructions for using chemicals are included with the product. One has to be careful not to use too much, thus burning the plants. Rotation of plants from year to year also prevents wearing out certain patches and if done properly restores the nitrogen and other elements which the previous crop removed from the soil.

• *Watering:* All plants require water in the natural process of using the sun's energy to manufacture food. An acre of corn, for example, uses enough water each month to supply a small village with all its domestic needs. At least one inch per week is needed for a garden plot. This is better supplied by soaking than by sprinklers.

• *Cultivation:* Hoeing to loosen the soil and destroy weeds is vital to the growth of healthy vegetables. This is not as big a job as it seems, though. A couple of hours a week is about all that is necessary. It is also good exercise, and you can't overdo it.

• *Pest Control:* Insects and plant diseases will be your enemies. In the case of insects, you can control these without chemicals by introducing certain kinds of friendly bugs like preying mantis, ladybugs, or Trichogramma that effectively eliminate all manner of harmful insects and moths. Earthworms also should be planted in the soil to help enrich it — and to provide fishing bait. Some insects and plant diseases can only be controlled by chemicals, and the information and means for this are readily available at any garden store.

Indoor Gardening

A great many vegetables can be started and even grown to maturity indoors. This can be done in jiffy cups, pots, boxes, trays, and other containers. Outdoor hot boxes, with glass enclosed beds, follow the same principle.

The containers should have holes in the bottom for drainage of water. Place a layer of gravel over the holes, then a layer of sterilized loam or commercial potting mixture. Seeds should be sown sparingly and planted simply by pressing into the soil. Water from the bottom up by placing the containers in a shallow tray of water if possible. Keep the soil just damp, not wet. Place trays in the sunshine behind a window until the seeds germinate, then maintain about sixty-five degrees temperature. Transplant sprouts to larger containers as necessary and then transplant into the garden when the soil is warm enough. Some things, like mushrooms, can be raised to maturity indoors.

Instructions for planting are always included in seed packets. Some vegetables best started indoors include broccoli, brussels sprouts, cabbage, cauliflower, eggplant, peppers, tomatoes, lettuce, cucumbers, squash, melons, and onions.

Folklore

• "Plant some for the worms, some for the crow, some to pull out, and some to grow."

• Use wooden clothespins to train climbing vines on fences and poles.

• A saucer of beer set out in the garden will attract snails and slugs, which will then fall in and drown.

• To grow the biggest pumpkins for entering state fairs, pinch all but one blossom off each vine, so the plant will use all its energy to produce one big trophy.

• Marigolds planted between rows of beans will repel some kinds of insects.

• Garlic and horseradish also repel invaders.

• Horseradish repels potato bugs and flying insects.

• Larkspur, onions, chives, and leeks hold off aphids.

• Marigolds fight off root nematodes.

• Mint repels flea beetles and cabbage butterflies.

• Garlic destroys aphids and onion flies.

• Nasturtiums repel aphids and cucumber beetles.

• Rosemary gets rid of cabbage maggots.

• Sage fights off carrot flies and cabbage bugs.

• Radishes repel cucumber beetles and spider mites.

• Pyrethrum defends against mites, aphids, and leafhoppers.

Signs of Spring

• When the trees split bark in winter, it will be a hot, dry spring.

• When snowdrifts face north, spring will arrive early.

• Thunderstorms before seven in the morning in April and May mean a wet summer.

Planting Moons

• *First quarter:* Phase is waxing new, increasing light. Plant leafy annuals like broccoli, brussels sprouts, cauliflower, cabbage, lettuce, leeks, onions, spinach, parsley, asparagus, and cereal crops.

• *Second quarter:* Gibbous, first quarter, and half moon. Plant beans, cereals, cucumbers, eggplant, watermelons, peas, peppers, cantaloupe, pumpkins, tomatoes, squash, and ones with integral seeds.

• *Third quarter:* Full but waning gibbous and decreasing light. Plant root crops, bulbs, perennials and biennials, such as beets, chicory, garlic, carrots, onions, parsnips, potatoes, radishes, rutabagas, peanuts, rhubarb, strawberries, turnips, grapes, and shrubs.

• *Fourth quarter:* Last quarter, old moon, decreasing. Plant nothing!

Sprouting Seeds

With farm-fresh fruits, vegetables, nuts, and livestock handy, the art of sprouting seeds was not much practiced in my youth. But in the off-season, and in parts of the world where the pantry was barren of such nutrition — such as on board the sailing vessels of the day on yearlong passages — it was common to carry seeds and sprout them to provide fresh salads and other dishes loaded with essential vitamins and minerals. Like many other practices, sprouting of seeds is enjoying a rebirth. Although we have a garden and also access to a number of neighborhood markets, we have a sprouting "vitamin factory" going in our kitchen all the time. It is amazing how much of your daily fresh greens can be obtained this way. A teaspoon of seeds, for example, provides us with a quart of delicious sprouts and greens in a few days' time. By using several quart jars and lids we can start a new batch every day for several days and thus have a new crop coming on constantly. The water used for rinsing the sprouts daily is saved for cooking, as it is loaded with vitamins and essential minerals.

Most health food stores, and some large rural supermarkets, carry the simple equipment needed for home sprouting. Actually all you need is a couple of mason jars and some perforated lids. These lids are also available in commercial kits at low cost, with different sizes of perforations for different size seeds. The seeds also are readily available from the same outlets (see appendix).

You simply place a teaspoon or tablespoon of seeds into a clean mason jar, screw on the appropriate lid, and run some rinse water over them. Set them in a lighted place, usually by the sink, but out of direct sunlight. Within a day you will see the seeds beginning to sprout.

For all seeds the water should be lukewarm but not hot. The ideal temperature for sprouting is between 65 and 75 degrees. We usually get good results with an average temperature of 60 degrees.

After the initial soaking and rinsing, repeat this process about twice a day until the sprouts are ready to eat. Save any excess greens by simply placing the jar in the fridge between meals. While seeds will keep indefinitely, the sprouts won't. They turn sour if not used.

The rinsing is to remove the chaff and seed hulls. These are not harmful, but removing them helps prevent molding and spoilage. Between rinsings place the jar on its side in a place where any moisture can drain out the perforated cap.

That's all there is to it.

• *Mung Beans:* Delicious in salads, chop suey, and soups. Can be grown in a shallow dish. Keep slightly moist for 3 to 5 days.

• *Alfalfa:* The popular old standby, packed with vitamins and minerals and high in protein. Super for sandwiches and salads. Takes 4 to 6 days to sprout. Can be eaten raw or cooked.

• *Lentil:* Very tasty, good for soups and stews. Can also be eaten raw as is. Excellent for exotic dishes and recipes. Grows like peas.

• *Fenugreek:* Eat fresh or cooked. Has a spicy flavor with a faint maple taste. Excellent for curries and other exotic recipes.

Other good sprouting seeds include rice, barley, wheat, oats, clover, corn, sesame, sunflower, pumpkin, lettuce, okra, turnip, garlic, parsley, almond, flax, pea, radish, spinach, celery, chard, broccoli, millet, buckwheat, cress, mustard, kale, and even weeds like sorrel, dandelion, peppergrass, plantain, or amaranth. Don't use tomato, petunia, or potato; they are toxic. Sprouting seeds can be obtained from most nature and health food stores, mail order seed catalogs, and purveyors of survival-type outdoor supplies.

The sprouts are superior to anything in the greens department. You can eat them raw, in salads, on sandwiches, as garnishes, and in soups, stews, casseroles, and bakery products. They can be used in flour making, as an additional nutritive, and blended into healthful beverages. They are a great source of vitamins, proteins, enzymes, minerals, and fiber. In fact, sprouts are virtually a complete source of natural essential elements. They are also low in calories and carbohydrates.

See appendix for chart of various seeds available and sprouting times.

Fresh Sprout Salad

2 tomatoes, sliced
1 c alfalfa sprouts
¼ c radish sprouts
¼ c sesame seeds
1 cucumber, chopped
½ c mung bean sprouts
1 c cottage cheese
herbs & spices to suit

Combine ingredients; toss with oil and apple cider vinegar. Lemon juice can be used; also other types of sprouts can be alternated.

Sprout Soup

Simply add your favorite sprouts to your favorite soup, whether homemade or store-boughten.

Don's Tomato Omelet

2 green onions
2 T fresh herbs
1 tomato
¼ c radish sprouts
½ c sunflower seed sprouts
salt, pepper, oregano, tarragon
6 eggs
¼ c milk
1 c alfalfa sprouts
½ c mung bean sprouts
dill weed flakes

Combine diced tomato and chopped onions with whipped eggs, milk, and herbs. Add rest of condiments. Cook in omelet pan with butter until it begins to bubble. Add sprouts. With fork make slits to let liquid run to bottom of pan. Fold over and cover. (Some cooks like to sprinkle cheese flakes on top before folding.) Cook over low heat until golden brown.

Planning the Family Garden Plot

Think of your backyard garden as a food factory. The size of this factory will depend upon how much space you have available, how large your family is, and how much of your annual food requirements you hope to produce — all interrelated factors.

As a rule of thumb, a plot 20 by 20 feet will provide a family of two or three with almost a complete supply of greens and vegetables, but it takes good planning and good management. The plot must be arranged and planted according to the growing times, so there will be a rather constant harvest of fresh produce as it ripens. The greens and fresh vegetables will be of first-class quality, rich in flavor, vitamins, and minerals. There is an added benefit much harder to put a value on — the fun, the good exercise, and the satisfaction of raising your own food.

The choice of vegetables is up to you and your family's preference, but in general plant a wide variety for best results. Studying the seed catalogs in winter and early spring is highly recommended — to say nothing of being a pleasant way to spend evening hours away from the boob tube. Select, first, plants that are known to do well in your locality and, second, plants that mature at various times so that you have not only vegetables like leaf lettuce and swiss chard that continue to produce as you crop them, but also vegetables that, harvested early, can be replaced with a later type. Early peas can be followed by broccoli, second peas followed by cabbage, early beets by escarolle, parsnip by early radish, carrots by chinese cabbage, beans by turnip. Early corn can be followed by late corn mingled with winter squash or pole beans. Herbs can be planted around borders; berries and dwarf fruit can go around fences and even around the house foundation.

For a family of four or five, a plot 30 by 40 feet will produce everything you can eat, plus a surplus of certain kinds of vegetables. It will also permit planting more potatoes for winter storage and more sweet corn, if you are partial to delectable roasting ears right off the stalk, before they begin to turn starchy — the only way to eat corn on the cob.

A large garden of about 50 by 100 feet will feed a family of eight and also provide a wider variety of vegetables, berries, and fruits. A garden this size will require one person to work a total of 16 to 20 hours a week. Divided among several family members this is a matter of only an hour or so a day — and most of us need the exercise anyway. With a garden this size, in addition to everything else you can raise several kinds of melons and other vine plants, and lots of potatoes and corn.

The garden plot should be selected for a southern exposure, be protected from heavy winds if necessary (a border of fruit trees and berry bushes will accomplish this), and have well-drained soil of a good type.

Without going into the chemistry of soil (you can find books on this if you want to pursue the subject further), the best type of soil is high in organic content — that is, the decomposed remains of plants and animals, as well as bacteria and small living things such as earthworms. The average garden soil will have about 5 percent inorganic material to 80 or 90 percent organic, with the rest composed of oxygen, water, and mineral salts. Clay soils have the most inorganic materials and the least organic matter and thus are the least desirable for raising a garden. Clay soils also have poor drainage, and water cannot percolate through them to feed the plant roots. Clay soil can be improved, however, with the intermixing of humus and peat with the inorganic matter, as well as sand. Sand is porous, drains extremely well, and dries out quickly. Sandy soil also warms quickly and is best suited for early crops. Mixing with humus or peat greatly improves it.

There is an old aphorism that goes with all this:

Sand in clay is money thrown away;
But clay in sand is money in the hand.

The ideal soil for gardens is *loam.* This is a mixture of sandy soil, clay, and silt of various kinds.

It might be well to mention that *topsoil,* or the upper layer of the ground, contains practically all the minerals and other matter that is vital to plant growth. Beneath this lies the deep stratum of *subsoil,* which is virtually useless for growing things. When hauling in soil to enrich your garden plot, be sure to get *topsoil* or *plant soil* and not earth that has been excavated from a basement site or a road-building borrow pit.

Soil-testing kits are inexpensive, easy to use, and available from most seed stores. These test mainly for acidity in terms of pH, which means a scale of “p” for parts and “H” for hydrogen ion concentration in grams per liter. Soil with a pH of 4.5 is very acid; a pH of 8 is very alkaline. Everything in between is arranged on a scale of quality.

To prepare soil for planting, select fertilizers that have been compounded to suit your soil conditions and to enhance the mineral requirements of the various vegetables you will be growing. There seems to be an endless variety of commercial fertilizers, but all of them list their chemical composition on the bottle, box, or bag. Consult with the seed store or nursery supervisor (not the part-time hired help, who may not know any more than you) and seek advice also from texts and manuals on the subject. One type of fertilizer that you can make at home is *compost.* In fact, no good garden is without a compost heap. This is simply a shallow pit in a shady spot into which are put layers of leaves and dead plants (not weeds), lawn clippings, vegetable garden waste from the kitchen, anything that will decompose. The layers are dusted with limestone powder and fertilizers and covered with three or four inches of topsoil. Build up the layers until the heap is three or four feet high, and keep it moist. If started in the spring it will be "garden fresh" by fall. It should then be dug out and spread over the garden plot and plowed or tilled into the soil before spring planting.

Rotation of crops is an age-old method of restoring to the soil the vital minerals removed by the last crop. As a boy I raised potatoes as a cash crop to help buy clothes for school and to have spending money. I didn't believe my dad when he told me that I shouldn't plant potatoes in the same place every year — until each crop turned out poorer than the last. At his suggestion I restored my field by planting alfalfa one year and plowing it under. The next year I had a bumper crop of early potatoes that made me temporarily rich.

This was called growing a cover crop, and the principle has been known for thousands of years. Cover crops are usually legumes, which have the quality of enriching the soil. With a lot of space you can grow cover crops on certain sections, rotating with vegetables and other plants each year. Not having this much space, you can carefully rotate the different varieties of plants, after studying their chemical and mineral requirements. In addition, use commercial fertilizers as a supplement.

Many gardeners depend upon manure from the horse or cow barn or the chicken coop. In Asia and other parts of the world, garden plants are fertilized with human waste or "night soil," an odiferous practice that is frowned upon here. Fresh or "green" manure can be obtained from farmers, most of whom are more than willing to let you come and haul it away. When you raise livestock you are usually up to here in manure and faced with the constant problem of disposing of it. The various manures have somewhat different qualities, but all of them should be turned under the soil with plow or tiller as soon as possible, not only to hasten decomposition but also to eliminate odor and flies.

Sugar, Honey and Health

One of our consultants in the preparation of this volume noted the seemingly high content of recipes calling for sugar. In this calorie-conscious, "natural health" era, plain old sugar has taken on a bad image. It almost seems at times that if sugar had just been discovered by medical science it would be banned by the U.S. Food and Drug Administration — or at least labeled, "This product has been determined by the U.S. Surgeon General to be hazardous to your health."

According to the Washington State Extension Service, Americans have been increasing their consumption of sweets to the point where more than one-third of a pound of sugar is consumed by each person per day. During the same test period (1960 to 1976) consumption of low-calorie sweeteners jumped from two to eight pounds per year!

Most sugars available in the store are made from cane and sugar beets, but more and more food processors are using corn sweeteners, including corn sugar (dextrose), corn syrup, and the new high-fructose corn syrup, which is much sweeter than cane or beet sugar and is used mostly in soft drinks.

Honey, molasses, and maple syrup are used in smaller quantities, about a pound and a half per person per year.

Two-thirds of all sugar products consumed are used by food processors and soft-drink bottlers. Only one-third is used by home cooks and restaurants. Most food products have some form of sugar in them, although the labeling required by law is confusing and often misleading. The sugar content might be disguised as "carbohydrates," or "dextrose," or "fructose," or some chemical form of sugar. But it's all sugar!

Sugar and sweeteners account for almost 20 percent of the calories in all foods and only a trace of minerals, with no vitamins or proteins. Even honey, which health faddists claim is "better for you" than mean, old granulated sugar, has only a trace of nutrients — and these are more easily obtained in other foods. Molasses has the greatest percentage of nutrients, with blackstrap molasses the most nutritious of all the sweeteners. However, it is bitter and often contaminated with nonfood residues.

Some facts about sugar and sweeteners:

Sugar *is* the leading cause of tooth decay. This is apparently, the only direct link to the ills of people living in modern, highly industrialized societies. There is no evidence that sugar causes any of the modern diseases, other than tooth decay. A person who eats too many sweets tends to be overweight, but this is because of overeating and underexercising — not the sugar.

Diabetes is *not* caused by eating sugar (something my mother always warned me about when she caught me raiding the cookie jar). It so happens I did develop diabetes in later life, years after I had cut my daily sugar consumption to a bare minimum (for weight reduction reasons). In my case it was determined by medical authority that it was heredity — my paternal grandmother had died of the disease at age thirty-eight, before insulin was invented. Diabetics, of course, are always put on sugar-free diets, but the reason is because the pancreas is not producing enough natural insulin to compensate. As my doctor told me, a person with normal function of the pancreas could eat five pounds of sugar and it would not show up in the urine or bloodstream. The natural functions of the body would take care of the excess sugar intake.

Medical science today also indicates that sugar has no direct link to atherosclerosis (hardening of the arteries) or to hyperactivity in children. Too much use of sugar, however, tends to replace complex carbohydrate foods like grain products and potatoes, which normally provide the vitamins, minerals, and fiber needed by the body. Hence it could be said that in this sense too much sugar is an indirect link to many illnesses and ailments. The National Food and Nutrition Board has warned that, "Increasing consumption of highly refined or fabricated foods substantially reduces the intake of essential micronutrients, which may lead to imbalances of trace element nutrition in the future."

Joggers and runners, and athletics in general, believe that honey or glucose can be used by the muscles for quick energy. Recent research shows that when glucose is taken just before exercise it provides little or no extra energy for the muscles.

Energy comes from the metabolism of body fat by oxygen. Training improves the oxygen uptake and the use of fat for energy. With exhaustion, the body's supply of carbohydrate is also used for energy. Carbohydrate is stored in the liver and muscles as glycogen. The supply of glycogen can be increased somewhat by "carbohydrate loading" for several days prior to strenuous exercise, but this is considered by doctors to be a dangerous practice.

A well-balanced meal is, in short, the best possible source of energy for anyone, athlete or not.

Sugar is a complex food and comes in different forms in different foods. That from sugar cane and beets is sucrose; that found in milk is lactose; in fruit it is fructose. Honey is a mixture of fructose and glucose, the simple sugar used by the body. Research has indicated that no one sugar is better for you than another. Some people cannot digest lactose; it seems to give them diarrhea, muscle cramps, gas, and other symptoms. These same people, though, can often tolerate dairy products such as buttermilk or yogurt.

Fructose has been promoted as a "safe" sugar for special diets, since some research in the past discovered that the body can absorb fructose without insulin. New research, however, proves that, in the case of diabetics especially, fructose must be counted as part of the carbohydrate intake, just the same as cane or beet sugar.

For centuries honey was the one and only sweetener used by mankind. It is one of the oldest food products. Honey bees have been kept at least since the days of ancient Egypt. It has always been a relatively rare and precious food, and over the centuries many myths have arisen around this product of the bees. In ancient times honey was also used for an alcoholic drink known as mead. The word for mead in the many obscure languages of ancient civilizations was, in fact, used as the key by etymologists and archeologists to decipher those languages. Many myths about the curative and even supernatural powers of honey also hung on for many centuries. Modern science, however, has determined that honey does not have any special properties not available in other foods. Moreover, honey is not more easily digested than other sugar. Some believe that honey tastes sweeter in proportion. This is apparently true, because honey is a mixture of three types of sugar, one of which — fructose — is two times as sweet as table sugar.

Raw honey from the comb is somewhat different from refined honey, having in it the pollen, which has small amounts of vitamins. The refining process removes the pollen *and* the vitamins.

Nutrition experts recommend that honey not be given to infants under one year old. Many honey samples have been found to contain botulism spores. In an infant's digestive system, these spores can produce botulism toxin, which causes infant botulism, a serious disease.

There is no evidence that sugar causes any kind of physical addiction such as alcohol or narcotic dependence. It can create a desire for more sweets, which is difficult to curb. And the more sweets you eat, the more food you eat and the more calories you consume. Nutrition experts recommend that people use less than 10 percent of their daily calories in sugar. For 3,000 calories a day (an active person), this means 300 calories of sugar, or about 6 tablespoons. They recommend becoming aware of the composition of various foods (see *The Composition of Foods* listed in appendix) and learn how to substitute natural foods for sugar — such as milk for soft drinks; whole grain bakery products, cheese slices, or fruit or vegetables tidbits instead of candy. Eat more cereal and grain products, potatoes, and vegetables, as well as fruits. Avoid replacing the sugar you cut down on with high-fat foods, alcoholic beverages, or cigarettes.

While this book is not intended as (nor are we qualified to prepare) a medical or nutrition text, it was felt the above information would help provide a better perspective. The following table shows the principle sources of sugar in foods:

Source	**Sugar**
Most vegetables	0–5%
Very-low-sugar cereals*	0–5%
Milk	5%
Dried peas, beans, nuts	2–7%
Most fresh fruit	5–10%
Soft drinks	10%
Bananas, grapes, sweet cherries	15%
Low-sugar cereals*	5–20%
Ice cream	20%
Canned fruits	20–30%
Medium-sugar cereals*	20–40%
Cookies	30–40%

High-sugar cereals*	40–55%
Jelly, jam, preserves	60%
Dried fruit	60%
Molasses	65%
Honey	75%
Brown sugar	96%
White sugar	99.5%

**Very-low-sugar cereals:* Puffed Wheat, Puffed Rice, Shredded Wheat, Cheerios, Wheat Chex, Corn Chex, Rice Chex, Post Toasties, Corn Flakes, Special K, etc.

Low-sugar Cereals: Grape Nuts, Rice Krispies, Wheaties, Total, Concentrate, Buckwheats, Grape Nuts Flakes, 40% Bran, Team, Life, All Bran, etc.

Medium-sugar Cereals: 100% Bran Country Crisp, C.W. Post Raisin Bran, Olden Grahams, Cocoa Puffs, Trix, Alpha Bits, etc.

High-sugar cereals: Cookie Crisp, Crazy Cow, Sugar Frosted Flakes, Cocoa Krispies, Corny Snaps, Sugar Corn Pops, Apple Jacks, Sugar Snacks, etc.

Butter Making

Butter making is a lost art today. Even most farmers and ranchers now buy all their victuals and fresh vegetables in town at the supermarket. Today, with television and instant telephone service, with modern pickup trucks, fancy cars, and even Piper Cub airplanes to get around in, most country folk live pretty much like city folk — including spending the winters in Arizona, Hawaii, or the West Indies and going on tours of Europe between harvest and planting time. I don't blame them. It's just a fact of modern day life. But I can't help thinking that something has gone out of our supersophisticated life-style.

Anyway, it's not likely that most of you will ever have a cow, even if you had the space to keep her. But if you like to daydream about the good old days and what it was like, here's how we used to make butter on the farm back then. (Even most folks in town kept a cow in the back shed.)

A large crock churn, with a wooden lid that had a hole in it about the size of a large broomstick, was the torture device used to divert us kids from the swimmin' hole or skating on the river ice. The crock was first scalded with hot water, then filled about half full with sour cream. A stick with two crosspieces on the bottom, called the dasher, was also scalded and sprinkled with salt. It was forced down into the cream and the wooden crock lid lowered so that the handle stuck up through the hole in the middle. The handle was manned usually by the most reluctant or recalcitrant member of the

A cornucopia of fine, wholesome foods that can be enjoyed by the average family with little preparation. The large crock in upper right corner is an old-fashioned butter churn such as the authors operated on the farm when growing up.

household, namely me, as punishment for some infraction. Even if there had been no infraction I was punished anyway, just in case I got any new ideas for getting into mischief.

The method of butter making was simple. You just pulled the handle up and pushed it down. You continued this thumping until the sour cream began to form butter. You could tell when this was happening because small particles of yellow began to come up through the hole along with the handle on the upstroke. The buttermilk formed first and then the lumps of yellow butter. When all the butter had formed that was going to, it was spooned into quart-size crocks and the liquid pressed out with a wooden paddle. Sometimes the butter was so soft that the crock had to be place in cold water for awhile. Cold water was also poured on the butter and then pressed out. When the surplus water came out clear, the butter was done.

The buttermilk that came out of the churn was about the most refreshing drink you could have on a hot day. I liked it that way, but I never could gag down the so-called buttermilk that is served in restaurants.

When set and ready, the butter was packed away (usually in the same crock with some salt worked into it) and stored in the root cellar while it was being used. A damp piece of muslin or cheesecloth was used to cover it.

One cow will provide all the butter, buttermilk, cottage cheese, and fresh milk a family can use. Two cows, and you have to start looking for customers to take the surplus.

Usually after the morning milking the raw milk was separated by pouring it through a sterilized cloth and straining it into stone crocks, leaving cream and skim milk. This was not like the cream and skim milk you buy in the market. The cream was so thick you had to spoon it — it wouldn't pour; and the so-called skim milk was richer than the so-called whole milk you buy today. The cream was spooned off the milk that had been strained into the big crocks. The sweet cream was used for coffee, cooking, and desserts; the rest was allowed to sour for butter making. The skim milk was just something we gave to the cat or fed to the pigs, although it was richer than today's whole milk. Some of the skim milk was used for clabber, by letting it turn sour and chunk up like the texture of custard. This was done by putting the milk into a stoneware kettle which was set on the back of the stove. As the skim milk clabbered it separated into chunks and globs of whey. Gradually chunks and globs of cheese would form along with the whey. The curds of cheese were then put into a cloth bag and allowed to drain until all the whey was removed. What was left was cottage cheese, which we called "clabber cheese" until we moved to town and got sophisticated.

All this produced the old country rhyme about Little Miss Muffett, and her curds and whey. . . .

For the table, the clabber cheese was mixed with sweet cream, seasoned with salt and pepper, and served as a salad at dinnertime.

As for buttermilk, you'll never really know what heaven is like until you've eaten buttermilk pancakes and buttermilk biscuits with your own home-churned product.

Black Iron Cookware

Many of the recipes in this book and in an earlier book *(The Old-Fashioned Dutch Oven Cookbook)* call for or mention cast-iron cooking utensils. In the olden days cast-iron or black-iron cookware was universally used. Even today many cooks prefer this type of utensil over the modern state-of-the-art space age materials like aluminum, stainless steel, and Teflon coatings. In fact, today there is a lively interest in these old-fashioned wares, and a brisk demand for them is reported by secondhand stores and antique shops. There are at least one or two small foundries turning them out from old resurrected patterns. They are not cheap. I priced a conventional dutch oven in a downtown hardware store the other day, and the price was $48 for the same size that I bought twenty years ago for $12. Even with the inflation factor this was a shocker.

The cast-ironware is in demand not only for nostalgia reasons but also simply because it produces the best and tastiest dishes. Cast-iron cookware is as old as iron-making and was originally designed for cooking over open fires outdoors and in fire-places indoors. In colonial America the cast-ironware brought over from Europe was improved and became standard kitchen equipment through the nineteenth century and into the early twentieth century, even after cooks moved indoors from the detached kitchens and began using fireplaces and finally cookstoves. We use our dutch ovens regularly atop our modern electric range!

In addition to the standard dutch oven there were huge, deep-frying pans, iron bean pots, skillets, popover pans, corn roasters, and stock pots. Some had legs and some did not. The legs were originally used on pots that were set on coals or kept warm on the hearth beside the fireplace. Most had heavy rimmed covers with hook handles or handles for suspending over the open fire.

Brass and copper were also used for utensils, but these were kept more for decorative reasons and for "company coming" purposes, while the black-iron or cast-iron pots were the real workhorses of the kitchen.

You will find that even today cast-ironware is hard to beat and worth what you have to pay for it. Once acquired it will last forever, handed down from generation to generation. It never wears out; indeed, it improves with age. It can be used on the highest heat, either on the stove or on an open fire, and once heated will hold its heat long after being removed from the fire. This is one reason cast-ironware is popular today, what with the popularity of wood stoves as an energy-saving device. When cooking bacon and eggs, for example, you can turn off the heat or remove the pan from the fire long before the bacon is done, and the retained heat will complete the cooking.

Not so well known is the alleged fact that cooking food in ironware adds minute amounts of essential iron to the diet.

Another fact, absolute, is that cast-ironware must be seasoned for best results. Put a new or restored utensil on the stove, fill with clean potato peelings, and boil for an hour. Then wash the utensil in clean soapy water. Do not use detergents on ironware. Dry the pot in a slow oven. Finally, rub the inside with suet, tallow (see tallow-making), lard, or vegetable oil and put back in the oven at 300 degrees for a couple of hours. Remove and wipe off excess oil or grease. With a new utensil this might have to be repeated several times for proper seasoning.

However, we usually find that making a batch of sourdough donuts and then merely rinsing the pot with hot soapy water afterwards provides excellent seasoning.

Other items of maintenance include removing rust if the kettle has been neglected. This is done by scouring with ashes or sand, then scrubbing with soapy water. Stuck food can be removed by soaking in soapy water and then using a brush, such as a toothbrush. Simmering the soapy water on the stove first also helps. Sometimes you will find a "burned" spot on the kettle. This appears as a rough, dark patch. Rub with steel wool or scouring pad, then scrub with soapy water and rinse well. A mixture of sand, ashes, and linseed oil also is excellent for this problem.

After using ironware, clean it and pat it dry with paper towels. Store it uncovered in a dry place.

In addition to the actual cooking utensils, other cast-iron accessories are of value today, including trivets, teapots, fireplace andirons, and kettle hooks or cranes. If you are not a knowledgeable antique buff, you may pass up many an opportunity to make a wise and profitable investment at garage sales, farm sales, flea markets, and auctions. Personally, we would not pass up a purchase like this, if the price seemed reasonable, even if we did not need the items. You can't lose money on it.

In our *Dutch Oven Cookbook*, ironware cooking was described in some detail, along with many recipes. To help you get started in the art of cooking with this old/new type of utensil, here are some recipes that can be used in a modern kitchen.

Cast Iron Popovers

1 c milk
1 c flour
3 eggs
1 T melted butter
¼ t salt

Grease and preheat a popover iron. Beat the eggs, then blend in milk and butter, adding flour sifted with salt. Spoon out batter into the cups until each is only ⅓ full. If batter is too thin, add some flour. Bake at 450 degrees for 15 to 20 minutes, then reduce heat to 350 degrees for another 15 minutes. Remove, puncture with a needle, and serve hot.

Dutch Oven Corn Bread

Mix 2 c cornmeal, 1 t salt, and 1½ c milk or warm water. Drop into preheated and greased dutch oven. Bake for 45 minutes. Let stand for a few moments and serve. For johnny cake, use 1 beaten egg stirred in, and decrease the amount of liquid; fry in a hot greased dutch oven.

Dutch Oven Apples

Wash and core 6 to 8 large apples. Fill holes with sugar, raisins, butter, and cinnamon. Put apples on a greased pie tin with a small amount of water. Place tin in preheated dutch oven. Set tin on props of bottle caps or pebbles to prevent scorching. Cover and bake 30 minutes.

Dutch Oven Potatoes

Fry ½ lb salt pork in an open dutch oven until crisp. Remove the pork and in the grease fry 4 medium onions, diced. Dice 8 medium potatoes and add to onion. Cook in covered oven until done. Remove the cover and brown. Add the salt pork, which has been chopped. Do not stir, but turn over with a fork when brown on the bottom. Season to taste.

Suet Pudding

Mix 1 c chopped suet, 3½ c flour, 2 c raisins, 1 c

currants, 2 t soda, 1 c molasses, and 1 c sour milk. Steam in dutch oven for 2 hours with lid on.

Tillamook Omelet

In a small skillet, prepare hashbrown potatoes in hot oil by chopping boiled spuds as they are browning. Beat together 3 eggs, 3 T cold water, 1 T butter, seasonings like oregano, salt and pepper, tarragon, parsley bits, and a dollop of Worcestershire sauce. Add chunks of cheddar cheese and turn into hot buttered skillet with the hashbrowns, which have been raked to one side to make room. Cook rapidly with cover on until cheese is melted, then remove cover, fold the omelet over and complete browning. Serve omelet and hashbrowns right out of the skillet, dotted with catsup if desired.

Tallow Making

The making of tallow is a lost art these days, but until about fifty years ago it was one of the world's most useful and used commodities. If there ever was a universal, do-it-all, ultimate material for improving one's life, this was it.

Tallow, according to *The American Heritage Dictionary*, is a "mixture of whitish, tasteless solid or hard fat obtained from the bodies of cattle, sheep, horses (or hogs) and used in edibles or to make candles, leather dressing, soap, and lubricants . . ."

It was a byproduct of animal husbandry, and the utilization thereof, from caveman days. It was not only a staple item of home manufacture for the family's own use but a worldwide commodity of trade, almost as common as money (or species). It was valuable; it was plentiful; and the uses for it were nearly endless.

Tallow was, and is, nothing more than rendered animal fat, although some forms were made from plants. To make it is simple. Ask your butcher for a bag of meat scraps, usually fat and gristle that is trimmed from cuts before the meat is wrapped and displayed. Start with 5 or 10 pounds. Place the scraps in a large kettle, along with a small amount of water. Put onto the fire to heat and let it simmer — not boil. Simmering will melt the fat (or suet), and it will float to the surface of the water. When no more liquid fat will come, skim off the residue of dirty scum, remove the unmelted chunks of bone and gristle, and discard. Strain the fat into a clean kettle and put on the fire to simmer for a couple of hours. Strain it off through a sieve — and what you have left is a pearly white, almost translucent paste that is ordorless, tasteless, 99 percent pure, and insoluble. Store it in a plastic container until ready to use, covered to keep out the dust and contaminants.

What you have is a product that is impossible to buy, even in the most complete specialty establishments. The only way to get it is to make it yourself.

What good is it? Well, tallow was used in ages past for making soaps, for medical salves, and as a binder or vehicle for mixing with other herbs and medicines in the treatment of dozens of ailments, injuries, and diseases. Some of these uses are reluctantly acknowledged by modern doctors to have a solid medicinal value. It was used for cooking — the first odorless, tasteless, pure cooking oil; for salads and soups; for the making of *pemmican*, the so-called Indian candy that kept for months at a time without refrigeration, even in hot weather, and was a nearly perfect food from a nutritional standpoint.

Pemmican is made by mixing dried wild berries and fruits with pounded or ground jerky (a dried red meat or dried fish) and binding it thoroughly with tallow — made in "them thar" days from bear grease, the finest fat of all. The finished product was then stuffed into pouches made of antelope or mountain goat hide.

Tallow was used in soap-making. In early days practically every family made its own soap — and at today's prices many ambitious rural families are making it again.

Tallow was used extensively for candles, which was the principle source of light (and in some cases, heat) in ages past.

Tallow provided the base for the finest lubricants of the day and was almost universally used for greasing wagon wheels and gears of grain and lumber mills, for coating and protecting firearms, and for all manner of cottage industries where a lubricant was used. It greased the ways of the great shipbuilding centers of New England that launched a thousand clipper ships and pushed the young United States into leadership in worldwide shipping. It was used for dressing harnesses, shoes, boots, and other items made of leather. Ropes were treated with a mixture of tallow and tar or linseed oil, especially necessary to protect against salt water on ships.

Tallow was also widely used for tools by mechanics, carpenters, and millwrights. My dad kept a tallow barrel in his shop, which I remember from childhood days. The tallow was taken out as needed and mixed with kerosene and mineral or linseed oil. It provided a lubricant and coolant when drilling holes in iron or sawing through oak timbers. A dab of this on the side of a saw blade made life twice as easy for cabinet makers and wheelwrights in the days before hand power tools. My dad always protected his sawing, cutting, and drilling tools from rust and corrosion, when not in use, with a generous coating of tallow and linseed oil.

References to tallow, always remind me of Capt. Joshua Slocum, who in the middle 1890s sailed his thirty-seven foot sloop, *Spray*, around the world alone. The doughty Yankee seadog, while working his way through the Straits of Magellan, came upon a shipwreck from which he spent days salvaging a cargo of tallow. He filled all the available spaces on the *Spray*, until the decks, cabins, and holds were completely covered with the slippery stuff. During the following months, wherever he made a port he would trade some of his tallow for food, supplies, and even money to help finance his circumnavigation.

Indeed, if ever an organic product could be called a friend of mankind, it is tallow — and, as one devoteé exclaimed, it is probably the only product in the universe that does *not* cause cancer, as defined by the U.S. Food and Drug Administration.

Next time you're at the market ask the butcher on duty if he will sell you a bag of scraps. Most butchers are friendly, cooperative types and likely will just give you a supply. Even if you don't think you'll have a need for tallow, making it is an interesting kitchen project for a rainy day — and it will help give you a sense of appreciation for a routine aspect of living in the good ol' days.

Beer Making

I probably should not admit this (my old Sunday school teacher is now gone and almost forgotten, God bless her, and I know she is enjoying the reward she earned on this earth) but in my early wastrel youth — as a lad of somewhere around the ripe old age of eleven — I learned the art of beer making from the town's neighborhood bootlegger. If this does not sound racy enough for you modern counter-culture freaks, just remember that I grew up in the decades of Prohibition with a capital Pro. I was taught from kindergarten on that booze of any kind was not only illegal by the laws of the land but was almost as sinful as playing pool in the Main Street parlor where the local loafers hung out.

Consequently, because it was *verboten*, I naturally was fascinated and was quick to research this evil in all its ramifications. The first one was: How do you make this devil's brew?

In the back lot of my dad's old blacksmith shop was the stone ruin of a former butchering operation, complete with dingy dark cellar filled with spider webs, lizards, and even bats. In this dungeon, as sinister as the catacombs of Poe's Cask of Amontillado, my buddy and I established the class of Thirty-Six's first underground bootlegging enterprise, with a 20-gallon pickle crock we snitched from his grandmother. We had no trouble finding the sugar needed, as every household kept barrels of it for home canning. We did have a little trouble buying the hops and malt. Hops and malt stocked by every grocery store, large and small, for one purpose only: making home brew. Of course, anyone buying these ingredients aroused a knowing smile and raised eyebrows from the clerk, especially if the purchaser was only eleven years old.

I don't remember what subterfuge we used, but we did acquire the ingredients, and we did start our first batch of what we called — in a blaze of marketing inspiration — Holm Brew. After seven days home brew is ready for straining and bottling. This is done by inserting a rubber syphon hose into the aromatic crock. (Aromatic! Our first batch contaminated the air for several blocks in each direction, and the only reason my dad did not investigate his back lot was because he attributed the souring mash scents that drifted into the blacksmith shop to the operations of Jake the Bootlegger, whose establishment was only two blocks beyond.) A suck on the other end of the hose started the syphon going, and the hose was then thrust into the open neck of a bottle previously scalded. The bottle was filled just to the bottom of the neck, after which it was capped and placed on the shelf to age for another week or so.

Sitting beside that crock, syphoning and bottling our first batch of Holm Brew, my partner and I took turns sucking on the hose to start the syphon. Each time, we absorbed a small amount of the sweet green brew, which had a deceptively innocent taste. By the time we had bottled our first pilot batch, both of us were strongly feeling the effects of almost pure alcohol.

We were, in short, crocked.

As our precious bottles aged in the blacksmith shop catacombs, we waited impatiently for the cure, after which we could begin marketing our product. Now and then during the week we would slip into the basement to inspect our stock, opening a bottle to test the concoction for quality. This always resulted in a mild high. We became a little careless handling the green brew, and when one of the bottles exploded and drove a chunk of glass into my buddy's leg we evacuated and stayed clear of the cellar until it was safe to handle the liquid TNT.

Somehow I survived one more potentially fatal childhood enterprise, and in the ensuing months we peddled Holm Brew at the Saturday night dances in the Park Pavilion and at barn dances in the surrounding countryside — at least until the local prohibs caught on and we were warned of the consequences that could result in a stretch in the reformatory at Mandan. At ten cents a quart we were well on our way during those Depression years to becoming relatively affluent. I always suspected that our competition, Jake the Bootlegger, blew the whistle on us to protect his own trade. Anyway, after we folded our operation Jake's price for a quart of beer soared to twenty-five cents.

Home brew is easy to make and contains none of the additives and adulterants found in the store-bought kind. What you need is:

Stone crock of 10 or 20 gallons
Hand bottle capper
Hydrometer
Wood lid for crock
100-150 bottles (dark or smoked)
Package of dry yeast
Sugar
Malt extract
Miscellaneous tools and utensils found in the kitchen

Malt extract comes in flavors like pale, light, regular, and so on. The crock and the bottles *must* be sterilized by washing, scrubbing, and scalding with hot soapy water and thoroughly rinsed. Do *not* use detergents or bleaches. Rinse first with a baking powder solution and follow with clear, clean rinse water.

Prop the crock up on ordinary cement blocks or tile.

In a large kettle, such as used for canning, heat 10 to 12 gallons of water. Add the malt and stir constantly until all is dissolved. Now stir in 5 lbs of sugar until dissolved, being careful not to boil the mixture. Pour into the crock. This should make around 8 or 9 gallons, so a 10-gallon crock would be sufficient. For larger batches, double the formula. Dissolve 2 pkgs. of yeast in lukewarm water and add to crock, stirring gently. Remember that the water and mixture should be warm, not hot. Test the mixture with the hydrometer. This will indicate the percentage of alcohol the finished batch will have — usually from 9 to 12 percent.

Cover crock with clean cloth and bind around edge or lip with a cord. If crock is set around a stove pipe or near a stove where it remains warm all the time, there is nothing else to do. To assure constant warmth, however, set under the crock a single bulb chicken-brooder light, obtainable cheap from Sears Roebuck or Monkey Ward. Let the brew "work" for up to a week, but start checking the batch after two days or so. Depending upon the temperature of the crock, the brew should be bubbling merrily and giving off a healthy aromatic yeasty odor. In two days try the hydrometer text again. The reading will sink lower and lower as the batch cooks. Check again the next day, and so on. When the hydrometer sinks to the bottom of the percentage scale, usually marked B, the batch is ready.

Remove the heat, assemble the bottles, caps, and bottling machine. Using about 6 feet of the versatile rubber hose (also noted for use in syphoning gasoline out of cars in the dark of night), stick one end into the brew well below the surface. Suck on the other end momentarily to draw some liquid, then quickly pinch the end between thumb and forefinger and lower into the neck of a bottle. Release the pinch, and the brew will begin coming down through the hose. Shut off the flow when the bottom of the neck is reached and insert into the next empty bottle. When all bottles have been filled, go back and bring the level of liquid in each bottle to the bottom of the neck. By this time the bubbles will have settled.

In the bottom of the crock will be several inches of dregs or mash. This has a by-product use, but I forget after all these years what it was. Certainly it is not bottled, although many a bootlegger product in the old days had a characteristic layer of sediment in the bottom of the bottle. In any case, the dregs are of no value and should be carefully separated from the beer in the syphoning process (this is the reason for syphoning).

Finally comes the capping. Do this carefully, pressing the cap on firmly. It should have a small dimple in the center if properly done.

It will take a few more days or a week for the green bottled beer to age properly. Keep in a cool, dark place and do not disturb until ready to drink. Do not shake the bottle when handling, and do not drink out of the bottle. To serve, handle bottle gently, open carefully with a bottle opener. There will be a small amount of sediment in the bottom of the bottle. Do not disturb this. Pour into a chilled glass, sliding the beer cautiously down the side of the glass. Discard the final inch of liquid on the bottom, which will have become mixed with sediment.

Before drinking, hold glass up to the light and savor the delicate golden elixir of the gods. Never again will you have a taste for the pallid, additive-adulterated — and costly — drink that comes from commercial breweries.

Home brew is an ideal drink for hot-weather work out of doors. It was always part of the refreshments offered to threshing crews. The brew had the quality of restoring to the hot, exhausted body the chemicals lost through excessive sweating, replacing body liquid and equalizing the metabolism. Sort of like nature's own air-conditioning system.

Now, clean up the mess you made, wash and sterilze the crock and other utensils, and get ready for the next batch. You'll be using it all again soon.

Home Remedies

It is always a source of inner satisfaction to me to stop and contemplate the period in human existence through which I, and my generation, have lived so far. As an eight-or-nine-year-old kid, I recall that an airplane passing overhead was an *EVENT*. Upon hearing the distinctive high and 'way off whine, practically everyone in the little village where I lived rushed outdoors to see the plane. I was usually the first one out and the first one to spot the two-winged speck on the far horizon. The whine would increase, with the pitch of the sound changing as the plane approached; then it would roar overhead and recede toward the opposite horizon. Sometimes the airplane was so low we could see the pilot's helmeted and goggled head peering down at us and perhaps see him waving. That people could actually fly, even better than birds, was regarded as a miracle by most and "the devil's doin's" by a few.

Fifty years later I sat in front of a television set (when I was a kid I had never seen or heard a *radio*) and watched live pictures of Neil Armstrong walking on the moon, his voice coming across space, "One small step for man; one giant step for mankind. . . ." My son who was born and grew up in a big city, watched this historic breakthrough in human achievement with momentary interest, then he yawned and went outside to resume his play.

But I never ceased to marvel at the great technical strides made by mankind during that ensuing fifty years. Truly this is the Technological Age. Through it all, however, some old things and old ways have remained true and undiminished, although in many cases it has been a matter of rediscovering them. As in food and cooking, many of the old ways have been proved unsurpassed by modern technology — including microwave ovens, freeze drying, and even refrigeration. Medical science now recognizes and admits that many of the old home folk remedies, including those of native Indians, have a valid scientific basis, discovered over centuries of crude experimentation and then refined. For example, it was long understood by primitives that letting a dog lick a wound stopped infection and hastened healing. It has been discovered by science that the saliva of the dog and many animals contains enzymes and microbes that do just that.

My mother's standard treatment for "croop," or grippe, was a dose of syrup of figs. For a really serious upset I always got a tablespoon of castor oil in a glass of orange juice. (The latter probably did more to help than the former.) For chest colds I was always treated with a mustard plaster (and it always worked). White liniment was a common treatment for muscular problems. It was also used for animals, but I don't remember just how. The worst part of it was the odor, which was so bad the treatment just *had* to be good.

Some people treated eczema with a mixture of hydrate of chloral and camphor gum, using a vaseline or wool-fat base and rubbing it on like salve. There were may treatments for sore throat, but one that was most successful and that I still use today, is warm salted water, gargled. In those days diphtheria was very common and often fatal. I think salt-water gargle probably was the best preventative, if not cure, for these germs. In those days, before penicillin or sulpha drugs, you either survived and built up a certain natural resistance, or you didn't live through childhood. In our family of eight children, two died — a boy and a girl — before reaching the age of one.

Goose grease and turpentine were also used as an

external treatment for sore throat and colds, rubbed on back, chest, and throat, then covered with a woollen sock. Mustard plasters were made with equal proportions of dry mustard and flour, mixed with water to make a paste and applied to the chest area with muslin. If left on longer than half an hour it resulted in burned skin. I used wool fat (the modern, refined version is lanolin) for many things, including burns, cuts, and abrasions. It was most effective for "pulling" slivers out of my bare feet. I would apply a heavy layer of wool fat and bind it up overnight. In the morning the sliver would be laying in the bandage and the wound healed. My dad always had a large supply of wool fat in eight ounce cans in his shop for treating cuts and infected hooves on horses.

Diarrhea was treated in many ways, including hot coffee with black pepper, or black tea with black pepper. A cup of boiled milk thickened with a little flour, with a pinch of salt and black pepper, was also used. Lewis and Clark reported that on their expedition they brewed tea from spruce needles.

I used milk from milkweed stems for treating warts, I don't remember whether it worked, but one thing that did work was painting the wart with iodine every day until it withered away. There is a sound medical reason for this, of course; a wart is a virus growth, and repeated applications of a strong disinfectant are bound to have some effect.

Messy axle grease could be removed from clothing by rubbing with lots of bacon grease or lard. When the axle grease was removed, strong soap was then used to removed the bacon grease.

Lots of folks, especially on the farm, made their own soap — at least the common laundry soap (this was before detergents). Soap was made from wood ashes, from which lye was extracted by pouring boiling water over them.

A large cast-iron kettle was used, outside over an open wood fire. Animal fat which had been saved was melted down and the ash lye poured over it. As this cooked, the fat rendered and was ladled out into wooden molds to harden. It was then cut into bars with a sharp knife and left to dry for a couple of weeks before using. An entire year's supply could be made, and the soap-making time was usually during or just after butchering time on the farm.

Homemade Soap

You can still make your own soap. Use about 6 cups of tallow, rendered from fat (see tallow making elsewhere in this book), and about 6 ounces of lye, which can be purchased at grocery stores. Dissolve the lye in a glass or plastic container with care — it is *very* caustic. Pour it over the melted fat or tallow. Water causes a chemical action when mixed with lye, so be careful! Stir the cooking fat and lye mixture until thick, using a wooden spoon, then pour out into boxes or flats lined with wax paper. Let stand for a day or so, then cut into bars. This is coarse laundry soap but is very effective for washing clothes. You can use it in a machine by scraping chips and slices and dissolving in water before putting into tub.

Use rubber gloves when handling lye. It any gets on the skin, wash off immediately with cold water. Avoid getting into eye or mouth. Vinegar will help counteract the chemical action of lye.

A good hand soap can also be made the same way — it just takes more refining, and also some perfumes or scents are used. Castile soap, originating in the Castila section of Spain, uses olive oil (olives were a common crop in that region) with tallow. This fine soap is almost impossible to buy these days — you have to make it. Use 26 ounces of olive oil to 60 ounces of refined tallow, 11 ounces of lye, and 32 ounces of water.

The rich, lathery coco-olive oil soap is made with 24 ounces of olive oil, 24 ounces of coconut oil, 38 ounces of refined tallow, 12 ounces of lye, and 32 ounces of water.

A mild soap, used for babies in the old days, was castor oil soap. It is a pale yellow and softer than any of the above but has a rich lather. If you add some vitamin E oil (now admitted by scientists to be a wonder drug in its own right), you will not only scent the soap and disguise the fatty odor but add to its medicinal qualities. Use 9 ounces of caster oil, 22 ounces of olive oil, 22 ounces of coconut oil, 32 ounces of tallow, 11 ounces of lye, and 32 ounces of water.

Mildest of all is vegetable oil soap. It does not use animal fat or tallow but the modern hydrogenated shortening used for cooking, such as Crisco. Use 44 ounces of olive oil, 17 ounces of coconut oil, 24 ounces of shortening, 10 ounces of lye, and 32 ounces of water.

Rose water is often used for scenting hand soaps. Add just enough to bring out a elusive odor.

Recipe For Plowman's Feet

Stumbling behind a walking plow and team of horses was not my idea of Saturday R&R, back in the good old days. It got you right in the feet. Here's how to restore those tired old bones after a long, hard hike, whether or not over a plowed field.

Mix 2 c of apple cider vinegar and 1 gal. of lukewarm (or slightly warmer) water in a basin. You might also spike it with ½ t of Purex or Clorox. Put feet in gently, wiggle toes, and lean back in your rocking chair, relax, take frequent sips of hot toddy, and exhale, "ah-ah-ah-ah!"

When water gets cold, pat feet dry, then rub briskly and massage with baby oil.

Garlic, the Natural Miracle Plant

When I was a kid in Velva, North Dakota, many of our neighbors were immigrants from Eastern Europe. I grew up with their kids, who were so thoroughly Americanized that even they referred to the old folks as "garlic snappers."

This was because old country cooking was liberally spiced with garlic in one form or another. The reason was not only for the flavor and gourmet properties but because garlic was and is the ancient cure-all. Garlic is known and used by almost every ethnic society around the world. It is a staple not only of fine European cooking but also of the best in the Orient and Middle East. The Chinese are probably the greatest garlic cooks; they use it in almost all their dishes.

Medicinally, garlic is claimed to prevent high blood pressure and heart disease, to prevent hay fever, ward off influenza, cure warts, and even protect you from insects. During a wide epidemic of influenza in Moscow, it is said, the spread of the disease was prevented by consuming tons of garlic flown in by air. Scoffers say the reason it worked was that those who did not have the flu kept their distance from those who used garlic, thus avoiding exposure to the germs. Scientists at the University of California, it is claimed, were successful in killing five species of mosquitoes using a crude garlic extract. Dogs have a great affinity for garlic, seemingly having an instinct for its wondrous properties.

German Garlic Pot Meal

3 slices bacon
10 oz. cut green beans, fresh
½ t salt
pepper to taste
1 c sliced onion
⅓ c water
3 c shredded cabbage
chopped garlic to taste

Saute bacon until crisp. Remove, drain, and crumble. Saute onion in bacon fat. Add beans, garlic, water, and salt. Cover and simmer 5 minutes. Add cabbage, cover once more, and simmer 5 more minutes. Season to taste and sprinkle with bacon bits. Serves 4.

A recent news item from Gilroy, California, reports that garlic-bulb snatchers stole more than 5,000 pounds of garlic from one grower's field. He was forced to hire security guards to protect the crop, one of the most valuable for the produce market — so valuable, in fact, that poachers will risk jail to steal the bulbs. Local Gilroy growers were reported to be considering a vigilante committee to deal with bulb snatchers in the same way that cattle rustlers were handled in the old days.

Also, in the largest study of garlic ever conducted, according to *Organic Gardening* magazine, Japanese medical scientists tested deodorized garlic extract on more than 1,000 patients at twenty-five hospitals and found a marked improvement in ailments such as neuralgia, heart and liver diseases, digestive problems, fatigue, aching joints, chills, and anorexia. Research in India showed that garlic effectively breaks up fibrin in blood vessels, a form of heart defect.

Stalking The Wild Mushroom

Wild mushrooms are a real treat — but also a real danger to amateurs who are not trained in identifying the edible from the toxic species.

Nevertheless, mushroom hunting has become a popular spring and autumn outdoor activity, and once you have been involved you'll look forward to going again. Stalking the wily mushroom is a lot of fun and can be enjoyed by the whole family, regardless of age or physical condition.

Mushrooms are a fungus and are found almost everywhere, even in the backyard, the school playground, fields, meadows, swamps, along country roads, or deep in the forest. They are especially noticeable after a warm rain, when they spring up seemingly from nowhere.

Some so-called foolproof ways of identifying edible mushrooms have been bandied about, but experts say these tests are not good ones. Even some edible ones can cause violent reactions — when taken with alcohol, for example. Amateurs should never attempt identification on their own. Go with an expert, or consult the local mycological society, of which there is one in every state. Often these societies hold public exhibits and fairs featuring local varieties of mushrooms.

One of the most popular of the edible mushrooms is the morel. This is a distinctive variety shaped something like a tall ice-cream cone, with a top that looks like a brain. There is no other variety that looks like the morel, so identification is easy. Morels grow in many places, on mountainsides and on islands or lowlands of river valleys, usually in groves of deciduous trees such as oak or maples or cottonwood. They grow in little colonies, suddenly popping up through the leaves after a warm rain. They should be harvested when young and tender, using a knife to cut off the stalk as close to the ground as possible. Never pull up a morel; this destroys the plant. If cut off, the morel will sprout again and again.

Gather them in pails and handle gently. To prepare, split them in two down the middle, wash well in cold water, and blanch. Deep-fry them in a suitable batter. Serve with a sauce. They can be frozen in plastic bags after cleaning and blanching and cooked later at your convenience.

Part Two

Summertime

Jack brought his wife and new baby home, and he and Maud set about farming in earnest. They fenced off the wild plum thicket which proliferated to the southwest of the cabin, protecting that most desirable resource from the depredations of roaming livestock. They planted crabapple trees and hardy apples, hoping that the shelter of the deep coulee would protect them from the freezing winds of winter. Hopefully, again, they planted gooseberry bushes, asparagus, rhubarb, horseradish — all food plants hardy enough to withstand the bitter weather. They worked up a large vegetable garden and planted the rich, black loam."

May Shipton Girard, *The Cruel Cold Land**

---

*Portland, 1980. *The Metropolitan Press.*

— 1 —

Signs of Summer

• When hay in the fields leans to the northeast, summer will be long and hot.

• Thunderstorms that come before 7 A.M. in April or May mean a long wet summer.

• A dry summer will follow a winter with few storms and blizzards.

In the summer of 1961 I returned to Velva on impulse for the 50th anniversary of our high school — a homecoming for every class that had graduated, all fifty of them, 1911 through 1961. Out of a total of about 1,500, an astonishing 800 or so showed for the weeklong festivities. With family members, the number of returnees far exceeded the town's permanent population. Of my class of '36, at least 16 returned. The entire class of 1911 was there — all two of them, both named Ruth!

The story of the reunion itself, which I produced in a book later at the insistence of the alumni committee,* has no place here, except to make a point or two about America and some little-realized elements that led to its becoming a great and dynamic nation.

Among the old grads of Velva were doctors, ministers, lawyers, judges, engineers, generals and admirals, inventors, musicians, stars of stage and screen, high and low government and political leaders, philosophers, industrialists, financiers, scientists (including one Nobel Prize winner), a medical researcher famed for cancer studies, a nuclear physicist, one of the inventors of the transistor,

---

**Reunion Summer*, Portland, 1965.

one who developed some of the components on the first spaceship to the moon, explorers, educators, and just plain folk, including authors.

They came from every state in the Union and a dozen foreign countries. One flew in from Calcutta just for the homecoming, another from Brazil, and so on.

Most of them still had families in North Dakota, descendants of the great waves of immigration in the middle and late nineteenth century and first two decades of the twentieth. These people had come from almost every country in the world seeking peace, opportunity, and freedom — and maybe a few were looking for adventure. They took up land on the treeless prairies and put down roots in the rich glacial loam, breaking the sod of ancient grasslands. They were lured there by the prospect of filing homesteads and buying cheap railroad grant lands — and the dream of every man becoming a squire or baron of all he surveyed. Soon they were producing not only the crops that made North Dakota the breadbasket of the world but kids, a surplus of kids, who in turn had to leave their homes and go out into the world to meet their individual destinies. Some of them made their way successfully indeed.

It is remarkable how the little obscure town of Velva, a village of about eight hundred souls at the southern bend of the Mouse River, in almost the exact center of the North American continent, could produce and send out so many to enrich the nation. This was true not just of Velva. It was a phenomenon of most small towns that were close to the soil, where times were often hard and kids acquired the work ethic early in life.

The contribution and influence of rural America in the growth and development of the nation is incalculable. But it is a heritage to be proud of.

The Westering America

Another phenomenon, or perhaps just a unique characteristic of America, was that the movement of people and economic and social dynamics was from East to West, from the Atlantic seaboard to the Pacific Ocean. This westering instinct was remarked upon by such perspective European observers as de Toqueville in the 1700s and Lord Brice in the 1800s, both of whom traveled extensively in the young United States. This westward expansion was mostly by railroads, which were given enormous grants of land to induce them to penetrate and open up the frontier. To a lesser extent, river transportation played an important role. For example, the most dependable means of hauling freight, people, and stock to North Dakota in the middle and late 1800s was by Missouri and Red River paddlewheelers. The campaign against the Sioux and related tribes in the 1870s was supplied logistically by steamboats that ran all the way up to the Bighorn in Montana. The dead and wounded from the Custer Massacre were brought down to Bismarck on one of these boats. My Great Uncle Ezra rode west to join the Seventh Cavalry on one, and my father first saw the homestead lands along the Missouri from the deck of a riverboat.

When the railroads pushed westward they crossed Dakota Territory and the central plains of Kansas, Nebraska and Oklahoma, with their twin iron rails being laid on rough-cut ties at almost the speed of the old covered oxen wagons. The rail lines were roughly 50 to 100 miles apart in a north-south direction, and from the main lines the tentacles of branch lines tapped large areas in between. At the same time the federal government, through the Homestead Acts, offered settlers the opportunity to file on 160-acre plots, which, when proved up by five years of theoretical occupation and cultivation, became theirs upon payment of a small filing fee. The railroads enhanced this by great advertising campaigns in the East and in Europe, often indulging in full-blown hyperbole — as is the nature of promotional advertising. As a result, eager settlers poured in with bag and baggage, belongings and machinery, bringing their kids, their heirlooms, and their native customs.

Dakota Territory — and other regions of the Midwest — became melting pots of many nationalities and religions. In North Dakota — it was Scandinavian, and Northern European, Icelandic, and Irish Catholic — and to some extent Italian and Balkan and Mennonite and Caspian, as well as second generation Americans from the Atlantic seaboard. First explored by French-Canadian fur traders in the early 1700s, Dakota country was an important primitive entrepôt long before there was a United States. This resulted in an indigenous group of mixed Indians and French-Canadians known as the *Metis*, who were probably the first to farm the lands, and who were mostly assimilated by the incoming railroad immigrants.

The lines of transportation and communication were east to west. North-south movement was — until the development of air transportation — difficult and expensive, if not impossible. Even roads and highways, to this very day, are best going east or west and less convenient going north or south.

When I was a kid, what citrus fruit we had came from California or Florida; apples, pears, and peaches came from Oregon and Washington. One of my fondest memories was going down to the railroad yard with the wagon, where, parked on the siding, were refrigerator cars full of delicious, juicy Pacific Northwest apples. Dad would select and purchase several boxes of Jonathans, Rome Beauties, and Golden Delicious for fall eating and winter pies and sauces.

North Dakota was not a ideal fruit-growing region because of the short season and the cold winters. Most settlers still brought in seedlings and graftings of various kinds, but the most successful appeared to be crabapples and plums. This seems logical, since the prairie coulees were usually choked with wild plum, crabapple, chokecherries, Juneberries, wild black currants, wild grapes, buffalo berries, and wild raspberries. Most families supplemented their garden produce with wild fruits and berries. In my youth I came in for a lot of picking expeditions, especially for chokecherries, which made the finest jellies and jams ever to top a buttered biscuit. When picking chokecherries we carried a lard pail hanging from the belt, and with two hands stripped the ripe, reddish black berries from the long panicles. Every other handful went into the mouth instead of the pail so that at the end of the day our face and hands were smeared a bilious purple.

All the wild fruits and berries had a characteristic tartness that resulted from the struggle for survival in the harsh environment, and it was this tartness and delicate, fragile flavor that made them so delicious and precious.

— 3 —

Summertime Living

Summertime living meant hot weather, long days, short periods of darkness, bugs and insects, and hours of hard work to accomplish everything that could not be done in the winter. It meant Saturday night barn dances in the country, Sunday church picnics in the riverbank parks, ice cream socials, baseball games, swimming in the sluggish Mouse, maybe Boy Scout camp on Lake Metigoshe, or fishing for walleyes and crappies at Strawberry Lake. It meant churning ice cream by hand in wooden tubs filled with ice sprinkled with rock salt; the ice was cut from Downing's Creek in winter and stored under mounds of sawdust in the barn until summer. It meant going barefooted and wearing bib overalls with nothing underneath.

Meals tended to be light, more frequent, with emphasis on fruits, vegetables, and fresh berries; on cold cuts of pork, beef, chicken, and turkey; on smorgasbords, iced tea, lemonade, garden salads, and boiled new potatoes with skins on.

When the wheat began to ripen the early harvest began. At first we cut and shocked bundles to be picked up later by the threshing-crew rigs. When combines were developed, the wheat was left standing in the fields longer to ripen, and the tedious shocking of bundles was eliminated, although shocking was a time when kids could make some cash money. We used to go from farm to farm to help — and to partake of the bountiful fare the farm gals provided. Shocking bundles was done mostly by kids, and often it was a lark that also put some money in your pocket.

Summer was also a time for making home brew and dandelion wine and doing a little bootlegging at the barn dances. And a time for excursions to other small towns and camp-outs in the old Chevrolet touring car.

Fruit Trees Earn Their Keep

Many things have changed over the years, but in a few cases not much. One of these is the availability of fruits and berries fresh off the trees and bushes. Farm and roadside markets dot the countryside everywhere, and most city supermarkets have extensive produce departments. U-pick fields surround most towns and cities. Exotic varieties from across the sea and from other regions are plentiful and readily available. The potential for enjoying such fresh foods is much better than it was during my youth.

In addition, anyone who has a backyard or a small plot of ground he can call his own, even temporarily, can grow his own fresh fruits and berries and enjoy wholesomeness and a much better quality than the store-bought kind — to say nothing of having them virtually free for the picking, rather than shelling out high prices at the market.

I have a friend who will not allow any tree or plant in his yard that does not earn its keep. With a small city lot, he has dwarf fruit trees loaded down all summer with apples, peaches, pears, apricots, and plums; several kinds of luscious berries; as well as a garden that provides almost all his fresh vegetables. And he doesn't have any grass to mow.

You can do the same.

Fruit Yield Chart

Kind	Age to Bear	Typical Yield
Regular apples	2 to 7 years	4 to 6 bushels
Dwarf apples	2 years	1 to 2 bushels
Apricots	3 years	2 to 4 bushels
Blackberries	1 year	3 quarts
Blueberries	1 to 2 years	12 to 20 pints
Cherries	2 to 3 years	8 to 12 gallons
Grapes	2 years	12 to 20 pounds
Plums	2 to 3 years	8 to 10 gallons
Rhubarb	2 years	3 to 4 bushels
Strawberries	1 year	1 quart

The yield chart shows the typical results that can be expected from average trees and plants. Other varieties have similar yields. Once started, the tending needed is negligible, and the only work is the picking come harvest time. In terms of dollars, the savings are dramatic; in terms of satisfaction and nutritious quality, the results are beyond calculation.

No matter where you live, there are fruits and berries suited for your locality which can be obtained from local nurseries and garden stores or from mail order catalogs. I even planted some good old North Dakota chokecherry and prairie plum trees on our place at Cape George overlooking the Strait of Juan de Fuca.

The Lowly Lovely Tomato

Tomatoes are not hard to grow but do require tender, loving care — at least until they get started right. They can be raised from seed on the sunny side of the house, but most folks start the seeds inside in pots or egg cartons and then set out the young plants as soon as the earth is warm and the season well established. From then on its a matter of proper pruning, watering, weeding, and training the exuberant growth, once you have selected the best varieties for your locality.

One year ours got a late start, and it was a cool, rainy summer. The poor tomatoes never did get ripe. Some of them were picked, wrapped in foil and brought into the house. In no time at all they ripened nicely. Most amazing was the discovery that green tomatoes are even more versatile than ripe ones. You can not only use them in salads but can also freeze, dry, or can them for later use. You can make green tomato butter, marmalade, preserves, mincemeat, pickles, and chowchow; broil and fry them in rings, stew them, bake them, make croquettes, use them in spinach and cheese loafs, casseroles, omelets, meat pies, and dozens of other goodies.

Here is a golden oldie that has delighted many generations:

Charbonneau's Chowchow

1 peck green tomatoes
6 peppers, red or green
salt
1 small cabbage
6 onions

Mince tomatoes and sprinkle handfuls of salt over

them. Let stand overnight and in the morning drain in a sack. Next make the syrup:

2 qts. vinegar **4½ lbs. sugar**
1 pkg. mustard seed

Mix and boil 7 minutes, add the chow mixture and boil 10 minutes more. Use scalded mason jars and seal hot.

Ripe tomatoes also are versatile and can not only be used in salads and sandwiches but made into delicious soups, stews, preserves, and relishes. A relish that goes well with hamburgers and can even be eaten alone comes from this old farm recipe:

Picnic Tomato Relish

24 large ripe tomatoes **12 large white onions**
8 large red or green peppers **3 T salt**
8 c vinegar **1 c brown sugar**

Grind peppers, mix all ingredients together, and boil until thick, about 4 hours. Can use raisins in the mix, too.

Hot Weather Aspic

Not many cooks bother with tomato aspic now, but it used to be popular with farm gals when too many had been picked for immediate use.

1½ envelope gelatine **1½ c boiling water**
¾ c sugar **½ c vinegar**
2 c tomato juice strained **salt**
stuffed olives (optional)

Dissolve gelatine in the vinegar, add sugar and salt, stir boiling water into mix; then add tomato juice and maybe some stuffed olives. Serve up a spoonful on a fresh lettuce leaf and see if you don't exclaim with delight.

*Myrtle's Green Tomato Marmalade**

2 qt. small green tomatoes, sliced
4 lemons, peeled, save rind
½ t salt
4 c sugar

Combine tomatoes, salt, chopped lemon rind. Cover with water and boil 10 minutes. Drain. Slice peeled lemons very thin, discard seeds, save the juice. Add to the tomatoes with the sugar. Stir over moderate heat until sugar dissolves. Bring to a boil, reduce heat and simmer until thick, or about 45 minutes, stirring. Seal in hot sterilized jars. Add ½ pkg. of pectin if desired.

*Myrtle's Scalloped Green Tomatoes**

2 medium green tomatoes, sliced
1 ripe tomato, chopped
1 c dried bread crumbs
salt and pepper
1 chopped onion
2 T brown sugar
1 T butter or margarine
½ c evaporated milk

Slice green tomatoes very thin. Combine with onion, ripe tomato, and condiments and cook covered in saucepan for 5 minutes, jiggling pan frequently. Put half of crumbs in buttered baking dish. Spoon tomato mixture over crumbs. Stir rest of crumbs in melted butter or margarine and spread over top. Bake at 400 degrees for 10 to 15 minutes or until brown.

Plowin' Time Tomato Soup

Real tomato soup cannot be bought, especially in cans. There is only one way to get the pure quill — the way the country gals used to make it.

1 bunch celery
6 large onions
1 peck ripe tomatoes
¼ c sugar
½ c flour
1 doz. whole cloves
2 green peppers
½ c butter
¼ c salt
seasonings to taste

Cook tomatoes until tender, strain, and mix with rest of ingredients. Boil 10 minutes and serve piping hot.

Tomato Juice Cocktail

4 c tomatoes
¼ c celery tops
¼ t Worcestershire
⅛ t pepper
4 or 5 cloves
1 c water
1 t salt
2 t lemon juice
1 T sugar
5 drops Tabasco

Mix all ingredients except lemon juice and boil slowly for 20 minutes. Strain through sieve, add the lemon juice, and chill before serving.

Northern Lights Cocktail

3 c tomato juice
1 small onion
1 t sugar
¼ t paprika
3 T lemon juice
4 whole cloves
4 celery leaves
1 t salt
¼ t grated lemon rind

Combine and simmer 5 minutes covered. Strain, cool, freeze like sherbert, serve in cocktail glasses. We used to set it out in a snowbank. you may use your fridge if you don't have snow.

Baked Tomato Cups

6 large tomatoes
2 T chopped parsley
1 c dry bread crumbs
½ t salt
1 c buttered bread crumbs
6 strips bacon
1 T chopped onion
¼ t celery salt
⅛ t pepper

Slice stem end of washed tomato, spoon out pulp to leave an unbroken shell. Saute bacon until crisp, break into small pieces. Add onion and parsley to fat and cook 3 minutes, adding cup of dry bread crumbs, celery salt, salt and pepper, bacon bits, and tomato pulp, mixing well. Fill the tomato shells with mixture and cover with buttered bread crumbs. Bake in shallow dish at 325 degrees until tomatoes are tender and crumbs are golden brown. Serve hot in the baking dish.

Old-Fashioned Green Tomato Preserves

2 qt. small green tomatoes
¼ lemon, sliced
½ t cinnamon
3 c sugar
½ t dry ginger

Clean and peel tomatoes, leave stem ends; cover with boiling water and then bring to a boil and drain. Sprinkle with sugar, set aside to cool. Add lemon slices and condiments. Boil until the tomatoes get glassy; let stand overnight. Pack in sterilized jars. Reheat the syrup, strain and pour over. Seal and process 15 minutes in hot water bath.

Breaded Tomatoes on the Side

For each quart of tomatoes:

½ c sugar
3 slices bread
pinch of salt
pepper

Mix all but bread and bring to a boil, stirring well. Turn heat down low. Pull 3 slices of bread into pieces and stir into the mixture. Cover and hold hot until ready to eat as a side dish.

Old Yaller Tomato Preserves

For each pound of yellow tomatoes:

¾ c water
½ lemon, sliced thin
¾ lb. sugar
1 small pinch ginger

Yellow tomatoes have a flavor and taste all their own. Bring to a rolling boil and continue for 2 minutes. Pour into scalded mason jars and seal.

*Tomato Mincemeat**

Slice some green tomatoes and sprinkle well with salt. Put into a bag and hang up to drip all night. Do not wash off salt. In morning take equal parts of sugar and tomatoes and cook until thoroughly done. To 7 lbs. of tomato mixture add 3 lbs. of seedless raisins and mace and cinnamon to taste. Cook a short time and put into jars. Need not be sealed.

*Myrtle's Chowchow**

1 small head cabbage
5 or 6 large onions
green tomatoes
brown sugar, vinegar, spices

Chop equal amounts of cabbage and green tomatoes, add chopped onions, and soak overnight in salt water. Drain in morning and add some brown sugar, vinegar and spices to suit. Boil 15 minutes.

Nest in the Garden of Eden

1½ c milk
1½ c fresh tomatoes, diced
2 c grated cheese
poached eggs
1½ c corn kernels
2 T butter
salt, pepper, paprika

Mix and heat in double boiler, cooking and stirring constantly until cheese is melted. Season with salt, pepper, and paprika. Serve on toasted garlic or melted butter sourdough or French bread. Top each slice with a poached egg.

Chokecherries — Fruit of the Gods

Readers may think the frequent references to chokecherries in this book unusual and puzzling, but it is only because this wild berry is much prized by those who grew up where it was common — and because more people are discovering that this shrub can be planted and raised in the backyard to provide a most versatile and delicious fruit for preserves, jelly, and wine. Improved varieties of chokecherry are available from most nurseries in the Midwest, and the plant will grow practically anywhere any other berry is successful.

Memories of picking wild chokecherries and other wild fruit in my boyhood have never left me. I especially remember the superb chokecherry jelly and jams, unmatched in my opinion by any other. Since most of my later life has been spent on the rainy side of the Pacific Coast mountains, I had long given up hope of ever again tasting chokecherry jelly on hot buttered sourdough biscuits. Then one day one of my readers, who happened to work in the composing room of my newspaper, read one of my nostalgia columns and dropped by my desk with a large sack filled with the biggest, juiciest chokecherries I had ever seen. Where did he get them? Why, he said, there were two big trees in the backyard of a house he had just bought in Gresham. He hadn't known what they were until that summer, when the blossoms set into a berry he had never seen before. A neighbor from North Dakota identified them as chokecherries.

For the next several years, in late summer he would bring me a couple of gallons of his chokecherries. I would return the favor by bringing him a fresh Chinook salmon caught out of the ocean. I think I got the best of the deal. After moving to the Quimper Peninsula on the Strait of Juan de Fuca, the first thing I did in the yard of our Cape George home was plant a couple of chokecherry trees obtained from a South Dakota mail order nursery.

The fruit usually ripens about late August, and you must protect the berries from birds, who also love them. The berries grow in clusters on a stem. You pick them by grabbing the stem and stripping the berries into a pail. They can be eaten when ripe but are quite tart and have large seeds. Also the juice stains the teeth and lips! At home, put the berries in a large kettle and cover with water. Bring to a slow boil for 20 minutes. Empty into a clean cloth bag and twist to extract the juice. A steam juicer can also be used. If making jam, save the pulp; for jelly, hotcake syrup, or wine-making, use just the juice. Proceed from there in the usual way, depending upon what you want to make.

— 7 —

The Egg and Me

Everyone has his prejudices and partialities. When it comes to food I'm partial to eggs in any form, shape, or size — while my bride, who was also born and raised on a farm, can hardly stand the sight of an egg, except when used as an ingredient in a recipe.

I think I came by my love for eggs when I was a young lad. One of my playmates, Milo Holstein, lived with an unmarried aunt in a cozy cottage on the edge of Wildwoods. I never knew what happened to Milo's parents, only that he was raised by his spinster aunt, a hard-working, gentle but shy woman, tall and skinny as a rail, who never stopped to rest. She was always busy, hoeing the garden, milking the cows, caring for the chickens. In fact, her place was a small chicken farm, and the hen house was almost as big as the cottage. She raised Rhode Island Reds, a good producer of big brown "farm eggs" and also a fine meat bird with an average weight of about six pounds.

We used to buy eggs from her, which she delivered fresh about once a week on her rounds. "Auntie" seemed to like me, and when I showed an interest in her chickens she gave me a setting hen and some fertile eggs. I made a nest of an old apple crate inside the back shed and kept some grain and water handy so the hen would not have to go far from the nest. For the next three weeks I looked in on her about twenty times a day. Finally I was rewarded by the first "peep peep" of a chick. I raised her gently from the nest to see a half-dozen little ones, just out of the shell and shivering in the cold, cruel world. I was elated. I had created life. It was a lesson I had learned myself and which I never forgot.

Eight of the dozen settin' eggs hatched out, which was about average, and five survived to become pullets and young roosters. I kept the pullets for laying hens, and we enjoyed Sunday dinners of fryers as long as they lasted. The next year I sent off to Arkansas and got fifteen certified, purebred Buff Orphington setting eggs. When they arrived I put them under my old Rhode Island Red hen, a wonderful "mother." She took to the eggs immediately, being just barely big enough to cover all fifteen eggs. She hatched an incredible twelve chicks, and a healthier bunch I have never seen before or after. The buffs grew fast, and, since they were allowed the range of the yard and garden and not cooped up in a pen, they benefitted to the fullest. All of these chickens grew to be big, fat, and healthy, but the best of the lot had to be one particular hen and one of the roosters. You never saw such magnificent birds. The rooster was two or three times the size of the average hen, erect, proud, and with golden iridescent feathers and rich, blood red comb. I mated him with the best hen, who was an ideal match — big, sure of step, and a fluffy golden tan color. That fall I entered the pair in the state fair in Minot and won the blue ribbon for best of show. The following year I still had them, and they won the best of breed.

My chickens were also good egg producers as well as for meat; the breed is known as "dual purpose" chicken. The hens would lay one big egg every other day or so, starting when they were about five months old. I always kept a couple of the best roosters for breeding stock and let them roam at will with the hens. This makes for the best and most nutritious eggs — but does not work for eggs to be stored. To store a winter's supply of fresh eggs I would separate the hens and roosters until I had enough eggs immersed in water glass to fill a big twenty gallon crock in the basement.

I sold the surplus eggs at the grocery store (in competition with Auntie), but we seldom had much surplus. The store eggs had to be candled to cull out the fertile ones, that is, the ones with little specks of blood in them. I candled eggs by holding them up to a light bulb. Fertile eggs are just as good to eat, but the sight of blood specks in the yolk repels most people. Fastidious cooks will always break eggs in a separate bowl. If a bloody one is found (a rare instance nowadays with store-bought eggs) it can be separated or the bloody speck carefully removed.

When recipes call for separate egg yolk or egg white, the usual way is to break the shell, hold one half-shell in one hand and the other half in the other hand and carefully transfer from one to the other over a bowl. The white or the yolk will gradually separate and fall into the bowl. You can also buy a gismo called an egg separator in stores that handle kitchenware. Another way is to use a large, slotted serving ladle, which holds the yolk while the white slips through. Another trick is to hold an egg under warm, running water from the faucet for a few moments. When the egg is broken, the white will run away cleanly from the yolk.

When beating egg whites, a pinch of cream of tartar or salt seems to make them fluff up better.

Although the egg has received bad publicity from alarmists in the medical profession, it is one of the most perfect foods — rich, nutritious, plentiful, versatile, and economical. Dollar for dollar and penny for penny you won't find a better buy in your grocery store. In my opinion the only ones who suffer from eggs are those who market them for a living. It takes a lot of expensive feed to produce a dozen eggs. In times when eggs are plentiful, often as not the grower does not make enough to pay the overhead. If you have room, and the local housing laws do not forbid it, you can raise your own chickens for meat and eggs.

There are literally hundreds of ways to cook eggs, such as Benedictine, Buckingham, goldenrod, a la reine, a la Lee, aux fines herbes, dozens of kinds of omelets, baked, scrambled, deviled, poached, in eggnog, boiled (hard or soft), and, of course, fried. Practically every pastry recipe calls for either the white or the yolk of an egg, often both.

Eggs were the mainstay of every breakfast when I was growing up, and we often had them for dinner or supper. Most often it was fried eggs, with bacon or ham if we had either, and always with fried potatoes. Eggs were fried in a wide, deep cast-iron skillet into which, when hot, was placed a chunk of lard or shortening. The eggs were carefully broken into the skillet one at a time so they did not touch or run together. Usually the pan was hot enough that the moment the egg touched the metal, the running stopped and the egg cooked in a nice round mound with the yolk unbroken. My mother would usually spoon a few drippings onto the top, especially if bacon was used for shortening, or carefully turn the eggs over just before serving to crisp the tops. I preferred to use a lid over the pan to steam the tops and not to turn them over, while my brothers always wanted the yolks broken and then turned over.

In the case of fried eggs, it was to each his own. I always seasoned my eggs after they were cooked and ready to serve, with salt and pepper and a dash of oregano or tarragon. They were served with bacon or ham and the fried potatoes. (These were cold boiled potatoes sliced for frying. If raw potatoes were used they were sliced very thin and browned on both sides quickly before the eggs were cooked.) I liked toast with my eggs, too, spread heavy with butter and topped with a generous pile of chokecherry jelly or wild plum jam. Usually for breakfast we had coffee for the grownups and milk or cocoa for the kids. If my mother thought we looked kind of poorly she would also serve us a dish of stewed prunes. Frequently we had a bowl of oatmeal, too, but I didn't care too much about mush.

When we were sick, the only food we got was poached egg on toast with a bowl of hot milk on the side. Sometimes my sickbed meal would be very-soft-boiled eggs, well seasoned, with a chunk of melted butter on top, and hot buttered toast.

We almost always had a whole hog and a half of beef, butchered in the fall after freeze-up and hung in the back stoop off the kitchen — nature's own deep freeze — and we literally ate high off the hog all winter. By break-up in the spring, however, most of it would be gone, and we'd be down to salt pork. Salt pork was always parboiled the evening before using and drained all night. At breakfast my mother would put on the big cast-iron skillet with a clump of lard, dip pieces of salt pork in flour and toss them into the pan. It was fried slowly to brown it crisp but not burn. While this was going on the coffee was made, the sourdough bread warmed and sliced, the eggs prepared, and often some previously boiled cold potatoes sliced up for frying. Maybe a bowl of stewed prunes or apricots was warmed up and the toast begun. With this lash-up, poached eggs were the usual fare. The eggs were poached in a pan with just enough simmering water to "float" them — never boiling water, which tended to shatter the broken egg. When the white part was done, the egg was removed with a slotted spoon.

Hard-boiled eggs were most often used for snacks or picnics, eaten cold. Breakfast eggs were always soft-boiled, about 5 minutes in a rolling boil. The problem with eating soft-boiled eggs is that they are too hot to handle when taken from the water and require a certain technique. I learned to put the egg in a saucer, hold it with the end of a napkin to keep it from slipping, and crack the shell sharply with a knife edge without breaking the yolk. Then, carefully pulling the shell away from the egg, I could slide the yolk and most of the white into the dish. With a knife I scraped the two halves of the shell to get the rest of the egg out. In a saucedish, I then crunched up and mixed the egg with a chunk of butter and salt and pepper. I could eat a dozen this way but usually had to stop with four or five. Served with toast and homemade jam or jelly, this made a fine meal that stuck to the ribs but didn't make you feel bloated and uncomfortable the first hour or two of doing the morning chores.

The next most popular way of cooking eggs in our house was scrambled — the old-fashioned way. Here again a cast-iron skillet was heated while the eggs were cracked into a separate bowl. Bacon grease or lard was dropped into the skillet and allowed to spread around until it began to smoke. Then the eggs, which had been stirred with a fork, were poured slowly into the skillet. While cooking, the eggs were again stirred with the fork, swirling them around as they stiffened. When the yolks and whites were marbleized, they were ready to eat They were usually served with hot biscuits, butter, and chokecherry or wild plum jelly, and sometimes with hot maple syrup.

Don's Omelet

My own specialty was the omelet, and my bride tells me that I still swing a mean spatula when it comes to whipping up a tasty omelet on a cold winter evening when we want a quick and easy meal before settling down to relax.

Here's how I do it:

Break 3 or 4 eggs into a bowl. With fork gently whip the eggs, adding a half-shell full of water for each egg. (Never use milk; it curdles.) As I whip the mixture into a frothy state, I add by guess and by God, from instinct or from long experience, a dash of oregano, a pinch of garlic powder, a shake of onion salt, a shake or two of Tabasco or maybe Worcestershire, black pepper, a little chive, maybe chervil, and a couple of flakes of parsley.

Meanwhile, in an omelet pan (if possible the kind that is hinged so one-half can be closed over the other) I put a big chunk of butter and let it warm on a medium stove. While this is going on I cut up cheese into small chunks (always yellow cheese, never white) or ready some bacon bits that have been previously browned. When all this is ready and the pan is beginning to smoke from the melted butter, I gently pour in the egg mixture so that it spreads evenly over the bottom of the pan (half in each side if using the hinged omelet pan). Watching closely, I break the bubbles with a fork and allow the eggs to spread down to the bottom of the pan. I run a plastic spatula around the outside to fold back the cooked part and let the uncooked mixture run down to the pan. Meanwhile I have dropped in the cheese chunks or bacon bits. When almost cooked, with no obvious runny parts, I flip the hinged half of the pan over and let cook for a minute or so to brown the omelet on both sides. If not using a hinged pan, simply and carefully with a broad spatula fold one-half of the omelet back over the other and brown.

Country Golden Rod

A favorite in most country kitchens is the Golden Rod egg:

4 hard-cooked eggs
2 T butter
salt and pepper
2 cups milk
3 T flour

Separate yolks from whites. Dice the whites. Make a white sauce with butter, flour, milk, salt, and pepper. Add diced egg whites and serve on toast. Garnish with grated egg yolks which have been pushed through a strainer. This serves about 6.

Ranch-Style Bacon Omelet

½ c diced bacon
1 c mashed potatoes
2 T milk
½ t salt
⅛ t pepper
1 t baking powder
4 well-beaten egg yolks
4 stiff-beaten egg whites

Fry bacon in iron skillet. Remove and pour off excess bacon drippings. Mix mashed potatoes, milk, baking powder, seasoning, and egg yolks. Fold in egg whites and pour into hot skillet. Sprinkle bacon bits over top. Cook over low heat until fluffy and browned, folding over to brown both sides. Garnish with parsley. Serves 4.

Prairie Baked Eggs

Break 6 eggs into a buttered baking dish. Cover with bread crumbs and then cream. Season well with salt and pepper and drop spoonsful of butter on top. Bake for 20 minutes. Serve piping hot.

Harvest Cookshack Eggs

6 strips chopped bacon
1 t salt
pepper
1 c bread crumbs
½ c milk
5 beaten eggs

Fry bacon crisply and remove from skillet. Add bread crumbs and crisp them until brown, then remove. Add milk and seasonings to eggs and scramble in the bacon drippings. Add bacon bits and crumbs when nearly done. Serves 6.

Old-Fashioned Deviled Eggs

6 eggs
1 T cream
⅛ t pepper
1 T salad dressing
¼ t salt
paprika

Boil eggs for 10 minutes, cool, then shell and cut in half lengthwise. Mash the yolks. Mix dressing, cream, and seasonings, and fold into egg yolks. Put this mixture back into the egg white halves and sprinkle with paprika. Serve as snacks.

Dainty Eggs

6 slightly beaten eggs
¾ t salt
6 slices crisp toast
⅓ c coffee cream
⅛ t pepper

Mix the eggs, seasoning, and cream. Cook in a double boiler until set. stirring frequently. Serve on the buttered toast. Serves 4.

Easter Eggs

No discussion of eggs would be best served without mentioning Easter eggs. These were always made in our house the day before Easter. On the prairies, spring was just beginning to stir, the pussy willows beginning to bud, and the crocuses pushing up through scattered patches of old snow. The ice was going out on the creeks where exposed to the sun. Honkers and sandhill cranes were beginning to wing northward across the sky in huge Vs.

My mother started early in the morning, with a huge kettle of water in which 2 or 3 dozen eggs were put to boil until real hard, about 20 minutes. Meanwhile, some bowls were collected (one for each color of dye) and filled with hot water into which the dye was mixed, along with a teaspoon of vinegar.

The eggs were next lifted carefully out of the boiling water with a big slotted spoon and lowered into a bowl of dye until the color took, then removed to a towel on the table to dry. Sometimes a dry egg would be lowered partway into a bowl of another color for a two-toned job.

This was all there was to it, except that the eggs were collected in big bowls to decorate the buffet. Sometime during the night they would disappear, and at first light on Easter morning we kids would jump out of bed and go hunting for the Easter Bunny and his eggs.

No one ever explained to me satisfactorily, how come bunny rabbits can lay eggs — especially colored ones?

P.S. Once all the eggs were collected, my mom took them to the kitchen and deviled them.

Summer Is Time for Salads

By the time school lets out in June, the first rewards from the spring planting are beginning to appear in the form of early vegetables, especially the leafy ones. Needless to say, there is no salad like a salad fresh from the garden, even with a speck of clean rich earth on it, merely rinsed under cold, clean water.

Even the most confirmed meat-and-potatoes eater will succumb to these crisp, summery recipes.

Tips for Saladiers

• To separate head lettuce, cut out core and run cold water into center.

• Lettuce is a base for most salads. If leaf is flat, split and lap over.

• Marinate cooked vegetables in French dressing for 1 hour to improve flavor.

• Fruits and vegetables should be thoroughly drained before using.

• Greens should be patted dry on towel after washing.

• Vary greens used. In addition to head and leaf lettuce, try endive, romaine, watercress, and what-have-you.

• Always use fresh crisp greens.

• Never *stir* salad ingredients; *toss* onto lettuce.

• Pull lettuce apart; don't cut.

• Arrange salad to look casual for more appetite appeal.

• Use uniform-sized pieces and avoid extremes.

• Simplicity is the rule for best-looking salads; if they look good, they taste good.

Salads for Six Days

First day: On saucer or salad plate serve shredded cabbage with diced celery and raisins.

Second day: Serve shredded cabbage with diced pineapple.

Third day: Use crushed pineapple and grated raw carrots in a lemon gelatine mold.

Fourth day: Try cooked green beans and beets, garnished with raw carrot strips.

Fifth day: How about stuffed tomatoes with chopped celery and cabbage?

Sixth day: Time for chopped or shredded carrots with diced celery and nuts.

Seventh day: A day of rest from labor and worry what to serve for salad, with time to reflect on the money you saved all week with these simple, nutritious, and inexpensive dishes.

*Myrtle's Cabbage Confetti**

Here is a little gem that is easy to make, inexpensive, and positively delicious:

Blend 2 parts shredded cabbage, 1 part finely cut celery (about ½ inch long), and 1 part chopped onion. Put about ⅓ cup water and 2 tablespoons butter or margarine into a fry pan. Heat until well blended, add vegetables, cover, and cook on low heat for about 5 minutes or until tender. Season with salt, pepper, and a little parsley.

Overnight Garden Salad

In a large nonmetal bowl place layers of the following:

1 small head washed, shredded iceberg lettuce
8 onions, sliced
8 radishes, sliced
2 stalks celery, sliced
2 c peas
1 c sliced almonds or water chestnuts

Spread 2 c mayonnaise over this and sprinkle with 2 T sugar, ½ c grated cheese, 1 t salad seasoning, and crisp crumbled bacon bits. Garnish with hard-boiled egg halves and chunks of fresh tomatoes. Set overnight in a cold place. Serve with garlic bread. Practically a meal in itself.

Cheesy Garden Salad

2 T gelatine
½ c boiling water
½ t salt
1 t onion chips
3 small pkgs. cream cheese
lettuce
¼ c cold water
¼ c sugar
2 T lemon juice
1 c grated cucumber
¼ lb. red cinnamon candy
canned pears

Soften gelatine in cold water, then dissolve it in boiling water. Add the sugar and cool. Add salt, lemon juice, onion, and cucumber. Soften cream cheese with ¼ c of the gelatine. Chill the remaining gelatine, then beat until foamy. Blend this with the cheese mixture, pour into a ring mold, chill until firm. Marinate pears in a syrup of the juice heated enough to dissolve the cinnamon candy in it. Turn the cucumber mold out onto plate, fill center with lettuce, and garnish with pears in crisp lettuce cups.

Alaskan Fruit Salad

1 pkg. lemon Jello
1 pkg. lime Jello

1 small can crushed pineapple
1 can fruit cocktail
1 pt. vanilla ice cream

Drain fruit and add water to make 3 cups liquid; add to the lemon and lime Jello. Let stand 30 minutes, then whip thoroughly and add the ice cream tablespoon at a time, beating well into the mixture. Whip in the fruit and mold it. Serve immediately.

*Fruit Salad I**

1 can sliced pineapple
2 lbs. grapes
a few Maraschino cherries
1 can white cherries
½ lb. shelled pecans

Serve with salad dressing.

*Fruit Salad II**

2 oranges
½ lb. Malaga grapes
12 walnuts
3 bananas
4 slices pineapple, cubed

Serve with salad dressing and/or whipped cream.

*Candle Salad**

On a salad plate arrange a ring of pineapple with half a banana stuck upright in the center. Use a slice of Maraschino cherry for the flame, with a spoonful of salad dressing on one side.

Cranberry Bog Salad

1 qt. cranberries
1 c chopped nuts
1 pkg. lemon Jello
½ c crushed and drained pineapple
½ c sugar
3½ c water
1 c white grapes

Mix berries, water, and sugar, and boil rapidly until mushy. Remove from heat and add Jello. Dissolve and cool, then add rest of ingredients and pour into mold. Serve on leaf of lettuce with mayonnaise or whipped cream.

Backyard Salad

4 thick slices bacon
2 T butter
1 t salt
4 T vinegar
black pepper to taste
½ c cream
2 eggs
1 T sugar
½ t paprika
dandelion greens

Collect some young dandelion greens and wash, picking over carefully.

Roll these in a cloth, pat dry, and put into salad bowl. set in warm place. Cut bacon into cubes, fry, and pour bacon and drippings over the greens. In a skillet, melt butter over low heat and add cream. Beat eggs and mix with warm cream, salt, pepper, sugar, and vinegar. Cook over high heat until dressing is thick. Pour over dandelions, blend well, and serve.

Icebox Pear Salad

Mix 3 pkgs. Philadelphia cream cheese with juice of 1 can pears, 3 T French dressing. Cut the pears into cubes and line a freezer ice cube tray. Pour the mixture over and freeze.

Raggedy Ann Salad

On a large plate place half a boiled egg cut lengthwise with round side up and small end at bottom. Make two eyes with cloves and a nose with a pimiento. Make body with thick slice of tomato, with stuffed olives for buttons. With a lettuce leaf make a skirt and decorate with a mix of tuna, grated chicken, macaroni, or what-have-you. For feet use a small sweet pickle, showing under the skirt. Make arms with celery hearts, and wrap each arm with a slice of luncheon meat. For hair shred some carrot into strips. Serve with hot rolls and dessert for a delightfully different hot weather meal.

Cottage Salad

1½ c hot water
1½ t vinegar
½ c salad dressing
4 chopped green onions with tops
¾ c cottage cheese
1 pkg. lemon gelatine
¾ t salt
¼ t paprika
½ c diced cucumbers
3 T chopped green pepper

In hot water dissolve gelatine, and add salt, paprika, vinegar, and salad dressing. Beat to blend and chill rapidly. Fold in rest of ingredients, and pour into mold. Chill until hardened. Turn out on crisp lettuce.

Old Bean Salad

3 hard-boiled eggs
1 medium onion
2 T pickle relish
1½ t salt
3 c cooked navy beans
2 T vinegar
⅔ c salad dressing

Chop the eggs and onion, mix with relish and beans, add salt and salad dressing. Chill before serving.

Old-Fashioned Picnic Potato Salad

3 hard-boiled eggs, chopped
1 qt. cubed boiled potatoes
1 t sugar
¼ c vinegar
½ c chopped onion
⅛ t pepper
1 raw egg
¼ c chopped raw carrots
1 t salt
4 slices bacon
½ c chopped green pepper

Cube and saute bacon. To this add onion and green pepper and cook 3 minutes. Mix vinegar, salt, pepper, sugar, and egg well beaten. Add and cook some more. Add the potatoes, carrot, and the hard-boiled eggs, chopped. Serve hot.

Simple Simon Salad

1 onion
2 T vinegar
sour cream
2 cucumbers
salt & pepper

Slice thin the cucumber and onion and sprinkle with salt. Place in serving dish with vinegar. Cover with sour cream and season with pepper. Serve cold.

Lime and Muskmelon Salad

1 cantaloupe
2 c boiling water
nuts to suit
1 pkg. lime Jello
1 pkg. cream cheese

Dissolve Jello in boiling water and cool until set. Cut ends off melon so it will stand on end. Scrape out seeds from top and fill with Jello. Leave in fridge for a couple of days and when ready to serve, peel the melon and cover with melted cream cheese. Sprinkle with chopped nuts. Slice across and serve on lettuce with whipped cream or salad dressing.

Suzie Salad

2 pkgs. cream cheese
10 marshmallows
2 T pineapple juice
2 T cherry juice
½ pt. whipping cream
2 T mayonnaise
1 small can cubed pineapple
1 small bottle cherries
⅛ t salt

Chop fine the cherries and marshmallows. Combine all ingredients except cream. Beat cream until stiff. Fold into mixture and freeze. Serve on crisp lettuce with mayonnaise or dressing.

California Cold Slaw

1 small cabbage
1 medium onion, minced
3 hard-boiled eggs
1 t sugar
1 t dry mustard
½ c whipped cream
2 winter apples, chopped
2 pimientos, minced
¼ t salt
⅓ c vinegar
1 T melted butter

Shred cabbage, blend with apples, onion, and pimiento. Make paste of egg yolks, add salt, sugar, mustard, and butter. Blend and stir in vinegar. Add whipped cream. Toss with cabbage mix and garnish with whites of eggs and parsley.

*Sour Cream Dressing**

1 c thick sour cream
dash paprika
¼ t prepared mustard
grated cheese (optional)
1 egg
salt
lemon juice or vinegar

Beat egg, salt, mustard, and paprika together. Beat sour cream until fluffy and stir into egg mixture. Add lemon juice or vinegar. Grated cheese makes it extra scrumptious. Serve with head lettuce.

*Delicious Salad Dressing**

Mix together 1 T Worcestershire sauce, 2 T catsup, 3 T vinegar, 6 T olive oil, and 1 finely chopped hard-boiled egg. Chill and serve on lettuce.

*Cooked Salad Dressing**

1 t salt
2 t sugar
1 egg
2 T butter or oil
1 t mustard
dash cayenne
2 T flour
¾ c scalded milk

Mix dry ingredients, add slightly beaten egg, add butter and slowly add milk and vinegar. Cook slowly until mixture thickens. Strain and cool.

Delicious with cold slaw.

Beekeeper's Dressing

⅔ c sugar
1 t mustard
1 t paprika
½ t salt
1 t celery seed
⅓ c strained honey
5 T vinegar
1 T lemon juice
1 T grated onion
1 c salad oil

Mix dry ingredients, then add honey, lemon juice, and vinegar. Pour oil over mixture while beating. The celery seed should be soaked first about 2 hours and drained. This makes a good dressing for fruit or lettuce.

Fruit Salad Dressing

¾ c pineapple juice
1 c sugar
½ lemon, juice and grated
2 eggs

Cook in double boiler until smooth and thick.

Grannie's Dressing

4 eggs
1 c sugar
1 c vinegar
2 T flour
1 t mustard
salt, pepper

Mix dry ingredients and add to beaten eggs, blending in vinegar and water. Cook in double boiler until thick. Keep in mason jar and use on fresh tomatoes and vegetables, or potato salad.

Holy Roller Dressing

1 T vinegar
2 hard-boiled eggs, mashed
½ t salt
1 grated onion
3 T salad oil
pepper to taste

Mix well with mashed eggs. Spread on lettuce and toss until well blended.

Light Meals for Busy Outdoor Summers

Except during the spring planting and fall harvesting seasons, when huge elaborate meals were the rule — especially if there were hired hands to feed or ravenous threshing crews to satisfy — the daily routine was pretty much daily routine, and meals were something to fix and take quickly between chores or other activities. At such times the cook was wont to whip up quick but tasty and nourishing meals to be eaten on the run, often for family members who came and went at different times. These meals were singularly easy to prepare of leftovers or of simple ingredients. Probably most important, they did not make a mess in the kitchen that had to be cleaned up afterwards. They were also meals that any member of the family could prepare himself or herself on an emergency basis when the regular cook was sick or in town on a well-deserved holiday.

Myrtle's 'teen-days kitchen notebook was full of these simple but delightful dishes. Here are some:

*Myrtle's Meat Loaf**

1½ lbs. ground hamburger
½ c tomato juice
chopped onion
1½ c dried breadcrumbs
1 egg
seasonings to taste

Mix thoroughly and bake in moderate oven. Add leftover peas, carrots, or beans if desired.

*Creamed Salmon**

¾ c milk
2 T minute tapioca
1 T butter
½ c water
¾ c salmon
1 egg

Heat milk and water, add tapioca, and cook for 10 minutes, stirring frequently. Add flaked salmon. Cook for 5 minutes, add butter, seasoning, and egg well beaten. Serve hot on toast or crackers.

*Scalloped Tomatoes**

1 qt. tomatoes
¼ t pepper
1 c grated cheese
¼ c butter
1 t salt
1 T sugar
1½ c cracker crumbs

Mix all ingredients except cracker crumbs. Butter a deep dish and sprinkle with ½ c cracker crumbs. Pour in tomatoes. Moisten 1 c cracker crumbs with melted butter and spread over the top. Bake until brown.

*Baked Corn**

Mix 2 pts. corn, 1 c milk, 1 T butter, 2 beaten eggs, salt and pepper to taste, and bake in a quick oven until done.

*Baked Beans**

Soak 1 qt. navy beans overnight; drain and add 1 t baking soda and scald. Drain, add fresh water, and boil 15 minutes. Drain and place in bean pot. Add 1 t ginger, 1 t salt, 1 t mustard, 1 T brown sugar, 1 T molasses, 4 or 5 c water, and bake 4 or 5 hours.

*Savory Beef**

4 lbs. beef rump
½ c vinegar
small piece of suet
1 lb. onions

Cut beef into cubes and put into deep kettle. Add vinegar, sliced onions, suet cut into pieces, and enough water to cover. Cook until meat is tender. Add salt and pepper to taste before done.

*Ham Rolls**

12 slices boiled ham	**3 c cottage cheese**
3 T minced onion	**paprika**

Mix cheese and onion and add enough paprika to give a slight pink color. Make into rolls, each containing 2 T cheese. Wrap with ham and serve with lettuce.

*Spanish Ham**

Soak thin slices of ham in lukewarm water for an hour. Drain, pat dry, and fry in a hot frying pan until slightly browned. Remove to a warm serving dish.

*Hungarian Goulash, Portal Style**

Peel and slice 2 medium-sized onions and fry in lard or shortening in hot pan. Let cook a few minutes, then add 1½ lb. hamburger or round steak, ½ c cooked rice, 1 c canned tomatoes cooked with ¼ c macaroni. Season with salt and pepper and cook slowly for one hour.

*Salmon Croquettes**

Mash 1 c salmon fine. Beat 4 eggs until creamy and add to salmon. Add 1 t salt and drop by spoonfuls into greased frying pan.

Country Egg Puffs

6 t baking powder	**6 T sweet milk**
1 t salt	**1½ c flour (approx.)**
2 eggs	

Break eggs into bowl and beat until smooth. Add rest of ingredients. Drop by spoonfuls onto greased pan and

Homemade sourdough pizza makes a light meal when served with wine or beer.

steam over hot water about 10 minutes. Serve with stew — especially good with chicken or beef-vegetable.

Little Piggies in a Blanket

1 lb. pork sausage
1 small onion, chopped
½ t salt
cabbage leaves
½ c uncooked rice
¼ t allspice
1 can tomato soup

Mix meat, rice, onion, and seasings. Wrap in cabbage leaves. Pour over this 1 can tomato soup mixed with ¾ can water. Bake for 1½ hours.

Cabbage leaves should be prepared by cutting out large rib and boiling for 8 minutes or until pliable enough to roll. Makes 12 large rolls.

Syrian Cabbage Roll

Use the heart of a large cabbage, boil in salted water until leaves are tender. Grind coarsely shoulder of lamb. Mix with drained rice in proportion of 2 parts lamb to 1 part rice. Season well. Mix gradually 2 stalks diced celery, 1 small finely cut onion, ¼ can tomatoes. Set bones of lamb in bottom of kettle. Roll mixture in cabbages leaves cut to size. Place in layers on top of bones. Cover with rest of the can of tomatoes. Cook ½ to 1 hour with mixture weighted with plate and kettle covered.

Logging Camp Stew

In the old days the best place to find this beef stew was in the Pike Street Market on Seattle's Skid Road. A big bowl, with crackers, cost only 10 cents, and you could live on it for a month for less than $5 if you were between stakes.

Cut beef into small squares and brown in skillet. Season well. Add water and simmer and then thicken gravy with flour and remove from heat. Pour meat and gravy into a baking dish with sliced potatoes. Season again and slice some raw carrots to top the potatoes; finally add a layer of sliced raw onion. Pour a can of stewed tomatoes over and bake for 2 or 3 hours.

Jamestown Tongue

Use 1 beef tongue, fresh or smoked, 1 t salt, 2 or 3 bay leaves, 6 whole allspices, 3 whole black peppers, 1 onion sliced, 1 carrot, 1 stalk celery.

Clean tongue well with brush and water. Cover with hot water. Add seasonings and vegetables. Simmer covered for about 3 hours. Do not boil. Cool in its own liquid.

Swedish Brown Beans

1 lb. red kidney beans
1 T vinegar
3 T brown sugar
1 T butter
1 t salt
1 T flour

Cook beans until well done, then add vinegar, butter, salt, and sugar. Thicken with flour paste and serve with pork.

Swedish Meatballs

1 lb. red kidney beans
1 T vinegar
3 T brown sugar
1 T butter
1 t salt
1 T flour

Cook beans until well done, then add vinegar, butter, salt, and sugar. Thicken with flour paste and serve with pork.

Mock Chicken Pie

6 T butter
3 cans milk
1 can peas
¼ t pepper
6 T flour
4 cooked carrots
¾ t salt
4 small cooked potatoes

Make a white sauce with flour, butter, milk, and seasonings. Add to other ingredients in a pan and top with biscuits made as follows:

2 c flour
3 t baking powder
¾ c milk
6 T shortening
1 t salt

Dressed up Fowl

Grind giblets of chicken, turkey, or goose. Break up dried bread into small pieces. Add butter, goose grease or shortening, allspice, sage, celery leaves, a small onion finely chopped, salt and pepper — all to taste. Beat 3 eggs and pour over mixture, with enough boiling water to soften the bread and make slightly doughy. Add ground giblets, mix and stuff into fowl and roast, or bake separately.

Summer Is Vegetable Time

All that exercise out-of-doors, tilling and weeding the garden plot, and all the other little chores that go along with a green thumb, do work up a healthy appetite, stimulated greatly by the sight of all those delectable growing things. Chances are your thoughts will weigh heavily on what's for dinner that day — picked at the peak of goodness.

Early Garden Delight

1 c celery
6 small carrots
1½ c white sauce
¼ lb. sharp cheese
1½ c fresh peas
1 small head cauliflower
¾ c rice
parsley to suit

Cut celery in 1-inch pieces. Cook all vegetables separately in salted water. Drain and blend with white sauce. Cook rice in boiling salted water, drain. Mold rice around bottom and sides of greased baking dish. Sprinkle with grated cheese and brown in moderate over. Pour creamed vegetables into this rice mold and garnish with parsley, Serve hot.

Prairie Fried Onions

1 c flour
½ c canned milk
1 egg white
3 onions
¼ t salt
2 T salad oil
6 T water

Slice onions about ¼ inch thick. Sift flour with salt, then add milk and egg white and beat smooth. Add enough water to make a thin batter. Separate onion slices into rings and dip in batter. Fry in deep fat at 375 degrees until a golden brown. Drain, sprinkle with salt, and garnish. Serve with meat.

Casserole Onions

8 onions
½ c buttered crumbs
salt and pepper to taste
1½ c white sauce
1 c cooked and ground ham

Boil onions in salted water until tender. Drain and place in buttered casserole. Cover with white sauce and ham, blended. Season to taste and sprinkle with crumbs. Brown in oven at 350 degrees.

Oven Onions

2 c small onions
1 can mushroom soup
2 T butter
2 c chopped celery
1 c bread crumbs
¼ t salt

Boil onions and celery in salted water until tender. Remove from water with slotted spoon and place in buttered casserole. Add soup to the water and then pour over vegetables. Sprinkle with bread crumbs and dot with butter. Bake until brown on top, about 40 minutes at 350 degrees.

Family-Style Onions

4 slices bacon, diced
1 T flour
2 T butter
1 c chopped mushrooms
salt
1 medium onion
1 can peas, drained
1 c canned milk
1/16 t white pepper

Saute diced bacon, add chopped onion, and cook until onions are soft. Blend in flour, add drained peas and milk, stir until thickened. Add melted butter to mushrooms and slowly cook about 5 minutes. Add to peas and onions and season well. Serve on potato patties or on hot biscuits.

Baked Carrots

2 c ground carrots
⅔ c chopped walnuts
pepper
3 beaten eggs
2 c bread crumbs
1 t salt
2 c stewed tomatoes

Blend together and pack in buttered loaf pan or casserole. Bake at 325 degrees and serve with sauce.

Cream Sauce

2 T melted butter
salt, pepper
2 T flour
milk to suit

Blend flour and butter, add heated milk, and bring to boil. Season to taste.

Scalloped Asparagus

1 pt. oysters
½ c cracker crumbs
1 c asparagus juice
salt and pepper
1 can asparagus
½ c cream
2 T butter

In buttered baking dish or casserole, alternate layers asparagus, oysters, and crackers, each layer dotted with butter. Add cream and asparagus liquid. Salt and season to taste. Bake at 350 degrees.

Schoolhouse Beets

⅓ c sugar
⅓ t salt
2 t cornstarch
½ c vinegar
2 T butter
2 c diced beets

Dissolve cornstarch in water. Drain beets and mix

juice with remaining ingredients. Bring to boil and pour over beets. Simmer and serve.

Baked Asparagus

1 can asparagus tips
1 c cracker crumbs
2 T butter
1 t salt
2 beaten eggs
2 c milk
1 t grated onion
pepper

Chop tips, mix all. Bake until set. Serve hot with parsley sauce.

Potatoes Au Gratin

1½ c milk
2 T butter
¼ lb. grated cheese
1 c buttered bread crumbs
2 T flour
1 t salt
4 c diced and cooked potatoes

Make a sauce of milk, flour, butter, and salt. Stir in cheese until melted. Place potatoes in a shallow greased baking dish and add cheese sauce. Cover with buttered bread crumbs. Bake until golden brown. Serve hot from baking dish.

Shoestring Spuds

Cut spuds into thin strips. Soak in salted water for 1 hour. Drain and pat dry. Deep-fry in shortening at 400 degrees until golden brown. Drain and sprinkle with salt.

Icehouse Soup

When I was a kid we did not have refrigeration but did have an old-fashioned icebox. The big chunks of ice came from the icehouse, an old red barn in the middle of the village. During the previous winter tons and tons of ice had been stored there in sawdust after being sawed from the pond behind the dam at the railroad bridge on Downing's Creek. The ice delivery wagon was a marvelous vehicle, especially on a hot summer day, as it creaked around on its errands, dripping cold water. We kids used to follow it, and at every stop the driver would let us collect the small pieces of ice broken off the blocks.

Which brings to mind Grandma Reed's favorite hot summer soup:

Dog Days Soup

2 cucumbers
1 small onion
2 tomatoes
4 c tomato juice
½ t salt
1 green pepper
1 avocado
2 c beef broth
3 T lemon juice
¼ t pepper

Chop onion fine, peel and cube tomatoes and avocado. Peel and chunk the cucumbers. Dice pepper, removing seeds. Mix well together and chill on ice. Serve mixture over ice cubes placed in a bowl. Top with a hot sauce.

Good on any day with an ambient outside temperature of 90 degrees or more.

*Stuffed Garden Pepper**

4 green peppers
½ c cooked rice
⅓ c soup stock
⅛ t pepper
1½ c cooked, chopped meat
¼ t salt
1 small onion, chopped
buttered cracker crumbs

Wash the peppers. Cut off tops and remove seeds. Stuff with the meat, rice, salt, pepper, onion, and stock combined. Cover with buttered cracker crumbs. Place in an uncovered casserole. Add ½ c water. Bake in a moderate oven, 350 degrees, 40 minutes.

Cream of Leek Soup

A leek is virtually unknown to the average American family, but it was popular with first-generation settlers from the old country. Happily, the leek is becoming popular today, as the seed catalogs and nurseries find there is a demand for it. A leek is something like a onion but with a more distinctive flavor. It has been a staple of gourmet cooking in Europe for centuries. Here is a good leek soup:

¼ c butter
4 chicken bouillon cubes
milk
10 leeks
4 potatoes
4 c water
salt, pepper

Slice and saute the leeks in butter in the soup pot. Peel and quarter potatoes; add to leeks, along with bouillon cubes and water to cover. Simmer over low heat 2 hours, adding water if needed. Season to taste. Thicken if necessary with milk.

Wholesome Country Soup

6 c diced parsnips
2 diced carrots
6 c chicken broth
1 c cream
garlic croutons
1 large onion diced
3 diced potatoes
1 t dill
½ t nutmeg
salt and pepper

Simmer the parsnips in a pot, with onions, carrots, potatoes, dill, and chicken broth. When vegetables are tender, cool and puree in blender. Return to pot and add cream, nutmeg, salt, and pepper. Serve with croutons. Enough for 8 people.

Chili Sauce a la Red River

18 ripe tomatoes
2 t salt
6 medium onion
1 c vinegar
1 t cloves
3 green peppers
1 c sugar
1 red pepper
1 t cinnamon
1 t allspice

Run through food processor and blend. Boil an hour. Fill jars and seal.

Garden Delight

1 small cabbage
1 red pepper
½ c salt
1 T mustard seed
3 c vinegar
1 green pepper
3 carrots
1 T celery seed
3 c sugar

Run vegetables through food chopper and sprinkle with salt. Let stand 2 hours and drain. Add celery seed, mustard seed, sugar, and vinegar. Pack in scalded jars and seal.

The Sandwich Is King in Summertime

The thought of cooking elaborate meals gets little enthusiasm in summertime, with kids out of school and most chores and activities being out-of-doors — to say nothing of impromptu picnics, fishin' trips, and just plain visitin' around. Anyway, there seems to be less time for regular, sit-down-at-the-table meals. For these times, the sandwich is at the head of the menu.

The sandwich was invented, so legend tells us, by the Fourth Earl of Sandwich (1718-92), so he could stay at the gambling tables without interruptions for meals. The earl's family name was taken (or vice versa) from the town in eastern Kent near the Strait of Dover, one of the most ancient of the Cinque Ports. The oldest or one of the oldest settlements on Cape Cod, Massachusetts, founded in 1639, also takes its name from its British beginnings.

Many of these sandwiches were put together by the farm gals and taken out into the fields for the hands at snacktime.

Petersburg Cathedral

1 loaf white bread
1 loaf wheat bread
1 loaf rye bread

Cut slices of various sizes with round cookie cutter. Use largest slice on bottom; butter and cover with jam. Cover the next slice with cream cheese and pimiento, the third with sliced tomatoes and cucumbers and a small piece of lettuce, the fourth with sliced meat of any kind or pieces of chicken or turkey, the fifth with anchovies, smoked herring, or caviar blended in a paste.

On top of the sixth slice place a olive speared with a toothpick.

Brown and White Sandwiches

Use one 3/4 inch slice of brown to two of white bread, with crusts cut off. Spread with butter, and cottage cheese mixed with pimiento, making two layers. Wrap with damp cloth and press under a plate with a flatiron or similar weight for an hour or so. Cut into 1/2 inch strips and serve with salad.

Hasty Sandwich Filling

In a saucepan break 3 eggs. Add a chunk of butter, some salt and a dash of red pepper. Scramble until dry and slightly smoking. Remove from heat, cool, and blend in some mayonnaise and a dash of paprika. Butter thin slices of bread and put a small lettuce leaf on under the filling. Makes about 15 sandwiches.

Variation: 1/4 lb. cream cheese, 1/2 c peanuts, 2 T salad dressing, and some cream. Grind and blend cheese and nuts coarsely. Add salad dressing and enough cream to make a paste.

Another: Use 2 hard-boiled eggs, chopped fine; 1 large can sardines, flaked; 1 small onion, grated, with mayonnaise and cream blended to form a thick mixture.

Still more: Use 1/2 green pepper, 1 small onion, 1 pimiento, 2 hard-boiled eggs, 6 small pickles, 1 pkg. cream cheese, salt, and paprika. Good for open-faced sandwiches.

Ragmar Roasted Rounds

1/2 lb. fried sliced ham | **2 large dill pickles**
1 large spanish or yellow onion | **1/2 c mayonnaise**

Blend ham, onion, and pickles in chopper and mix with dressing. Spread on white bread, then roast in broiler

Or: Fry some sausages, dip in hot fat, place two on each slice of bread and cover with slices of tomatoes topped with slice of cheese. Broil until cheese melts.

Or: Cream 1 pkg. sharp cheese with 1 well-beaten egg, 1 T Worcestershire sauce, 1/4 t salt, 1/8 t mustard. Spread on bread slices about 1/2 inch thick and top with a slice of bacon. Roast in oven until done.

Barbecue Sandwich Filling

1 lb. lean boiling beef
1 lb. lean pork
1 bunch celery
3 onions
1 T brown sugar
2 T chili powder
2 green peppers
1 c tomato catsup
1/2 c vinegar
soy sauce or A1 sauce

Cook the pork and beef in onion water until tender and almost mushy. Add water as needed during cooking to make 2 c stock. Shred meat with two forks while cooking and add celery, pepper, and onions that have been chopped or ground. Add the catsup, brown sugar, vinegar, chili powder, soy sauce, and salt and pepper to taste. Cook in meat stock until thick, adding shredded meat. Spread on hot buns or toast.

Don't Forget Desserts

Garden Rhubarb Pudding

1 T butter
½ c milk
1 c flour
½ t salt
½ c sugar
1 egg
1 t baking powder
rhubarb and brown sugar

Mix batter and pour into buttered casserole over layers of raw rhubarb sprinkled with brown sugar. Bake 45 minutes at 350 degrees. Serve hot or cold with cream.

Garden Rhubarb Shortcake

1 c sugar
pinch salt
1 c butter
½ c milk
rhubarb
1 egg
1 t vanilla
2 c flour
4 t baking powder

Grease pan and fill with cut raw rhubarb sprinkled with sugar. Cover with mixed batter and bake at 350 degrees for 1 hour. Serve hot or cold with cream or topping.

*Baked Apple with Nuts**

Peel and core apple, fill center with nuts and a little lemon peel and sprinkle with cinnamon. Put in pan with a heaping T sugar and ½ c water to each apple. Bake slowly.

*Fruit Sherbert**

2 oranges
2 bananas
3 c water
3 lemons
3 c sugar
3 egg whites

Extract the juice from lemons and oranges. Mash bananas and rub through sieve. Add water and sugar and stir until sugar is thoroughly dissolved. Stir in stiffly beaten egg whites, after quick-chilling other ingredients. Then freeze.

*Marshmallow Salad**

Cut up 1 lb. marshmallows and pour over them 1 can pineapple. Let stand overnight. Add 6 sliced bananas, ½ lb. chopped walnuts, ½ pt. whipped cream.

*Icebox Dessert I**

Put a layer of vanilla wafers in a pan with a layer of crushed pineapple. Sprinkle with walnuts. Add a layer of whipped cream, then another layer of wafers. Let stand 24 hours.

*Icebox Dessert II**

1 c graham cracker crumbs for each person. Mix in chopped walnuts, marshmallows, and dates. Moisten with enough cream to make a loaf. Let stand in icebox 24 hours. Serve with whipped cream.

*Simple Dessert**

Crushed pineapple topped with whipped cream on top of a graham cracker or a vanilla wafer.

*Pineapple Sherbert**

1 can crushed pineapple
1 pt. water
3 egg whites beaten stiff
1 pt. sugar
1 t lemon juice
1 t gelatin

Mix; add the beaten egg whites; freeze.

*Strawberry Mousse**

1 box strawberries	**1 c sugar**
¼ box or 1 T gelatine	**2 T cold water**
3 T boiling water	**1 qt. cream**

Wash and hull berries and let stand 1 hour sprinkled with sugar. Mash and rub through fine sieve. Add gelatine which has been soaked in cold water and dissolved in boiling water. Set in ice water and stir until it begins to thicken. Fold in whipped cream. Freeze 4 hours. Others fruit may be added, including dates.

*Baked Apple Tapioca**

3 c water	**2 T lemon juice**
3 tart apples, pared and sliced	**½ c tapioca**
1 c brown sugar, firmly packed	**1 t salt**
¼ t mace	**3 T melted butter**

Combine water and lemon juice and pour over apples in greased shallow baking dish. Cover and bake at 375 degrees for 15 minutes. Mix tapioca, ¾ c sugar, salt, and mace. Sprinkle over apples, mixing thoroughly. Add butter. Continue baking for 10 minutes. Stir well, sprinkle remaining sugar over apple mixture, and bake 5 minutes longer. Serve hot or cold with cream. Serves 6.

*Pudding Topping**

Heat and thicken canned cherries with cornstarch and sugar, a little butter, and dash of cinnamon. Chill and serve on tapioca pudding.

*Pineapple Tapioca**

Add ¼ c tapioca and ⅛ t salt to 1 pt. pineapple juice and water. Cook in double boiler 15 minutes or until tapioca is clear, stirring frequently. Add ¼ c sugar and pineapple. Serve with whipped cream. Serves 4.

*Cream Tapioca Pudding**

2 c milk
¼ c sugar
⅛ t salt
2 eggs
½ t vanilla
2 T tapioca

Combine tapioca, sugar, salt, egg yolk, and milk in the top of a double boiler. Bring to a scalding point, 5 to 7 minutes, and cook 5 minutes while stirring. Remove, fold a small amount into beaten egg white. Add to tapioca and blend. When cool add vanilla and chill.

*Baked Custard**

Scald 1 pt. milk in top of double boiler. Beat 2 or 3 whole eggs, add ¼ c sugar, mix, and add a little of the scalded milk. Add ¼ t cinnamon and ¼ t salt. Pour into individual molds which have been rinsed in cold water. Bake in a very moderate oven. When puffy on top and an inserted silver knife comes out clean, they are done.

Original Cold Water Butterscotch Pudding

2 eggs
1 c cold water
1 t vanilla
2 T flour
2 rounded T butter
1 c brown sugar

Blend sugar and flour. Add water and stir over fire until thick. Add eggs yolks, butter, and vanilla. Make meringue of egg whites for topping.

*Maplenut Ice Cream**

Bring to a boil 1 c maple syrup. Pour this over the beaten yolks of 3 eggs. Cool. Beat the whites of 3 eggs stiff. Whip 1 pt. cream, add 1 c milk and a pinch of salt. Mix all together and freeze. When partly frozen, add nuts and continue freezing.

Congregational Recipes of Yesteryear

Most recipes in bygone days were handed down orally and by example and demonstration from mother to daughter. No doubt there was considerable innovating and editing along the way, according to individual skills and personally, as recipes were adapted to the family's taste, convenience, and available ingredients. This constant evolution sometimes turned up some astonishing variations — and some clever improvements.

From time to time the local ladies' aid society or the church mothers would get together and solicit favorite recipes from church members and friends, collecting them in simple, often hand-lettered (before the Mimeograph machine) cookbooks. These were usually produced as part of a fund-raising project. Our research files contain many of these from all over the country, most of them more than fifty years old and some well over a century old. Sources include church organizations like the Baptists, Lutheran, Mennonite, Methodist, Catholic, and Presbyterian.

Few of these old recipes are fancy — but all are well proved and wholesome. To all those hundreds of anonymous ladies who contributed to these obscure collections, we owe many thanks.

Prairie Chili Sauce

3 small green peppers
9 large ripe tomatoes
1 T ginger
1 t salt
2 T sugar
1 medium onion
2 c vinegar
1 T allspice
1 T cloves

Chop up peppers and onions with remaining ingredients. Cook slowly for 1½ hours. Seal hot in jars.

Springtime Pudding

1½ c flour
1 c suet
1 c currants
1 c grated carrots
½ t soda
1 c sugar
1 c raisins
1 c grated potatoes
1 t salt

Mix and cook in steamer for 3 hours. Serve with hard sauce.

Root Cellar Pudding

6 medium apples
2 c bread crumbs
cinnamon, cloves, allspice
2 eggs
1 c brown sugar
butter to suit

Mix all ingredients and place in shallow baking dish, with small pieces of butter dobbed on top. Bake ½ hour. serve with whipped cream.

Old-Time Cabbage Rolls

8 large cabbage leaves
2 c mashed potatoes
½ c tomato juice
3 T vinegar
1 lb. sausage
1 t salt
2 c boiling water
2 T sugar

Blend the meat, potatoes, and salt. Pour boiling water over cabbage leaves and let stand a few minutes. Dry with paper towels. On each leaf put meat blend and roll from stem end, folding in the sides. Tie with string and place in kettle. Cover with tomato juice and boiling water, vinegar, and sugar. Simmer until done.

Country Hot Slaw

Here is an unusual dish seldom prepared these days, but an old-time favorite on the farm:

Shred some cabbage fine and crisp it with cold water. Beat the yolks of 3 eggs with 2 T cold water, add 1 T butter, ½ c vinegar, salt to taste, and cook until thick. Pour dressing over the drained cabbage. Heat and serve.

Yummy Yummy Applesauce

Assemble some applesauce and sliced, cooked sweet potatoes and place in a casserole in layers, one layer of sauce to one layer of sweet spuds, until dish is full. Dot the layers with globs of butter. Top with a layer of bread crumbs, sprinkle with salt, and bake in moderate oven ½ to ¾ hour.

Quick and Easy Pudding

1 c molasses
2 t soda
3½ c flour
1 c currants
1 pt. sour milk
⅔ c chopped suet
2 c raisins

Mix and cook in steamer for 2 hours; serve as desired.

Farmer Brown's Cornmeal Bread

1 c cornmeal
1 c sweet milk
½ c flour
1 t soda
1 c raisins
1 c graham flour
1 c molasses
½ c sour milk
¼ t salt

Mix well and cook in steamer for 2 hours.

Plowshare Doughnuts

1 c sugar
2 t butter
2 eggs
1 t nutmeg
3½ c flour
1 c sour milk or buttermilk
2 T sour cream
1 t soda
pinch salt
1½ t baking powder

Mix well and roll out on floured board. Cut and fry in hot fat. Lay out to drain on paper towels before eating.

Old-Time Vinegar Pie

This was a real favorite in the old days but is seldom heard of nowadays.

First, make your favorite pie shell. For filling:

3 egg yolks, beaten
¼ t salt
1 c sugar
1 ¾ c boiling water

Blend the above in the top of a double boiler. Then combine:

¼ c apple cider vinegar
¼ c cold water
¼ c corn starch

Add this mixture to the double boiler, stirring smoothly. Cook over boiling water about 12 minutes, stirring constantly. Remove from heat when thick, add 1 t lemon extract, and pour the mixture into a baked pie shell. Let cool a few minutes. Spread generously with meringue. Bake at 350 degrees for 10 to 15 minutes or until topping is a golden brown.

For the meringue:

3 egg whites
¼ t salt
¼ t cream of tartar
½ t vanilla

Blend in bowl and beat until frothy. Add 6 T sugar and beat until thoroughly smooth and totally blended.

*Sweet Potato Pie**

5 boiled sweet potatoes
½ c brown sugar
⅛ t nutmeg
milk or cream
½ c pecans
1 T butter
1 pkg. marshmallows

Mash potatoes, add sugar, butter, nuts and nutmeg, and beat until creamy. Add liquid to moisten. Place in buttered baking dish and bake until brown. Cover with marshmallows and brown again.

This is one of my all-time favorites, indulged in almost daily during a winter spent in the Rio Grande Valley of Texas.

*Farmhand Fried Potatoes**

Heat 2 T butter in a frying pan. Peel and slice into the butter 4 uncooked potatoes and 1 onion. Hash them together as they cook.

The One and Only Lemon

Why the word "lemon" has taken on a connotation of something bitter, a mistake, a poor example, and undesirable, is a puzzle. This citrus fruit is one of mankind's best friends. It is one of nature's wonders. Lemons can be harvested every month of the year, and it is common to see ripe fruit on the same tree with new blossoms. Fresh lemon is sodium free, and a whole one contains only forty-four calories, while providing 87 percent of the daily vitamin C requirement for adults.

Although lemonade is as American as baseball, apple pie, and the Fourth of July, this fine beverage was invented by the Mongols in about A.D. 1299.

Lemon is used not only in a beverage but also to provide citrus juice and garnish for hundreds of different recipes. It is almost a necessity for salad dressing and seafood seasoning. It adds that special zest to vegetables, cooked or green. It is used to prevent discoloring of other fruit such as bananas, pears, apples, peaches, and avocados. It is used in many ways as a mild beaching agent, including keeping white vegetables white. It has been used for writing in invisible ink by spies and lovers.

It is one of the most versatile of fruits; every part of the lemon is used for something. Distilled lemon oil is used in soaps and cleaners, in floor and shoe polishes, in household sprays. It is commonly used in the best furniture polishes.

It contains pectin, a plasma fluid extender with astounding lifesaving properties when used as a blood substitute to improve circulation of a victim in shock.

Almost all lemons today come from California and,

to a lesser extent, from Florida and the lower Rio Grande Valley. Fresh lemons of high quality have thick, fine-textured skins. Those with coarse, hard, or spongy skins are of poor quality and undesirable. Some may be old, dried out, and infected by rot at the core. These should not be used for cooking.

Part Three

Autumn

He that will have a cake out of the wheat
Must needs tarry the grinding.

Wm. Shakespeare, *Troilus and Cressida*

— 1 —

Hot Days, Chilly Morns, and Indian Summer

After the dog days of late summer, when the sluggish Mouse River ran a bilious green in the backwaters and the high sun blazed unmercifully out of a pale blue, scalded sky, there came a gradual change: The days began to shorten almost without notice; the sun rose a little bit less to the north of the equator and set just a little bit earlier and lower.

Mornings (which meant daylight on the farm) carried a fresh new tang, and there was an absence of the usual heavy dew. Out across the prairies the endless fields of grain had been shocked — the bundles left by the harvester or mower had been stacked in neat rows of shocks of eight or ten bundles each. These would await the arrival of the contract threshing crew on its regular circuit from farm to farm.

The garden crops were being picked and readied for canning and preserving. School was not far off. There was an increased bustle of activity. Autumn was a time of harvest, of preparing for the coming winter, and of scurrying to do all the chores and repairs and projects that cannot be done after the freeze-up. It was time to shake off the languid slothfulness of summer and get the blood boiling again. It was a time for farm auction sales, for barn dances, and for heeding all the urgencies of nature. From the north country, the first of the endless migrations of ducks, geese, and other waterfowl began to appear, the first small flocks stopping leisurely to rest in the ponds and potholes being freshened by the first fall rains. All the wild fruits and berries were well-ripened by now, and there would be a flurry of picking and jelly-making. On the prairie and in the tree-filled coulees and along the creeks and fencerows the wild creatures, too, were preparing for the winter they knew instinctively was rapidly approaching. There was building of nests and burrows and storing of seeds and nuts. The new fresh breezes from the north and west carried the brittle scents of a vast land now losing the lush green vitality of the growing season.

There was no time to be wasted.

— 2 —

Harvesttime Was Circus Time

In farm country, especially in grain-growing country, harvesting the rolling, waving fields of wheat, barley, oats, rye, and other grain crops was the event of the year. It was the time when the fruition of a year's labor was anticipated; a time when the farm family would know whether it had made it through another four seasons — and if so, how well they would live through the winter until the next planting time. For the farm-related services and businesses, such as the implement store, the oil distributor, the grain elevator, the blacksmith, general store, and all the others, it was a time for settling up debts and accounts they had carried for months. Like the traditional Jubilee of the Jewish faith — when every fifty years all one's debts and accounts are settled and the slate wiped clean for starting over — the annual fall harvest on the farm was a renewal of faith, hope, and charity.

In my youth, harvesttime meant that point in late summer when the grain was cut with a harvester and bundled with binder twine. The bundles were then stacked together or "shocked" in clusters for drying. The grain was cut while still green and then dried or ripened in the shocks. One advantage of this was that it forestalled loss by disease, although the crop was vulnerable to grasshoppers. Later, when combines were developed, the grain was left standing until ripe, maybe a month or so longer, and then in one operation was cut and threshed to remove the kernels from the chaff. For the old shocking method, the climax of the operation came when the threshing crew arrived with the thresher and wagons and related equipment. The thresher was still being powered with steam when I was a kid, but steam was soon replaced by gasoline engines. The steam- or gasoline-powered tractor had a massive flywheel which was connected to the threshing machine by a huge, slapping belt of leather and provided power to operate all the Rube Goldberg system of beating and winnowing that went on inside the ungainly-looking threshing machine.

"Pitching bundles" was a hard, demanding job. Each pitcher (sometimes two hands worked together) with a team of horses and a wagon, fanned out along the windrows of shocked bundles and pitched them onto the wagon. Then the wagon was brought to the threshing machine, and the bundles were pitched into the hopper. The enormous leather belt slapped and whipped; the tractor rumbled, barked, or hissed, depending on whether it was steam or internal combustion; the threshing rig clattered and whined and shook; and a great cloud of chaff spewed out of the rig exhaust stack, floating downwind to form a rising mound of straw.

This operation went on from daylight until dark, which on the prairies in the autumn meant from about 5 A.M. until 7 P.M. I remember some years when the threshing was not completed until late October, occasionally when there was already snow on the ground. Before you went out in the morning you had first to take care of your horses and harness them to the wagon, always before you headed for the cookshack for breakfast. You were expected to be on your way to the field by daylight. At some farms where I worked, we went out into the field and worked for a couple of hours *before* breakfast, came in and ate a huge meal, then went out again until noon or "dinnertime." Otherwise we had a midmorning snack brought out to the field by the farm gals, came in for the noon meal, went out again, had a midafternoon snack brought out, then knocked off about 7 P.M. Then we had to take care of the horses and stable them for the night before washing up and going in for supper. After a huge meal we headed for the barn and dropped exhausted onto the fresh hay in the mow to grab a few hours' sleep.

It sure kept one busy and out of mischief.

Few farmers, even those with a section of wheat, could afford to maintain complete harvesting and threshing equipment. Most of the harvesting and threshing — later combining — was done by specialists. These were contractors who had the equipment and who started in the winter wheat fields of Kansas and Nebraska and worked north until they wound up operations about November along the Canadian border.

These contractors generally supplied not only the machinery and sometimes the horses but also living quarters and other equipment for their permanent crews. The crew was usually supplemented by local help as needed, including the farmer's family members. At most places where I worked as a kid, the farmer supplied the cookshack and living quarters in the barn, at least for the local help, and quite often the horses and wagons.

It was a sight to see the threshing entourage approaching, coming down the old country road to the next farm like a circus come to town. The caravan rumbled into the farm lot, spreading out like a gypsy camp. The threshing machine would be towed out to the first field, while the crew readied the rest of the gear. The arrival meant a sort of holiday to the isolated farm; for the girls in the family it was a chance to flirt with the strange men who had come from far-off places, and there was a good deal of sparkin' going on before the actual work started.

But my most vivid memories of threshing are centered

around the cookshack and the enormous and incredible meals served up by the farm women, often including neighbors who got together and helped each other while the threshing crew was in the neighborhood.

It was a culinary miracle how so much food and such wholesome meals could be turned out for so many hands seemingly without effort. Of course, it was not effortless. It actually meant long, exhausting hours for the women. They had to be up long before the men, as early as 2 A.M., to start the baking, stewing, and preparing of breakfast, which might include not only mountains of flapjacks but bushels of bacon, eggs, and potatoes, vegetables of several varieties, sirloin steaks, homemade sauces, farm butter, hot maple syrup, steaming oatmeal, canned peaches, piping hot breads, biscuits, rolls, barrels of fresh raw milk, reservoirs of coffee and tea, platters of cold meats, sausages, cheeses. . . .

Midmorning snacks were also bountiful, packed in clean lard tins and carried out to the men in the field.

"Dinner," the noon meal, was a main event, for which the breakfast feast was only a prelude. Supper, the evening meal, was a virtual banquet and ended with fresh-baked berry pies, tarts, and sumptuous layer cakes with homemade ice cream made with ice from the icehouse down by the creek.

These meals benefitted from the backgrounds and skills of many woman of different ethnic and national backgrounds, blended together for a few days each year. The result was an incredible bounty that I believe has never been equalled before or since.

For the women behind the scenes there was the inevitable drudgery of cleaning up after each meal, acres of pots and pans and utensils — to say nothing of collecting and preparing the ingredients for the next meal. They worked long hours, even longer than the men. Workdays often stretched to twenty hours — then after a few hours of drugged sleep, the woman started the day all over again.

Probably few people would want to return to that kind of life-style after sampling the comforts and conveniences of modern living, but neither will most of us enjoy that kind of eating adventure again.

The nearest we can come to sampling that kind of food nowadays is to grow our own vegetables and fruits, and in some cases even keep a cow or some chickens, possibly a pig. The next best thing is to go out into the countryside and purchase produce and farm products either at roadside farm markets or from the growers. This is the principle source of fresh vegetables and fruits used by homemakers these days for continuing the fine old tradition of putting up food in the autumn.

Threshing Crew Salad

As the threshing crews moved north from Kansas and Nebraska starting in the early spring, winding up in North Dakota or Saskatchewan in late fall, they had a chance to sample the best of farm cooking. Indeed, it was the farm circuit that kept them coming back every year for the 100-day season of backbreaking, dawn-to-dusk work, seven days a week, for an average wage of $3 to $5 a day. In 1934, for example, I was paid $3 a day for pitching bundles twelve hours a day, taking care of the horses and wagon on my own time.

At each farm the wives and daughters of the family and neighbors tried to outdo themselves. America lost one of its greatest gastronomical assets when the modern combine was invented and cold-blooded contracting syndicates took over the harvesting.

One of the arts not lost, however, was this fine recipe:

2 slices home-cured bacon
2 eggs
3 T cider vinegar
salt and pepper
3½ T sugar

Cut bacon into small squares and brown. Stir other ingredients in a bowl or earthenware crock, with the bacon and drippings. Thin if necessary with canned milk or real cream. Use as a salad dressing on leaf lettuce right out of the garden, or for dandelion greens, fresh-picked spinach, or potato salad.

Dandelion leaves should be picked only from the first plants of spring and cooked until tender. Same for the spinach. Leaf lettuce should be pulled into large chunks, placed in bowl, and the dressing spread on it while warm. Early spring potatoes should be boiled and cooled, cut into small chunks, mixed with chopped hard-boiled eggs, sprinkle with seasonings, and topped with dressing.

Harvest Time Chili Con Carne

In the fall, the harvest crews began arriving in the north country, after starting earlier in the year on the Texican border and working the fields northward as the wheat and oats and rye and barley ripened. The harvest hands usually worked for a contractor who went from farm to farm with his equipment, portable bunkhouse, and cookshack. But many of them were free-lance workers who hired out to the farmer and came and went as they pleased (usually leaving when they had a stake to spend, before hiring out again). These were motley crews, of many origins and customs. In the early part of the century my dad was a blacksmith with one of these crews one fall, and my mother ran the cookshack. The recipe for chili she used in later years probably was acquired from the Texican hands and originated south of the border.

1½ lb. hamburger or ground beef
1 large onion, chopped
1 small green pepper, chopped
½ c ketchup
1 can mushrooms
1 T crushed red pepper
1 small stalk celery, chopped
1 clove garlic, chopped
1 can tomatoes
1 can tomato soup
1 can kidney beans
salt and pepper to taste

In a large kettle mix celery, mushrooms, tomatoes, tomato soup, and ketchup. Let cook over a slow fire while preparing the rest. In a frying pan, brown the chopped onion, pepper, and garlic with a large chunk of butter. Add the meat and keep mixing until meat loses raw color. Combine this with the mixture in the kettle, add seasonings, and cook, thickening with beans before removing from fire. Serve with salted crackers.

(Note: This is not a "hot" chili — more of a pot meal.)

*Rib-Stickin' Beef Stew**

Real country beef stew is always good, always appropriate, and always rib-stickin' nourishment. Good fer what ails ya, as the old-timers say.

1 lb. beef
1 T lard
¾ t salt
1½ c water
¾ c carrots
½ c tomatoes
3 small onions
pinch pepper
3 T flour
1½ t parsley

Cut beef into cubes. Sprinkle with flour and brown evenly in pan. Add water, tomatoes, and parsley. Simmer 1 hour. Add rest of the vegetables, salt, and pepper. Simmer 1 hour longer. Mix 1½ T flour with ¼ c water. Stir to a paste and thicken the stew. Serve hot.

— 3 —

Home Canning and Food Processing

Long after the REA (Rural Electrification Administration) brought electrical power to even the most isolated farmhouses, the annual fall canning and food processing would begin with the general harvest. Indeed, home canning has regained its popularity, due to the renewed interest in the land and the old ways and an almost universal search for goodness that seems to have been lost in the sophistication of the computer age. Happily, the equipment available for this very satisfying home-kitchen activity is today much more efficient (and safer) than in the old days. It is doubtful that home canning today is more economical than store-boughten products, but the quality and nutritious value of the home-packed foods makes up for this.

I can remember that for days on end our kitchen, back stoop, dining room, and root cellar would be caught up in an air of organized confusion, as boxes and boxes of mason jars, lids, and seals were prepared; crates and crates of vegetables, fruits, and berries were gathered; and newly butchered cattle and hogs were assembled. Firewood was chopped, and scuttles of local lignite coal were stacked handy. On the kitchen stove, great kettles would be bubbling or throwing off clouds of steam. Everyone was part of the canning crew, including all my brothers, with my mother leading and directing.

Before the week was out the cellar shelves would once again be jammed from floor to ceiling with jars of canned fruit, vegetables, meat, fish, preserves, jams, and jellies. This would be the main winter's supply of food for the family — and then some.

There is nothing quite so satisfying as having your basement shelves full of home-canned and preserved food. Since this is a major subject in itself, our purpose here is to introduce readers to it and to some of the ways it has traditionally been done. The authors wish to emphasize that readers should pay strict attention to directions for using home-canning equipment, as provided by manufacturers. County agricultural agents, state university extension services, and the U.S. Department of Agriculture can provide free information suited to local food products and conditions.

However, there are no great mysteries connected with home canning, nor is any great skill required. Exercise reasonable care and follow directions exactly, and you'll be successful and have a lot of fun doing it.

RULES FOR SAFE HOME CANNING

1. *Botulism:* This is a rare but usually fatal poison which has occurred in both commercial and home-canned *low acid* foods such as corn, green beans, beets, mushrooms, peas, and, potatoes, and meats, including fish. Low-acid foods should always be processed in a pressure canner at the recommended pressure and time. Be sure the pressure gauge is working properly

Cans of both commerical and home-processed low-acid foods that you even remotely suspect should be discarded. You cannot detect botulism bacteria by smell or visual inspection The taste test is like playing Russian roulette; it is just as deadly as eating tainted food, even though you don't swallow it. Botulinus bacteria can be destroyed by boiling the food 10 to 15 minutes (some say 25 to 20 minutes) in an open vessel before tasting. If it then does not smell or look okay, discard without tasting.

2. *Molds and Yeast:* The main cause of food spoilage

is the growth of these microorganisms, but they are not necessarily toxic. A few minutes' boiling will stop their growth.

3. *Bacteria:* There are many different kinds of these microorganisms, and some are more resistant to boiling than others. Acid foods like tomatoes and fruit inhibit the growth of bacteria, but, generally, simply heating or cooking food is not enough to destroy them. Only by boiling or processing in a pressure cooker for the recommended time can you be sure.

4. *Enzymes:* These are numerous proteins produced by living organisms which function as biochemical catalysts and which can cause discoloration, loss of flavor, and texture in raw fruits and vegetables. Enzymes can be neutralized by proper processing in canning and drying. Fruits, tomatoes, rhubarb, and pickled vegetables are best processed in a boiling-water bath-canner. All else *must* be pressure cooked.

Fruit and Vegetable Yield Chart for Home Canning

Kind	*Fresh*	*Canned*
Apricots	1 bu.	20 to 24 qt.
Apples	1 bu.	16 to 20 qt.
Berries	crate (24 qt.)	12 to 18 qt.
Strawberries	crate	12 to 16 qt.
Cherries	1 bu.	22 to 32 qt.
Peaches	1 bu.	18 to 24 qt.
Pineapple	2 whole	1 qt.
Plums	1 bu.	24 to 30 qt.
Tomatoes	1 bu.	15 to 20 qt.
Asparagus	1 bu.	11 qt.
Lima beans (pods)	1 bu.	6 to 8 qt.
Snap beans	1 bu.	15 to 20 qt.
Beets	1 bu.	17 to 20 qt.
Brussel sprouts	1 lb.	1 pt.
Carrots	1 bu.	16 to 20 qt.
Sweet corn (cobs)	1 bu.	8 to 9 qt.
Eggplant	each	1 pt.

Kind	*Fresh*	*Canned*
Kale	1 bu.	12 to 18 pt.
Okra	1 bu.	17 qt.
Peas (pods)	1 bu.	12 to 15 qt.
Pumpkin	50 lb.	15 qt.
Spinach	1 bu.	6 to 9 qt.
Summer squash	1 bu.	16 to 20 qt.
Sweet potatoes	1 bu.	18 to 22 qt.

STORING HOME-PROCESSED FOOD

Canned foods should be stored in a cool, dark, dry place, usually the basement or root cellar, at a temperature below 68 degrees F. Before storing, remove the screw bands that hold the seal on the jar. Wash jars in warm soapy water, rinse and dry. Do not allow canned foods to freeze.

Dried foods can be stored in sealed plastic bags; or better, in mason jars with caps. They do not have to be pressure sealed.

Pressure Canner

Altitude	**Canning pressure**
2,000- 3,000 feet	11.5 pounds
3,000- 4,000 feet	12 pounds
4,000- 5,000 feet	12.5 pounds
5,000- 6,000 feet	13 pounds
6,000- 7,000 feet	13.5 pounds
7,000- 8,000 feet	14 pounds
8,000- 9,000 feet	14.5 pounds
9,000-10,000 feet	15 pounds

Boiling Water Bath

Altitude	**Increase the time***	**Increase the time****
1,000 feet	1 minute	2 minutes
2,000 feet	2 minutes	4 minutes
3,000 feet	3 minutes	6 minutes
4,000 feet	4 minutes	8 minutes
5,000 feet	5 minutes	10 minutes

Altitude	Increase the time*	Increase the time**
6,000 feet	6 minutes	12 minutes
7,000 feet	7 minutes	14 minutes
8,000 feet	8 minutes	16 minutes
9,000 feet	9 minutes	18 minutes
10,000 feet	10 minutes	20 minutes

*If time called for is 20 minutes or less.
**If time called for is 20 minutes or more.

Warning

All vegetables except tomatoes and all meats, poultry, and fish canned at home must be boiled in an open vessel for 10 to 15 minutes before tasting or eating.

Boiling Water Bath Processing Times

Kind	Pints	Quarts
Apples	20 minutes	25 minutes
Applesauce	25 minutes	25 minutes
Apricots	20 minutes	25 minutes
Berries	15 minutes	20 minutes
Cherries	20 minutes	20 minutes
Cranberries	10 minutes	10 minutes
Currants	20 minutes	20 minutes
Dried fruits	15 minutes	15 minutes
Figs	90 minutes	90 minutes
Fruit juices	10 minutes	10 minutes
Grapefruit	20 minutes	20 minutes
Grapes	20 minutes	20 minutes
Nectarines	20 minutes	25 minutes
Peaches	20 minutes	25 minutes
Pears	25 minutes	30 minutes
Pineapple	30 minutes	30 minutes
Plums	20 minutes	25 minutes
Rhubarb	10 minutes	10 minutes
Strawberries	15 minutes	15 minutes
Tomatoes	35 minutes	45 minutes
Tomato juice	15 minutes	15 minutes
Stewed tomatoes	55 minutes	55 minutes

Note: For half-gallon jars add 10 minutes to the above.

Pressure Canner Cooking Time and Pressure

Food	**Pints**	**Quarts**	**Pounds**
Asparagus	25 minutes	30 minutes	10
Green wax beans	20 minutes	25 minutes	10
Lima beans	40 minutes	50 minutes	10
Beets	30 minutes	40 minutes	10
Broccoli	25 minutes	40 minutes	10
Brussel spouts	45 minutes	55 minutes	10
Cabbage	45 minutes	55 minutes	10
Carrots	25 minutes	30 minutes	10
Cream-style corn	85 minutes	—	10
Whole kernel corn	55 minutes	85 minutes	10
Eggplant	30 minutes	40 minutes	10
Greens (all)	70 minutes	90 minutes	10
Hominy	60 minutes	70 minutes	10
Mushrooms	30 minutes	35 minutes	10
Okra	25 minutes	40 minutes	10
Onions	40 minutes	40 minutes	10
Shelled peas	40 minutes	40 minutes	10
Bell peppers	35 minutes	35 minutes	10
Pimiento peppers	10 minutes	—	5
Pumpkin	60 minutes	80 minutes	10
Irish potatoes	40 minutes	40 minutes	10
Rutabagas	35 minutes	35 minutes	10
Soybeans	80 minutes	80 minutes	10
Summer squash	25 minutes	30 minutes	10
Winter squash	60 minutes	80 minutes	10
Sweet potatoes	55 minutes	90 minutes	10
Turnips	20 minutes	25 minutes	10

Pressure Canner Cooking Time and Pressure

Food	**Pints**	**Quarts**	**Pounds**
Lamb	75 minutes	90 minutes	10
Veal	75 minutes	90 minutes	10
Beef	75 minutes	90 minutes	10
Tenderloin	75 minutes	90 minutes	10
Ham	75 minutes	90 minutes	10
Sausage	75 minutes	90 minutes	10
Pork	75 minutes	90 minutes	10
Chicken	75 minutes	90 minutes	10
Birds	75 minutes	90 minutes	10
Turkey, duck	75 minutes	90 minutes	10

Food	Pints	Quarts	Pounds
Venison, (deer, elk)	75 minutes	90 minutes	10
Geese	75 minutes	90 minutes	10
Fish (all)	100 minutes	100 minutes	10

Processing Pickles in Boiling Water Bath

Kind	Jar	Minutes*
Bread and butter	qt.	10
Bread and butter	pt.	5
Chutney	pt.	5
Cross cuts	pt.	5
Dill green beans	pt.	5
Gherkins, sweet	pt.	5
Piccalilli	pt.	5
Onion-pepper relish	pt.	5
Corn relish	pt.	15
Watermelon	pt.	5
Dill, whole (fermented)	qt	15
Dill (unfermented, fresh)	qt.	20
Sauerkraut	qt.	15

*Start counting time when water starts to boil and *after* jars are placed into kettle.

HOW MUCH TO BUY OR HARVEST

Produce	Unit	Weight	Canned
Apples	box	40 lbs.	15-18 qts.
	pounds	2½ lbs.	1 qt.
Apricots	lug	25 lbs.	15-18 qts.
	pounds	1½ lbs.	1 qt.
Asparagus	pounds	3½ lbs.	1 qt.
Snap beans	pounds	2 lbs.	1 qt.
Beets	pounds	3 lbs.	1 qt.
Berries	crate	10 lbs.	6 qts.
Broccoli	pounds	1 lb.	1 pt.
Brussel sprouts	pounds	1 lb.	1 pt.
Cabbage	pounds	6 lbs.	2 qts.
Carrots	pounds	3 lbs.	1 qt.
Cauliflower	pounds	1⅓ lbs.	1 pt.
Cherries	pounds	2 lbs.	1 qt.
Corn husks	pounds	4 lbs.	1 qt.
Peaches	lug	24 lbs.	10 qts.
	pounds	2-3 lbs.	1 qt.

Produce	Unit	Weight	Canned
Pears	pounds	2-3 lbs.	1 qt.
Peas, pod	pounds	3-6 lbs.	1 qt.
Plums, prunes	crate	20 lbs.	10 qts.
	pounds	2 lbs.	2 qts.
Strawberries	crate	8-9 lbs.	4-5 qts.
	12 pints	1½ lbs.	1 qt.
Tomatoes	lug	25 lbs.	10 qts.
	pounds	3 lbs.	1 qt.
Pumpkin	pounds	3 lbs	1 qt.
Squash, summer	pounds	2 lbs.	1 qt.
	For Juice		
Apples	3 lbs.		4 cups
Blackberry	3 lbs.		4 cups
Cherry	3 lbs.		3 cups
Grape	3½ lbs.		4 cups
Plum	4½ lbs.		4 cups
Strawberry	4½ lbs.		4 cups
	Jam or Jelly		
Blackberry	4 lbs.		4 cups.
Blueberry	2 lbs.		4 cups
Cherry	3 lbs.		4½ cups
Rhubarb	2½ lbs.		4 cups
Plum	2½ lbs.		4½ cups
Peaches	4 lbs.		4 cups
Strawberry	2 lbs.		4 cups
Chokecherry	3 lbs.		4 cups

Pickled Carrots

2 to 3 bunches carrots
1 c sugar
1 t salt
1½ c water
2 T pickling spices
2 t dried rosemary
2 c vinegar

Cook carrots in a little water until tender. Drain, and scrape skins. Small carrots are left whole; large ones sliced lengthwise. Mix sugar, water, vinegar, and salt in a large pan or kettle. Put the spices in a bag and add.

Myrtle Holm is completing a batch of dried vegetables to be used in the winter for soups and stews.

Boil 5 minutes. Pack carrots into hot, sterilized jar. Leave about ¼-inch head space.

Remove spice bag. Heat syrup to boiling and pour over carrots. Use lids and process in boiling water bath. Makes about 3 pints.

*Sweet Pickles**

Use medium sized cucumbers with skins on. To each quart of sliced cucumbers add 1 large sliced onion and 1 sweet pepper, chopped fine. Sprinkle lightly with salt and drain in colander for 3 hours. Add to drained liquid 1 t tumeric, 1 c sugar, mustard seed, and 1 doz. cloves with soft heads removed, 1 t grated horseradish, and enough vinegar to cover. Heat to the boiling point, pour over cucumbers, and seal while hot.

Wholesome Homemade Dills

5 lbs. small cucumbers
2½ qts. water
¼ c salt
3 c water
fresh or dried dill heads
5 cloves garlic
½ c salt
2 c vinegar
2 T sugar
1 T mixed whole pickling spices
2 T whole mustard seed

Wash cucumbers. Mix ½ c salt and 2½ qts. water to make a brine. Pour over cucumbers and let stand overnight. In morning, drain. Mix vinegar, ¼ c salt, 3 c water and pickling spices. Bring to a boil. Strain and remove pickling spices. Pack cucumbers into hot pint jars. Add a dill head to each jar, plus 1 t whole mustard seed and 1 clove garlic. Pour hot vinegar mixture over cucumbers to within ½ inch of top. Make sure the rim is clean and dry, and adjust the lids. Process in boiling water bath for 20 minutes. Remove and cool. Makes 5 pints.

Corn Relish

12 ears corn
5 red peppers
1 bunch celery
1 head cabbage
8 onions

Chop cabbage and sprinkle with salt and some water. Let stand for 1 hour and boil until tender. Cook corn and cut kernels from cob. Combine corn with cabbage, peppers, onions, and celery in a kettle. Mix and add the following:

3 c vinegar
1 T mustard
½ c flour
2 lbs. brown sugar
1 T tumeric

Boil until thickened. Pour all into scalded jars and seal.

Pickled Crabapple

7 lbs. crabapples
3 lbs. sugar
1 t cinnamon
1 qt. vinegar
1 t whole cloves

Wash crabapples and prick with needle. Pack in scalded jars. Make a syrup of rest of ingredients, boiling spices in a bag. Pour over apples and let stand overnight. Pour off liquid and boil; pour over apples again and let stand overnight. Boil with apples third time. Seal hot.

Watermelon Pickles (My Favorite)

7 lbs. watermelon rinds
3½ lbs. sugar
¼ t oil of cinnamon
½ t powdered alum
1 pt. vinegar
⅛ t oil of cloves
2 t salt

Cut rind into fingerlike chunks, cook in water with

salt and alum. When tender, drain. Make a syrup of sugar, vinegar, and oils, and pour boiling hot over rinds. Let stand overnight, then drain off syrup, bring to a boil again, and pour back over rinds. Let stand another day. Then drain off syrup and bring to a boil. Pack rinds in scalded jars, cover with hot syrup, and seal.

Bread and Butter Pickles

25 pickling cucmbers
2 peppers
5 c cider vinegar
2 T mustard seed
½ t clove
8 white onions
½ c salt
5 c sugar
1 t tumeric

Wash and slice cucumbers crosswise, as thin as possible. Chop onions and peppers. Mix with cucumbers and salt. Let stand 3 hours and drain. Combine vinegar, sugar, tumeric, clove, and mustard seed in large kettle. Bring to a boil. Add cucumbers, onions, and peppers. Heat until well blended, but don't boil. Pour into scalded jars and seal.

Beet Pickles

Cook and skin beets. Pack in jars and cover with the following syrup:

4 c sugar
4 c vinegar
4 c water
2 T pickling spices in bag

Boil well and fill jars. Makes 6 qts. Use in salads or as table vegetable.

Chowchow

1 peck green tomatoes
6 onions
1 small cabbage
6 red or green peppers

Chop tomatoes, combine with chopped cabbage, onions, peppers, and spread with 3 handfuls of salt. Let stand overnight. Drain in a sack. Prepare a syrup as follows:

2 qts. vinegar
½ c mustard seed
4½ lbs. sugar

Boil 7 minutes. Add chow and boil 10 minutes. Seal in jars while hot.

Sweet Mustard Pickles

small cucumbers
¼ c brown sugar
2 T salt
¼ t saccharin
1 qt. vinegar
2 T ground mustard
1 t mixed spices

Pack pickles in scalded jars and pour liquid over. Seal.

Spiced Rhubarb

7 lbs. rhubarb
1 pt. vinegar
½ t ground cinnamon
3 oranges
7 lbs. sugar
½ t ground cloves
2 lbs. raisins

Grind raisins; grate and juice oranges. Combine with rhubarb and sugar and let stand overnight. Add rest of ingredients and boil until thickened. Add nuts if desired. Scald jars and seal.

Rhubarb Jam

2 c rhubarb
1 lemon
2 c sugar
1 orange

Chop rhubarb. Combine with sugar and juice of lemon and orange. Let stand until juice forms. Boil until thick. Add nuts if desired.

Pear Delights

24 pears
4 oranges
sugar
1 c pineapple
1 bottle cherries

Chop fruit into small chunks. Add ¾ c sugar to 1 c fruit. Let stand overnight. Steam until it jells. Add cherries last. Color with cherry juice if desired.

Tomato Jelly

1 envelope gelatine
¾ c sugar
2 c tomato juice, strained
stuffed olives
1½ c boiling water
½ c vinegar
½ t salt

Dissolve gelatine in vinegar. Add salt and sugar, blend in boiling water. Add tomato juice and, if desired, some stuffed olives. Let set and cool. Serve on lettuce leaf.

Raspberry Conserve

1 pt. raspberries
1 lb. raisins
2 oranges
1 lb. sugar to each lb. fruit
1 pt. rhubarb
1 lb. walnuts
2 lemons

Cut and slice lemons and oranges into very thin slices. Mix all ingredients and cook 2 hours in open kettle or until jelled.

Strawberry Preserves

1 qt. strawberries
5 c sugar

Collect berries in a colander and pour boiling water over them. Follow this by boiling slowly with 2 cups sugar for a couple of minutes. Add the rest of the sugar and boil 5 more minutes. Cool and set for 24 hours, stirring occasionally.

Two-by-Two Marmalade

2 oranges
2 lemon
2 T cornstarch
2 c cold water
2 c sugar

Chop oranges in food grinder. Add the juice and pulp of lemons, and the water. Cook until orange rind is tender. Mix cornstarch with sugar and add. Cook another 5 minutes.

Pumpkin Butter

6 lb. pumpkin
2 lemons, sliced thin
4 lb. sugar

Peel pumpkin, cut into small chunks, combine with sugar and lemons. Let stand overnight. In the morning boil slowly until thick. Store in mason jars, sealed.

Four-Fruit Jam

12 peaches
1 orange
12 pears
1 can pineapple

¾ cup sugar for every cup of fruit. Simmer until thickened.

Pepper Relish

No country home was ever without a pepper relish jar on the table. Here is the basic formula: Select several varieties of peppers fresh from the garden, such as a dozen sweet ones for red color, a couple of dozen Sweet Banana peppers, and two or three hot peppers. Remove seeds and membranes and grind with 7 onions. Mix 2 cups sugar, 2 tablespoons mustard seed, 3 cups vinegar, and 2 tablespoons salt. Add to peppers and onions and boil 30 minutes. Pack and seal in scalded mason jars.

Preparing Horseradish

Harvest roots in the cool of the evening, or in the fall or spring. Scrape and peel, then run through grater until you get the consistency you want, either chunky or smooth. Add some sour cream and/or a little white vinegar and blend well.

For a hot mustard, blend some raw horseradish into regular table mustard to suit taste.

Store horseradish in small jars, sealed, in fridge.

Rhubarb Marmalade

1 lemon
4 lbs. rhubarb
3 lbs. sugar
2 oranges
1 lb. raisins

Juice the lemon and oranges, and blend the juice with chopped rhubarb. Add chopped lemon and orange rind, and chopped raisins. Mix and let stand 1 hour. Add sugar and bring to a boil. Simmer for 1 hour, stirring. When thick, pour into hot, scalded jars and let stand until cool. When set, seal with melted paraffin.

Cherry-Rhubarb Jam

Pit cherries and slice into pieces. Cut and wash rhubarb and put on to boil with cherries. When soft, add jell and bring to a boil. Add sugar and bring to a rolling boil for 1 minute. Pour into hot jars and seal at once.

Green Tomato Jam

For every cup of chopped green tomatoes add 1 cup sugar. Add 1 lemon to every 6 cups. Add cloves, cinnamon, nutmeg to taste and boil. When ready pack hot in scalded jars.

Gooseberry Conserve

5 c gooseberries
1 c chopped raisins
1 t cinnamon
6 c sugar
2 oranges
1 t cloves

Chop and juice oranges. Boil all together until thick. Pack in jelly glasses. Seal with wax.

Wintertime Jam

2 c dried apricots
2 c shredded pineapple
7 c sugar
juice and rind of lemon

Soak 'cots overnight. Cook slowly ½ hour, adding pineapple and sugar. Boil a few minutes until thick, adding juice and rind of lemon. Pack hot and seal with wax.

Garden Potpourri Relish

2 c green tomatoes
2 c sliced onions
2 red peppers
2 c diced celery
3 c sugar
1 can lima beans
1 c salt
2 c cucumbers
2 green peppers
2 c diced carrots
3 c vinegar
3 t mustard seed
1 can kidney beans

Dice tomatoes, cucumbers, onions, peppers. Soak overnight in 1 quart of water with 1 cup salt. Drain well. Cook carrots and celery separately. Drain. Make a syrup of vinegar and sugar, with mustard seed. Add green vegetables and boil in syrup until done. Add cooked celery, carrots, and drained lima and kidney beans. Bring to boil and seal in scalded jars.

Pickled Peaches

12 to 16 peaches
2 c cider vinegar
6 sticks cinnamon
whole cloves
2 c sugar

Use firm peaches. Remove skins. Press 4 to 6 cloves into each and drop into boiling hot syrup made from sugar, vinegar, and cinnamon. Boil until peaches are tender, about 10 minutes. Pack in scalded jars to within ¼ inch from top of jar. Pour on hot syrup , and seal.

Sausages and Kings

The lowly sausage comes down to us from earliest recorded history. At various times this salted and preserved form of meat has been reserved for royal use only, for religious festivals, and for military campaigns. The word comes from the Latin *Salsus*, meaning salted and preserved meat. It was a common staple of Roman life. Sausage, however, predates the Roman Empire by centuries and is probably as old as civilization — perhaps older.

Homer mentioned sausage in the *Odyssey;* Caesar used precooked sausage in his military expeditions — which could be called the earliest K-rations. In the Middle Ages sausage was an important part of the daily diet, especially wurst, which was — then as now — served with beer and wine. Germany and Italy were centers of sausage-making, and the old Butchers' Guild handed down the art for generations. Various types of sausages were named for the towns where they were originated, such as frankfurters, weiners (Vienna), bologna, thuringer, romano, salami.

Sausage is also a major staple for consumers of meat, according to the U.S. Department of Agriculture. About 10 percent of the total meat supply today is in the form of cooked and smoked sausage. Home sausage making has also become increasingly popular in recent years, with the equipment readily available at low cost from specialty food stores and suppliers.

Salome's Salami

4 lb. lean hamburger **½ lb. pork sausage**
¼ c Tender Quick or Adolph's Tenderizer

Mix well, cover and refrigerate overnight. The next day add:

2 T liquid smoke **2 t garlic powder**
2 t fresh ground pepper **½ c dry red wine**

Mix well and shape into 3 long rolls. Wrap each roll tightly in nylon netting. This keeps meat from spreading out. Place on broiling rack in oven. Bake at 225 degrees for 4 hours. Remove from oven and place on paper towels to absorb the excess grease.

— 5 —

Harvesting the Wild Ones — Fish and Game

It was taken for granted when I was growing up that our menu would be supplemented with wild game when available.

The most desirable bird around our place was the ring-necked pheasant, which had been introduced into the United States — first in Oregon's Willamette Valley — by Judge Owen Denny, then consul general in China. These fine birds took readily to America and quickly spread across the northern tier of states. At one time North and South Dakota were the Chinese pheasant capital of the world.

These are big birds with golden flesh. My mother always skinned the birds and cut them into serving pieces to be fried.

Ducks and geese were so plentiful in the fall that our back stoop was usually jammed with gunnysacks full of birds waiting to be cleaned. After the first freeze we could clean them more or less at our convenience. The first thing to do is clip the wing tips and remove all the coarse feathers, until only the fuzzy down is left. Melt a package of paraffin in a pail of water and immerse the bird in the hot liquid. Remove and dunk in cold water to harden the wax. Peel off the coating of paraffin, and the feathers and down will come with it, leaving a clean, naked bird. Next, open up the pelvis and draw all the innards.

Soak the birds in cold salted water overnight if possible but for at least 2 hours. Do not parboil, as this will ruin the taste.

Roast wild duck without dressing but with a large

The author, Don Holm, with a fine cock pheasant taken during a hunting trip to Idaho.

onion, carrot, or unpeeled apple in the cavity and strips of bacon or salt pork on the breast. Cook in a hot oven for ½ hour, then reduce heat to 325 degrees until bird is done, or about 1 to 2 hours, depending on the size of bird. Baste frequently and don't overcook.

Venison, which means any red-meated wild animal such as deer or elk, can be prepared in many ways. Roasts are done, the same as with beef, by searing in a hot oven for ½ hour, then at reduced heat for about ½ hour to the pound. Deer meat is very dry, and *all* the fat should be removed and discarded. Baste or moisten with beef suet while roasting, and put in onions for the last hour or so.

How to Cook Venison

The word venison technically refers to all hoofed wild animals but is most commonly applied nowadays to deer meat. The same processing of venison, however, applies to moose, caribou, reindeer, elk, bighorn sheep, mountain goat, or antelope.

Venison not only has a different taste and texture than domestic meat but has many not-so-subtle differences that will affect any recipes or meals produced from it. First, the animal usually has been feeding on graze that tends to make the meat "strong," unlike beef animals that are fed and fattened on domestic grains developed for that purpose. Moreover, domestic beef is always aged after butchering, which improves the flavor and cooking qualities.

Assuming that the wild animal has been properly cared for and butchered after killing, the meat can be of excellent quality if a few tips are followed:

1. *All* fat and gristle should be removed, leaving only the lean. Discard low-quality parts.

2. Do not *overcook*. Venison has short fibers that

quickly become tough while cooking. Do not use extreme high temperatures. Venison should be served medium well done, never rare or very well done.

3. Unlike beef, venison with no fat is *not* low quality, and this should be taken into account when cooking. Tender cuts like loin or tenderloin should be broiled or grilled. Less tender cuts like round should be cooked with moist heat, by stewing or pot-roasting. Venison burger, ground meat, is a popular and excellent way to use wild game. Most experienced cooks mix a little pork sausage with the ground venison to add flavor and moisture.

4. For storing, venison should be protected from further drying by wrapping in foil, using a cooking bag, or covering with bacon strips.

5. When cooking, use beef or pork fat or cooking oil for shortening. Never use venison fat.

6. Disguise the flavor, if necessary, with spices, herbs, and seasonings. Marinades, soy sauce, and barbecue sauces are fine.

7. "Tame" the wild flavor by combining venison with domestic meats and vegetables in stews, soups, and burgers.

8. Try to expand your repertoire of venison dishes so as to provide variety — individual tastes vary with wild game just as they do with domestic meats.

9. Venison should be aged like domestic meat before using — except for the liver, which may be cooked and eaten with relish as soon as cooled after butchering.

Pheasant

Skin (don't pick) the bird and cut into serving-size pieces. Brown in butter or suet. After cooking until nearly done, cover with sweet or sour cream and continue frying on low, even heat until tender. Make gravy from drippings, adding onions and mushrooms if desired.

Rabbit

Clean and wash animal and wipe well. Cut into serving pieces. To 1 slightly beaten egg add 2 T water, ⅛ t pepper, 1½ t salt. Dip pieces into egg mixture and roll in 1 c fine, dry bread crumbs. Brown in about a half inch of hot fat or oil. Reduce heat, cover, and cook slowly for 30 minutes or until tender. Serve on a bed of boiled rice and brown gravy:

Brown Gravy

Drain off all fat in pan except about 3 T. Blend in 3 T flour, ¾ t salt and ⅛ t pepper. Cook until brown, stirring constantly, then boil 2 minutes. Stir in 1½ c water or rabbit stock.

Roast Venison

Wipe meat with vinegar-soaked cloth and dredge with salted and peppered flour. Put strips of bacon over meat, fasten with toothpicks. Hang onion rings over toothpicks. Put in hot oven for about ½ hour, then reduce heat and bake slowly for ½ hour to the pound. Before serving pour tomato soup over roast. Cover and put back in oven for a few minutes. Remove and make gravy or Spanish sauce from liquid, to be served with meat.

Bread Stuffing

4 c bread cubes
1 t salt
¼ t poultry seasoning
⅓ c melted butter
3 T chopped onions
¼ t pepper
sage
hot water or stock

Combine bread, onion, seasonings, adding butter and liquid to moisten. Toss to mix gently. It takes about 1 c stuffing for each pound of poultry or game birds.

Variations:

Add 1½ c chopped celery.
Add chopped, cooked giblets and use giblet stock for liquid.
Add ½ pt. drained, chopped oysters, heated in the butter.
Add ½ c seedless raisins.

"And the Bullfrog in the Pool. . . ."

Bullfrogs were common throughout the Midwest, their natural habitat. They are also common over most of the continent now, but most people are unaware that they were *transplanted* and introduced by homesick pilgrims to many areas, such as the Rocky Mountain states. In Idaho, for example, the bullfrog was brought out from Missouri about 1895 by a man named William H. Ridenbaugh, who was superintendent of the stage company and Wells Fargo agent in Boise. He was the guy, also, who introduced the largemouth bass to local Idaho waters, another popular transplanted citizen of the West.

Bullfrogs are classed with game fish in most states, with a bag limit, usually 12 a day. An amphibian, not a fish, the bullfrog is nevertheless classified with the fishes for legal and administrative purposes. The Roman Catholic Church, confronted with this biological anomaly, has for religious reasons, decreed that the bullfrog is a fish.

Whatever the bullfrog is called it has legs that are a gourmet's delight. When I was a kid, we used to catch frogs with a long-handled net, something like a butterfly net, and we also raised them in ponds in the backyard for sale. The bullfrog, though, can be caught on hook and line just like a fish. A long pole with a short line attached is very effective, dangling a small piece of red cloth or an old artificial fly. Cast anywhere near a bullfrog, it invariably results in lightning fast leap and a hook-up.

Frogs can be kept alive indefinitely in a backyard

pond, provided there is cover, food (insects), and protection from predators (besides man) such as fish, hawks, cats, and kids.

Frogs can be "butchered" by a quick thrust of a icepick through the throat. While the frog is pinned to a plank, cut off the legs with a sharp knife and skin them.

Frog Legs Royale

Remove legs from frog and skin them. Wash and cover with boiling water, letting stand for a minute or so. Dry on paper towel. Beat the yolks of 3 eggs. Add 1 t lemon juice. Dip legs in this and roll in grated crumbs. Shake and dip once more. Drop in hot oil and deep-fry quickly. Don't overcook. Serve with slice of lemon and sprig of parsley.

How the Indians Cooked 'Em

Dried Indian Pumpkin

When Lewis and Clark made their famous trek to the Pacific Ocean and back, they were surprised to find many of the Plains tribes cultivating gardens, including pumpkins, squash, and many other vegetables. One of the pumpkin dishes they recorded was this:

Cut a pumpkin into rings about 1 inch thick, removing strings and seeds. Hang rings in the sun on a cord or on a stick, rod, or bar. Let dry and dehydrate naturally, until they get brittle. Take in at night and set out in the morning to keep dew off. When all moisture is gone, store in sealed jars.

For a delicious dish, boil the rings, sweeten with brown sugar and bake.

Indian Chokecherries

The tribes of the mountain areas of the West gathered wild chokecherries in late summer and early fall, prior to the gathering of pine nuts. The cherries were washed and rubbed through a basket sieve to remove the pits. The juice was saved. The mash was formed into patties and dried for the winter supply. When used, the patties were first soaked in water, which restored the wild chokecherry flavor. In more recent times the juice was used for making jelly and wine.

Indian Oak Tree Soup

Collect wild acorn nuts from the oak grove, shell them, and pound the nutmeat into a meal. Put in a clean cloth and strain with fresh cold water. Add the meal to any soup broth before bringing to a boil.

Indian Fried Bread

3½ c flour
3 t baking powder
½ t salt

Mix with enough lukewarm water to make a batter. Let stand while heating oil in a deep kettle. In a bowl blend more dry flour into the dough to make it very stiff. Knead it thoroughly, shake off loose flour, and form into flapjack-size cakes, about ¾ inch thick. Deep-fry in 350 degree fat until golden brown. Serve with butter and syrup or jam.

Northern Lights Pudding

1 qt. milk
4 T sugar
3 eggs
1 T butter
½ t ginger
2 T corn or grain meal
1 t salt

Amounts are not critical; use your own judgment. Boil the milk in a double boiler, stir in the meal thoroughly. Cook for about 10 to 15 minutes, while stirring. Beat the eggs and blend in salt, sugar, and ginger. Stir butter into milk mixture. Pour this over the beaten eggs. Bake in slow oven for 1 hour. Serve with a buttered syrup, hot.

Frontier Recipes

Before the pioneers came, the West was well crossed by obscure, independent characters known as mountain men — traders, trappers, and nonconformists of another century on a wild and half-explored frontier. Some of the fixin's they enjoyed have been passed down, but most are lost. Here are a few:

Tradin' Post Pemmican

First obtain some meat like moose, deer, elk, bear, mountain sheep, goat, antelope, or what have you, even a stray beef or so. After butchering and cleaning, cook by roasting or boiling, then grind or pound into small bits. Grind up onions, wild or otherwise, and season with anything you've got. Mix well with melted suet or meat stock and pack in a container (they used a pouch of hide or a hollow horn or buckskin bag), pressing down firmly and sqeezing out juice. Cover with melted suet or lard. Cool well and store in a cool place. You can also add to the mix, dried and pounded fruit and berries. Use a lot of spices, if you have them handy. This is a very nourishing, long-lasting food. Very good for packing on the trail, as no refrigeration is needed.

Bear Fat Pastry

The fat of the black bear is probably the best, most nutritious there is, especially if the animal has been feeding on wild berries. It makes a superb pie crust. Use 1 c bear fat or mix 50-50 with deer or elk fat, 4 c flour, and salt to taste. Use milk to make the dough, and roll out for pie shells in the usual way.

Frontier Soap

Bear fat also makes an excellent soap. Render it out like tallow and follow directions on a can of lye, usually available in old-time stores. Or use 1 lb. of lye and 3 or 4 lbs. of tallow with water. Simmer over low flame until solids have melted. Remove pot from heat, keep stirring, and cool in cold water. Pour into molds while still liquid. Let age a few days and slice into slabs for use. If covered with soda ash, scrape this off before using. Old-timers did not have lye handy; they made soap with ashes, which had the same effect.

Pickled Deer

2 c coarse salt
2 t black pepper
½ t saltpeter
1 c brown sugar or molasses
2 t soda

This is enough to cure a half deer carcass or quarter of elk. Butcher meat into convenient pieces and sprinkle with the above mixture, packing tightly in a crock. Weigh down with a crock lid or plate so all is submerged in liquid. Brine for about 1 week before serving. It tastes like ham. No cooking is necessary.

Boiled Milkweed

The trappers got this from the Indian maidens:

Collect milkweed pods early in the morning before the sun comes up. Boil the young plants with salted water. The pods are very sweet and can be used for sugar.

All-Day Stew

Butcher deer, elk, or bear and cook venison in bear fat rendered in boiling water. Add rice, onions, or any-

Art Lacey, Milwaukie, Oregon, friend of the authors, is preparing to bone out and butcher a deer carcass.

thing else you have. Stir in a little flour. Cover and, if using a dutch oven or cast-iron pot, set on bed of coals and let simmer all day until the evening meal. Serve with bannock or sourdough biscuits.

How To Preserve Wild Berries

Pick berries and spread out on canvas or mat of woven rushes. Let dry in sun. Take in at night and set out in morning after dew is gone. When dry, store in clean, dry, dark place for winter use.

Wild tiger lily bulbs are pulled up by the roots after the flower has dropped. Wash off dirt and boil with blueberries or huckleberries.

Horse Soldier Stew

Cut meat in pieces and roll in flour with salt and pepper. Make a pastry of 1 lb. flour, 1 t soda, 1 t cream tartar, and chunk of butter, with milk to make paste.

Divide dough into two parts, one large and one small. Roll out larger piece into a scone-type pastry. Put pieces of meat in center and turn up edges all around. Sprinkle with a little water. Roll out small piece and put on top. Knead together and tie in cheesecloth. Boil for 3 hours.

Portable Soup

An entry in the army quartermaster records of May 30, 1803, shows a purchase at the request of Capt. Meriwether Lewis by Israel Whelen, purveyor of public supplies for the United States by order of the Secretary of War, of 193 pounds of "portable soup at 150 cents per pound" for a total of $289.50. This was a lot of money in those days, especially since a total of only $1,500 had been allocated by Congress for the forthcoming Lewis and Clark Expedition. Whelen, incidentally, was a ancestor of the late, famed big-game hunter, outdoor writer, and editor, Col. Townsend Whelen, author of many books on fishing, hunting, and firearms.

The portable soup was one of many items purchased in Philadelphia at the beginning of the expedition. It was sold by François Baillet, a cook at 21 North Ninth. It was actually a dried soup, a form of what is now called dehydrated and freeze-dried rations. The enlisted man then had about the same regard for it as veterans of modern wars have for K-rations.

The records of the expedition show that the only time the expensive portable soup was used on the grueling trek was in the game-scarce section from Lolo Hot Springs in Montana to the Clearwater River in Idaho. On September 18, 1805, Captain Lewis wrote that the men had killed their last colt for food and had nothing left but a few cannisters of portable soup, some bear oil, and candles.

Portable soup was not new in 1803. For years something called Extempor Broth was used by naval forces and on long voyages of discovery. This type of soup is found in many old recipes, including those of the British Admiralty. Apparently this was a sort of bouillon cube, dried and compressed, which needed only water to reconstitute. A German chemist, Baron Justus van Liebig (1803–1873), invented the first "official" commercial concentrated meat and bouillon cubes. All he did, probably, was refine a recipe that had been known for decades by wives of whaling ship captains and military purveyors.

This is the way it was done by François Bailet and others:

In a large cast-iron kettle or dutch oven, place several pounds of beef with bones broken up. Cover with cold water and bring to a boil. Skim off the slurry, add a little more cold water, and continue to boil and skim until the broth is clear, or from 8 to 10 hours. Cool and remove the meat and bones. To the broth add 1 T peppercorns. Bring to a boil and simmer again, skimming off any fat. Continue this until reduced to the consistency of syrup, testing it with a spoon to see if it will turn to jelly. Continue simmering until it does, then pour into a shallow pan the thickness of about ½ inch. Cut into small cakes and keep in a warm, dry place for a week or so, until completely dry and hard.

To reconstitute, simply add water and bring to a simmer. The amount of water used will determine the thickness.

These portable soup cakes will keep for years without refrigeration.

Jerky the Easy Way

The oldest form of food processing is probably the drying of meat, nowadays known as jerking. It isn't much of a mystery how it started: prehistoric humanoid predators, with a fresh kill they could not eat at one sitting, left it hanging in the sun. When they returned a few days later the carcass was perfectly preserved.

On the frontier, jerky was a staple item, not only of the fur traders and explorers but of pioneer families, settlers, and the army on the march. With a bag of jerky you could march for days, needing only water and what fresh berries you could pick along the way. Jerking or drying meat was the only way to keep it from spoiling, at least away from towns where ice was available. It is still a good way to preserve meat for later use.

The word "jerky" comes from the Spanish *chirque*, meaning "dried meat." Naturally.

What kind of meat? Any lean, red-blooded meat such as domestic beef, buffalo (yes, you can buy buffalo meat), deer, elk, horse, bear, or cougar; and also fowl such as ducks, geese, pheasant, chicken, and turkeys.

The secret of good jerky is good, nonfat cuts of meat. All fat and gristle should be removed. Cut the meat across the grain into strips from ¼ to ½ inch thick. If you like it chewy, cut it with the grain. Place the strips in the bottom of a deep pan or casserole. Sprinkle with salt and pepper and spices to taste, such as oregano, garlic, onion salt, or whatever. Place another layer crosswise over the first layer and repeat the seasoning. When the pan is full, add a mixture of ¼ c liquid smoke and ¾ c water. Work this mxture into all layers with the blade of a knife. Add enough to barely cover the meat. Place a small plate (not plastic) on top to weight down the layers. Store in fridge for 24 hours, then pour off the liquid. Place the meat strips close together on an oven rack. Cook at lowest heat, about 150 degrees. Leave oven door ajar so moisture can escape. Place foil or cookie sheet under the strips to catch drippings. Leave in for 6 to 8 hours, or overnight. When meat is dry but not brittle, turn oven to 200 degrees for 20 minutes. Store in plastic bags or jars in fridge. Freeze for longer storage.

The Rose Hip Connection

The state where I was born (some say it was a state of confusion), North Dakota, the first one north of South Dakota, is the Flickertail State — a flickertail being the ubiquitous little gopher. The state flower is the wild rose. This also happens to be the name of our boat and my nickname for my bride, who was born and raised not far from a little prairie settlement known as Wild Rose, which is still on the map, although with fewer residents.

The wild rose grew in profusion along fencerows, in coulee thickets, almost everywhere. In the spring its delicate pale pink to crimson flowers brightened up an otherwise drab landscape. I didn't know it then, but the wild rose, with its so-called "hips," is a valuable source of vitamin C, along with other elements.

There are maybe six to eight species of the wild rose (*Rosa gymnocarpa*) along the northwestern tier of states out to the Pacific Ocean. This dainty rose generally has five petals, about one to three inches in diameter, growing on a shrub from one to six feet high. It bears a bright red fruit about the size of a small marble. The rose fruit, or rose hips as they are called, was discovered just before World War II to be one of the richest sources of vitamin C, although Indians and early trappers had used them long before for making *pemmican*. During the war, in Europe and England, wild rose hips were harvested extensively for a vitamin supplement when citrus fruit was scarce. Rose hips make excellent jams and jellies. The Indians and early settlers made hot tea from the leaves and hips. A hot beverage was also made from the roots and was said to be good for colds,

The ubiquitous wild rose, so common along fencerows in farm country.

colic, and assorted aches and pains. The straight stems of the plant were used for arrow shafts. Animals and birds of all kinds also find the rose hips a source of food. In the wild state, the berries left on the bushes provide emergency food for wildlife all winter long.

The fruit or hip is a bright red or orange, ranging in size from pea to walnut. The hips are dried for use, generally harvested after the first frost. In addition to vitamin C, rose hips are high in iron, phosphorus, and calcium. The seeds also contain vitamin E, a very important one.

The dried and ground hips can be used in soups, stews, or teas or made into jams and jellies (the latter from the fresh fruit, of course). The petals are nice to use in salads or in Jello. In addition, the petals have been used to make a very delicate jelly and even wine. The plant is truly one of nature's wonders, in addition to being cheerful and beautiful.

Rose Hip Sauce

2½ c water
5 medium apples
4 c rose hips
1 c honey

Wash hips. Peel and core apples, slice. Cook apples in water over medium heat to a heavy consistency. Blend the hips slowly in a food processor. Add the apples to the hips and blend well, adding honey gradually. This makes about 4 cups. The seeds, incidentally, can be strained out with a cheesecloth if not desired in the sauce. You may want to do this, especially if you wear dentures.

Dried and finely ground rose hips can be used to spike other hot beverages to add a mildly sweet and delicate accent.

The hips can be gathered in the autumn almost anywhere north of the Mason-Dixon Line. City dwellers who never get out into the country will find the hips readily available at most health food stores.

Nasturtium Pods

Nasturtium, like the wild rose, also provides a nutrituous food. The seeds are picked when fully formed and the petals dried. The seed pods are soaked in cold salted water for 2 days, then drained and rinsed with fresh water, soaking one more day. The seeds are drained once more and put into scalded mason jar, covered with boiling vinegar, and scalded. The pods can be used in salads or as pickled capers for seasoning.

The Great Lakes Fish Boil

My immediate forebears came from the Great Lakes region. Wisconsin, and Minnesota. Probably one of the most notorious members of the family was Uncle John, also known as Black Jack Holm, a rough, tough woods boss in the Duluth lumbering industry. Another was a two-term governor of Minnesota on my paternal grandmother's side. Included in the early family were circuit-riding preachers and sea captains.

It was during the immigrant period of the middle 1800s that the "fish boil" tradition originated. It is said that the early settlers and lumberjacks, finding the lakes almost choked with trout and other species (such as what was locally known as whitefish) quickly developed a simple way to prepare a nourishing meal out of doors in a large pot that left very little clean-up. The custom probably began with the Scandinavian immigrants who settled around the Great Lakes and built sawmills and founded small settlements with a general store, boardinghouse, blacksmith shop, a church, and camps for the workers. If on the lake, there would also be a boat dock or fishing wharf. My grandfather was a blacksmith, an immigrant from Sweden, and my dad apprenticed in his shop at the age of nine. My grandfather came over with three of his brothers, leaving two brothers and a sister back in the old country. One of those who came to America became a soldier in the Seventh Cavalry on the western plains and died in the Old Soldier's Home at Fort Snelling. Another, with his entire family, survived the holocaust known as the Hinkley Fire, which in 1871 swept over Wisconsin, part of Minnesota, and Michigan.

The family gathered around the well in the backyard and stayed under blankets kept wet with pails of water while the fire swept through the town.

To get back to the fish boils, any large species of fish such as trout, salmon, halibut, snapper, bass, hake, sea perch, cod, tuna, steelhead, haddock, or whitefish can be used. It doesn't matter how bony they are. You need a large kettle, into which you place 15 medium potatoes, 8 qts. of water, 2 c salt, and 12 lbs. fresh fish cut into steaks. Add some onions, butter, parsley, and lemon. Bring the water with potatoes to a boil. Add 1 c salt and the onions. Continue boiling for 20 minutes with the kettle partly covered (regulate the boil with the cover). Next place the fish in a wire basket and lower into the boiling water. Add another cup of salt, cover again, and boil for 12 more minutes. Test the condition of the potatoes with a fork. Also spear a piece of fish. When done, the fish will be flakey. Be careful not to overcook.

Drain and serve immediately with drawn butter, lemon juice, and parsley sprigs.

Note that I did not mention seasonings. This is a matter of local or personal preference. I like to place peppercorns, bay leaves, and whole cloves in a cloth bag (in the old days, a clean Bull Durham tobacco bag was used) and add to the boil at the time the fish are put in.

You can also add additional potatoes, which can be saved for a breakfast fry the next morning. The potatoes will not have a fishy taste. They also make good shoestrings.

To top off the fish-boil party (the above serves 12), provide cold slaw, garlic bread buttered generously, pickles, and homemade pie — maybe with homemade ice cream.

Great Lakes Salt Cod with Potatoes

My dad, being a second generation Swedish immigrant to Minnesota, inherited a love of fish dishes. As long as he lived his eyes would light up at the mere mention of one like this.

½ lb. salt dry cod
(this was imported from New England in wooden kegs)

6 large potatoes	**1 T vinegar**
2 oz. salt pork	**2 T whipping cream**
2 onions	**butter the size of an egg**

Rip cod into small pieces and soak in cold water overnight. Peel potatoes and cut into strips. In the morning remove fish from water and cook potatoes in the water the fish soaked in. When partly done, add the fish and cook until spuds are tender. Drain, put on platter, and spinkle with seasoning. Dice the pork and brown in frying pan with butter. Add sliced onions and stir until brown. Stir in butter, vinegar, and cream, heating slowly to prevent curdling. Pour over fish and potatoes.

Loaves and Fishes

Don's Secret Seafood Sauce

For years, family members and friends have been tantalized by the author's "secret" sauce on shrimp, clam, crab, and lobster, as well as fish. Truth is, even the author doesn't know exactly how it works. It was a recipe concocted in sort of an ad lib fashion down through the years. This is as close as he can get to putting it down in writing:

4 T tomato catsup
1 t Worcestershire
1 T lime juice
1 t black pepper
1 T coarse horseradish
½ t Tabasco
1 t mustard

Combine and stir with fork until streaks blend and disappear. Place on table in saucedish for each individual plate.

Nova Scotia Crab Quiche

¾ lb. crab meat
1 T butter or margarine
3 eggs beaten
½ t salt
¼ c sliced almonds
½ c chopped onions
1½ c Swiss cheese, shredded
1½ c whipping cream
dash cayenne
1 T flour

Saute onions in butter. In a 9-inch unbaked pie shell toss flour and cheese. Blend eggs, cream, salt, cayenne. Mix crab meat and onion and spread over cheese; pour in egg mixture. Garnish with almonds. Bake in preheated 425-degree oven for 15 minutes. Reduce heat to 325 degrees and bake for 30 minutes longer.

Myrtle (left) and Don Holm enjoying an outdoor meal on a camping and fishing trip to Curlew Lake in Northeast Washington State.

Don's Crab-Legged Eggs

1 c crab meat cooked
¼ c mayonnaise
1 t finely chopped onion
dash Tabasco
chopped parsley
6 hard-boiled eggs
1 T sour cream
¼ t lime juice
½ t paprika

Slit eggs lengthwise. Remove yokes, and run through coarse grater. Fill white egg halves with all the ingredients thoroughly mixed with crab meat. Spread over with grated yolk. Sprinkle lightly with paprika. Garnish with parsley sprig.

Oregon Mussel Feed

I got this on the Oregon coast, from a commercial fisherman who was a descendant of a long line of old country fishermen.

Saute some chopped onions, green pepper, and garlic in olive oil. Add oregano, basil, and fresh chopped parsley and continue cooking for at least 5 to 8 minutes. Add white wine and washed mussels in the shell. Cover and cook for 5 minutes. Eat out of shells.

Royal Chinook Salmon Poach

There are two ways to poach salmon. One is to net or spear one illegally out of season; the other is to use Tom Vaughn's secret recipe for cooking one. Vaughn is the longtime curator of Oregon's magnificent Historical Society, and I think this recipe must have been handed down in the distant past from the Hudson's Bay Company post across the river at Fort Vancouver. Anyway, here is his prize recipe:

2 c water
½ c dry white wine
¼ t thyme
1½ t dried chopped onion
½ c canned clam juice
½ c dry vermouth
1 envelope dried vegetable soup

Bring liquid to boil on top of stove. Meanwhile preheat oven to 350 degrees. Use a special poaching pan, usually of cast iron or black iron, about 16 inches long, 4 or 5 inches deep, and 6 to 8 inches wide. It has a rack to hold the fish off the bottom of the pan — or you can use a couple of small trivets.

Wrap salmon in cheesecloth and lower gently into preheated pan. Fish should be covered about halfway with the poaching liquid. Cover and cook 6 minutes per pound. Do not let the liquid boil; it should merely shimmy and shake with anticipation.

When done, remove fish, drain, remove skin, and serve hot or cold with a sauce, as follows:

One: Combine 1 c homemade mayonnaise, 1 c sour cream, and 1 T lemon juice.

Another: In a blender mix 4 egg yolks, 3 T lemon juice, ¼ t salt, ⅛ t coarse pepper. Gradually add ¼ lb. hot melted buter. When thick remove from blender and stir in 1 t dried tarragon, 2 t minced chive, and 2 t minced parsley; then 1 T capers. Serve hot with poaching liquid but don't boil. Strain rest of bouillon and use later for chowder.

Lake Pontchartrain Boogalee

From good friends in New Orleans, Ralph and Mardell Morgan, at whose home I have enjoyed some fine Southern hospitality, I have obtained my favorite barbecued shrimp recipe — real Louisiana boogalee. The shrimp is caught by Ralph, who has a small shrimp boat he tows down to nearby Lake Pontchartrain.

To make boogalee, the shrimp are washed and veined and placed in a pan. Salt and pepper is added to taste. The juice of 1 lemon is then squeezed over the shrimp. In a saucepan melt 1 stick of butter or margarine. Add

3 T A-1 Sauce and 5 pieces of garlic. Pour half of the mixture over the shrimp and broil for 10 minutes. Turn shrimp over and repeat the process, using the rest of the mixture and broiling for another 5 to 7 minutes.

Serve on platters with hot French garlic bread and pitchers of cold beer or the wine of your choice.

As Mardell says, "Bon appetit!"

I second the motion.

Balls of Fish

Here's a way to prepare fish for fish-haters. They'll love it and won't even suspect they've been had.

2 eggs
3 carrots
1 c water
3½ lb. fish
1 t white pepper
3 T cracker meal
3 onions
4 potatoes
1 T salt
3 T butter
3 T shortening
2 t chopped parsley

Bone fish and cut meat into small pieces. Put through grinder with 2 onions, the cracker meal, and the seasonings. Blend well, then add eggs and mix thoroughly.

Grease a large baking dish. Cut the carrots and potatoes into ¼ inch strips. Slice remaining onion thin. Line the bottom of the dish with layers of carrots, potatoes, and onion. Shape mixture into balls and place in pan. Add hot water. Plop a blob of butter on top of each ball. Bake at 300 degrees for 1 or 2 hours. Serve hot with light milk gravy or sauce. Fish can be any kind or any combination.

— 11 —

Halloween and the Old Outhouse

In my day there was a popular comic character known as Chic Sale, and his trade mark was the crescent sliver of a waning or waxing moon. His name was quickly adopted into the vernacular to mean any backhouse, outhouse, or privy, which every family had — even in town, where there was a sewer system. "Privy" means "private," so it was only logical that this more delicate name should be applied also to the latrine. In Middle English, privy meant secret, private, acquainted with; in Old French, privé meant the same thing, originally taken from the Latin *privatus.* Of course, the privy, latrine, Chic Sale, or backhouse had a lot of less delicate and unprintable names, too. As a kid, one of the greatest joys on Halloween was roaming around in gangs and tipping over backhouses — sometimes with the occupants still inside.

One of my worst memories is having to trot out to the backhouse on a cold winter night through the snow and minus-10-degree air — after having been given a dose of syrup of figs — and putting my bare bottom on the frosty seat. Wiping was just as bad, as the Montgomery Ward or Sears Roebuck catalog, which was used for toilet paper, was also cold, frosty, and slippery. I wonder if the present executives of these two old and huge companies, when they slip away to the exclusive executive rest rooms in their supermodern, state-of-the-art office buildings, ever think about the contribution their firms made to the sanitary welfare of Middle America.

Anyway, as one modern environmentalist wrote the other day, "If you eat, you defecate." So, what with large sections of the country unsuited for septic tanks because the soil won't perc, and with sewage disposal plants operating at maximum capacity in many communities, the privy is returning. The National Wildlife Federation a few years ago did a complete study of this rebirth of outhouses in a report entitled: *In Praise of the Privy.**

The Farallones Institute at 15290 Coleman Valley Road in Occidental, California 95465, has published a study of composting outhouses for rural homes that is very efficient and economical. Plans are available in Tech. Bulletin No. 1.

Actually, modern sewer systems are not as old as one might think. It was not until after World War II and the housing boom that municipal sewer systems and treatment plants really became common. Then in the late 1960s there was a great revival of the outhouse or privy among the back-to-nature people, this time with modern progressive engineering techniques being applied. The underlying theme was sanitation and the conservation of energy and resources, plus the additional benefit of recycling valuable wastes, mainly for fertilizers but also for various combustible gases.

Scandinavian countries for a long time have designed their privies for composting and probably have developed the art to its highest state. In our country there is a lot of resistance from county and city health departments, to say nothing of esthetic objections from the uniformed populace. We are in no danger of outhouses replacing sewers all over the country, but in rural areas, where not prohibited by zoning laws, the modern version of the privy could be entirely practical.

---

*National Wildlife Federation, 1412 16th St., N.W., Washington, D.C. 20036; May 15, 1979, Vol. 44 No. 10.

Some Old Favorites on the Farm

Here are a few old-timers that are easy to prepare and ideally suited for the guy who's batchin' it while the womenfolk are in town shopping for the holiday season coming up. They are tasty and filling enough to get you through the day's chores, until the regular cook gets home and takes over.

Prairie Creamed Beef

½ lb. dried beef
1 c milk
1 T flour
1 T green pepper, chopped
2 T butter
1 c grated cheese

Cut dried beef into patches. Brown with pepper in hot butter or fat, adding flour and milk slowly, until thick and smooth. Add cheese and seasonings. Serve on toast when cheese is melted.

Saucy Macaroni Loaf

⅓ c uncooked macaroni
1 c cracker crumbs
½ c grated cheese
1 T celery chopped
2 eggs, beaten
1 c milk
¼ c melted butter
1 T pimiento, chopped
1 t salt

Add cracker crumbs to macaroni when cooking. Blend in the pimiento, cheese, celery, butter, and salt. Add milk to eggs and blend into rest of mixture. Pour in buttered baking dish. Set in pan of hot water and bake at 350 degrees F. for 45 minutes.

Sauce:

1 lb. cooked and diced veal
1 can mushrooms
3 T butter
3 c milk
1 jar stuffed olives, sliced
6 T flour

Bring milk to boil, thickening with paste of flour and butter. Add veal, olives, and mushrooms, stirring until smooth. Pour over loaf on platter and serve immediately.

Welsh Rarebit

Welsh rarebit is not rabbit and has nothing to do with Wales. We used to make it at home thus:

2 T flour
2 T butter
2 c milk
⅛ t pepper
1½ c grated cheese
1 t salt
1 egg
½ t mustard
pinch cayenne

Make a white sauce of the milk, butter, and dry ingredients. Add the cheese, then a well-beaten egg. Serve hot on toast.

Stratified Hot Dish

2 c raw potatoes
1 c diced onion
1 lb. hamburger
½ t salt
2 c diced celery
½ c diced green pepper
2 c tomato
⅛ t pepper

Place layers of meatballs and vegetables in baking dish and season. Bake in moderate oven until meatballs are done.

One-Dish Dinner

4 T shortening
2 green peppers
2 c fresh cut corn
¼ t pepper
½ c bread crumbs
1 medium onion
1 lb. hamburger
1½ t salt
2 eggs
3 tomatoes

Dice pepper, slice onion, and fry until brown or crisp. Mix in the meat and seasonings. Remove from heat and beat in eggs. Put corn in a buttered baking dish, cover with layers of meat and vegetables. Top with bread crumbs and bake in moderate oven until meat is done.

Red Hot Mexican Chili

¾ lb. ground veal | **¼ lb. ground pork**
¾ c water | **1 c peeled tomatoes**
½ lb. potatoes | **1 t garlic chopped**
1 6-oz. can tomato sauce | **½ t oregano**
4 jalapeno peppers | **2 T jalapeno pepper liquid (from can)**
¾ c diced pimientos | **fresh ground pepper**
salt

Place the meat in a saucepan with just enough water to cover. Bring to a boil, breaking up lumps with a tablespoon. Cover and simmer for 30 minutes. Blend in tomatoes, salt, pepper; add peeled and cubed potatoes, garlic, tomato sauce, pimientos, oregano. Split the jalapeno peppers in two and discard the seeds. Dice and add to mixture with pepper juice. Cover and cook 15 minutes or until potatoes are tender. Serve in warm bowls with a glass of milk. (You'll need it.)

*Baked Meat Croquettes**

2 c chopped meat | **1 small onion minced**
salt and pepper to taste | **1 egg**
4 shredded wheat biscuits | **2 T melted fat**
parsley | **soup stock or water**

To meat add onion, salt, pepper, and egg. Roll biscuit fine. Combine with meat mixture and add enough soup stock or water to make shape. Form into cones. Place in well-greased baking dish, brush with fat, and bake 20 minutes in a 425 degree oven. Serve with a sprig of parsley stuck in top of each cone and surround with hot tomato sauce if desired. Serves 6.

*Baked Chicken**

1 chicken, cut up
flour
½ c fat for frying
½ lb. mushrooms
milk
salt and pepper
1 T onion, chopped fine
2 c hot cream or top milk

Dip the pieces of chicken in milk, then in seasoned flour. Fry the chicken pieces until nicely browned. Remove to a deep baking dish. Fry mushrooms in fat about 2 or 3 minutes. Sprinkle mushrooms and onions over the chicken pieces. Pour on the hot cream. Bake in a moderate oven until chicken is tender and cream is thick sauce.

Colonel Sanders, eat your heart out.

Browned Rice

1½ c rice
3½ c water
sliced olives
1½ t butter
1½ t salt

Do not wash rice. Place in a frying pan with butter and stir over moderate fire until rice is an even brown. Turn fire very low, add salt and water, let come to a boil, then cover and place pan in moderate oven. Cook 30 minutes. Serve with sliced olives. Serves 5 or 6.

Scalloped Corn and Links

Cut 6 pork link sausages into 1-inch lengths and fry until lighly browned. Arrange in a baking dish in alternate layers with ¾ cup fine cracker crumbs, 2 c canned corn, and 1 c white sauce made of 2 T butter, 2 T flour, and 1 c milk. To each layer add seasoning of salt and pepper. Cover with a layer of buttered cracker crumbs and bake 30 minutes in a moderate oven.

*Salmonburgers**

2 c canned salmon
1 egg, slightly beaten
2 T butter
¾ c coarse cracker crumbs
1 small onion
3 large buns

Drain and flake salmon. Mix with cracker crumbs and egg. Mince onion and fry lightly in half the butter. Add to salmon mixture and season to taste. Shape into 6 thin cakes and brown quickly in remaining butter. Split and toast the buns and place a hot salmon cake on each half. Garnish with dill pickles and onion rings and serve with chili sauce.

*Wax Beans en Casserole**

1 c wax beans
4 slices bacon

Drain beans. Put in a casserole. Cover top with bacon slices. Bake in hot oven, about 400 degrees, for 20 minutes or until bacon is crisp. Serves 4.

North Dakota Pizza

Here's one I invented myself for those late winter evening snacks after the basketball game:

On bread slices arrange 1-inch squares of American or cheddar cheese and, on top of the cheese, staggered squares of bacon about the same size.

Place on cookie tin in a hot oven and leave the door ajar. Broil until bread toasts, cheese melts and runs, and bacon curls up crisply.

Better figure on at least 2 or 3 per person.

Squash Burgers

3 acorn squash
½ c cooked rice
1 T minced onion
3 T bacon drippings
⅛ t pepper
2 c cooked ground beef
½ c tomato juice
¾ c bread crumbs
½ t salt

Wash and bake whole squash, then cut in halves and remove seeds. Brush with butter or bacon drippings. Cook onions in drippings for 3 minutes. Add meat, salt and pepper, rice, and tomato juice. Fill squash halves with mixture and sprinkle with bread crumbs soaked in drippings. Bake 15 minutes at 375 degrees.

Baked Winter Squash

Cut squash into 2-inch chunks and remove seeds. Place in pan, sprinkle with salt, brown sugar, molasses, lemon juice, and paprika. Dot with butter. Bake in covred dish for 30 minutes at 375 degrees. Serve in shells.

Get Out the Pot and Make Some Stew

One of a litter of six, I was usually left to my devices around home, to amuse myself by reading, pounding nails in boards, making sailboats out of wood roof shingles, or concocting things on our old kitchen cookstove, which was always hot. My mother tolerated my messes left over from fudge-making and other experiments. Maybe she saw in me the makings of a chef like her younger brother, who was head chef on the Great Northern's prestige train, the *Empire Builder,* for years.

Most of my experiments were disasters, but one that wasn't I still use today when I am batching on the boat or camping out. I call it:

Don's One-Pot Banquet

½ can stewed peeled tomatoes **2 or 3 canned peeled potatoes**
butter or margarine **1 egg**
3 or 4 slices Walla Walla sweets or any Spanish-type onion
seasoning to taste

In a small saucepan, saute the onion rings and the potatoes, cut into small chunks the size of acorns. When brown and sizzling, slowly add the stewed tomatoes and bring to a nice happy simmer. Put cover on saucepan. When steaming and piping hot, break egg over top. (Don't break the yolk.) Season sparingly with herbs, salt and pepper, dash of Worcestershire or Tabasco — not too much to overpower the onion. Put cover back on and poach the egg in the bubbling sauce for a minute or so, or until ready.

Remove from heat and serve at once. This is a tasty, filling meal for one, but it can also serve two with lighter appetites by poaching two eggs on top. Some hot homemade garlic bread and a glass of cold milk will go nicely with this.

Can you think of a tastier, more nutritious, simpler meal to make for less than you would have to pay for a bottle of beer or a pack of cigarette?

Bull-Cook Beef Stew

The "bull cook" in logging and construction camps, according to writers who never worked there, was some sort of kitchen wizard. Actually, the bull cook was a sort of janitor, handyman, guy who made up the bunks, dispensed laundry, and swept up the place. He was not a cook at all.

Nevertheless, I call this old-time recipe, "Bull Cook Beef Stew," because I always associate it with the camps I worked in as a youth while roamin' around after high school. Unlike the bull cook moniker, it is no joke.

⅓ c flour
¼ t ground pepper
4 T shortening
1 t Worcestershire
2 bay leaves
12 small carrots, diced
8 small peeled potatoes
1 t salt
2 lb. stewing beef with bones
1 T lemon juice
1 sliced onion
¼ t allspice
12 small white onions

Cube meat and roll with flour, salt, and pepper. Melt shortening in cast-iron kettle or dutch oven with cover. Add beef a little at a time to brown, then remove to make room for more. When done, return all meat to pot and pour in 4 c boiling water. Blend in juice, Worcestershire, onions, bay leaves, and allspice. Reduce heat and simmer 1 to 2 hours, until meat is tender. Add vegetables and cook 20 minutes or so. Can also be improved with dumplings.

Borsch or Russian Soup

In our prairie community there were a lot of folks known as "Rooshians." Actually, they were people of German stock who immigrated first to the Ukraine and then to America — bringing with them the old-fashioned recipes like Borsch.

5 qts. water
2 T salt
1 onion, shredded
2 carrots, shredded
3 c shredded cabbage
1 can tomatoes
bay leaves
1 chicken
pepper to taste
1 beet, chopped
potatoes
1 T lard
3 T sour cream

Put chicken in water with carrots, beet, salt, and pepper and cook for 1 hour. Add some potatoes to thicken, 3 c shredded cabbage, and cook for 25 minutes. Fry shredded onion in 1 T lard until brown, add 3 T sour cream and fry a few minutes, then add 1 can tomatoes and simmer for 5 minutes or so. Add a few bay leaves, combine with rest of mixture in the kettle, and cook for 30 minutes.

Bull-Cook Chili

2 lbs. lean flank steak
5 T suet oil
6 T chili powder
1 T oregano
1 T crushed red pepper
2 cans tomato sauce
1 T salt
1 T cornmeal
3 lbs. lean ground beef
2 c finely chopped onions
4 cloves garlic
1 T ground cumin
1 can beef broth
1 can tomato paste
1 T black pepper
1 lb. small kidney beans

Wash and soak beans overnight just covered with water, to which a teaspoon of salt has been added. In the morning cook slowly until beans are tender, adding water as necessary. In a large dutch oven or black iron kettle, simmer the onions for 20 to 30 minutes in hot oil. Add meat gradually, searing until starting to crisp. Add beef broth, tomato sauce and paste, with garlic, stirring at the same time. Continue stirring and add chili powder and other condiments. Cover and cook for about 4 hours at lowest heat. Add the beans, blended well. Serves 10 to 12. Dish out in warm bowls, with chopped onions or grated cheese sprinkled on top.

Pea Soup

We lived one whole miserable Depression-Dust-Bowl winter on nothing but pea soup; I came to hate it. Then, years later, I had a nostalgic revival and remembered that wonderful aromatic dish my mother put together to keep our family alive. It was as follows:

1 c split peas
3 stalks celery
1 ham shank
2 raw potatoes, sliced thin
1 large onion, minced
¼ c pearl barley

Peas were soaked overnight.(Actually there was a pot of peas soaking all the time.) In morning water was poured off and peas were covered with boiling water. Vegetables and ham were added, and the whole cooked slowly for 3 hours. The ham was removed, and, if there was any meat on it, this was diced and returned to the soup. Generous seasonings were the rule.

Another Pea Soup

½ c navy beans
4 large potatoes
2 small onions sliced
seasonings to taste

Beans and potatoes were cooked separately; then everything including seasonings was combined with enough milk to make a soup of desired consistency, which was brought to a boil. A big chunk of butter was added before serving.

Sparerib Soup

1½ lb. spareribs
1 large onion, sliced
1 c chopped celery
2 T salt
3 qts. cold water
1 pt. dried peas
½ t pepper
1 large potato, diced

Soak peas overnight in salted water. Drain and cover with boiling water. Add spareribs, vegetables, and salt and pepper, maybe a dash of paprika. Perk slowly for 1 or 2 hours.

Mouse River Tomato Soup

My favorite Tomato soup!

2 c milk
¼ t baking soda
1 c tomatoes, stewed
salt and pepper

Put tomatoes and milk in separate saucepans. Add part of the soda to the milk and part to the tomatoes. Bring milk to boiling, add to tomatoes, and bring to a full boil. Remove and add seasonings.

Dumplin' Soup

An all-time favorite:

2 lbs. veal
1 c green peas
1 c diced celery
pepper
1 t salt
1 c diced carrots
½ t ginger
paprika

Boil meat in 1 qt. water, then simmer a couple of hours. Strain broth, add vegetables, bring to a boil again, and drop in dumpling batter by spoon. Cover and simmer for a few minutes.

Dumplin's:

1 egg
½ t salt
1 c flour
½ c milk

Beat egg and mix with rest, blending well.

Sea Shanty Chowder

½ lb. salt pork
2 qts. water
¼ t pepper
4 crackers
1 T butter
2 onions
6 potatoes
1 pt. clams with juice
1 pt. cream, fresh or canned
1 t salt

Dice and crisp pork. Add onion and saute. Add water and potatoes and boil about 1 hour. Add chopped clams with juice and boil 15 minutes. Add crackers, butter, cream, and seasonings. Simmer a moment and serve.

Meat Dumplin's

A variation of vegetable dumplin' soup.

1 soup bone
1 c stewed tomatoes
⅓ c parsley
¼ c chopped onion
1 c chopped carrots
1 c chopped celery
3 T uncooked rice
salt and pepper

Combine and simmer in 4 qts. water for 2 or 3 hours, covered. Remove soup bone and add dumplin's.

Dumplin's

½ lb. ground pork
1 egg
⅓ t sage
¼ t pepper
½ lb. ground beef
1 c bread crumbs
1 t salt
dash paprika

Blend and form into balls and drop into boiling soup. Cook covered until done.

Country Corn Soup

1 small onion, minced
2 T butter
celery salt
1 pt. milk
½ can corn
salt, pepper, paprika

Simmer minced onion in melted butter. Add corn, milk, and seasonings. Serves 4.

Conventional Corn Chowder

1 pt. boiling water
1 pt. milk
½ t salt
2 c canned corn
pepper, paprika
1 qt. diced raw potatoes
1 T diced salt pork
1 onion, chopped
2 T chopped parsley
1 t chopped celery

Boil potatoes for a few minutes in the pint of water. Saute pork with onion, add to corn and potatoes. Cook until potatoes are done. Add milk and seasonings. Bring to boil, add parsley and celery. Serve in hot bowls.

*Hot Potato Soup**

Heat 1 c water in saucepan. Peel 1 small potato and cut into small slices. Peel and slice 1 small onion. Cook potato and onion rapidly, 8 minutes. Add 1 c rich milk and a lump of butter. Salt and pepper to taste. Heat and serve.

Ribble Soup

Here's a real old-fashioned soup, wholesome, delicious, and rib-stickin':

Cover a soup bone or chunk of boiling beef with cold water, season well to personal taste, and cook until meat is done. Put meat into covered pan in oven and keep hot until ready to add to soup stock.

Boil soup stock and stir into "crumbs" made from 2 c flour into which an egg has been broken and the mixture kneaded until it becomes crumbly. Stir these "ribbles" into soup until it is well thickened. Boil all for 15 to 20 minutes, adding carrots, celery, parsley, onion, cloves and seasonings as desired. Add meat and serve.

Winter Prairie Chili

1½ lbs. ground beef
1 clove garlic, chopped fine
½ c flour
2 T chili powder
1 small onion, chopped fine
1 small can tomatoes
salt and pepper to taste

In frying pan with melted suet, brown meat which has been floured and sprinkled with salt and pepper. Add garlic, onions, and tomatoes. Make a thin paste of chili powder and water and add to rest of ingredients. Cover and cook slowly for about 1½ hours, adding water if necessary. Serve over Mexican or kidney beans, or on half of hot bun.

Line Shack Pie

Cowboys hated sheep, but they didn't mind eating lamb — especially when prepared like this:

1 c cooked lamb, diced
1 can kidney beans
1 t Worcestershire
1½ c gravy (stock)
pepper and seasoning to taste
3 c mashed potatoes
1 c chopped celery
1 c diced carrots
½ t salt

Blend all into a casserole. Make a thick paste of 3 c mashed potatoes and blend around the meat and vegetables. Bake 30 minutes at 350 degrees.

Basque Lamb Stew

The Basque sheepherders of the high western desert country brought this recipe over from their homeland in the Pyrenees Mountains of Spain:

3 lb. lamb stew meat
1 t garlic salt
1 c tomato sauce
bunch parsley
4 diced celery stalks
3 T lard
3 T flour
¼ t pepper
1 bay leaf
1 large onion diced
3 carrots
wine or water

Cube lamb into 1-inch chunks. Dredge in flour and seasonings. Brown quickly, adding rest of ingredients. Blend in enough water or wine to make a thick stock. Cover and simmer in dutch oven for 1 hour.

Winter Lamb Pot

1 lb. split peas
3 lb. lamb chops
1½ lb. turnips
1 gal. water
1½ lb. carrots
salt and pepper

Boil the peas 2 hours and put through sieve. In a saucepan boil lamb chops, seasonings, carrots, turnips until vegetables are tender. Add the strained peas and boil 10 to 15 minutes longer.

Farm Scalloped Chicken

Cut a 4 or 5 lb. chicken into pieces. Season stalks of celery with salt and pepper and cut into small pieces. Simmer chicken and celery, with the kettle partly covered, until meat is tender. Remove meat from bones and return to broth. Add 1 or 2 c of milk, 3 beaten eggs, and a small green pepper, finely chopped. Place mixture in casserole or baking dish and break crackers over top. Press crackers down into liquid until moist. Add globs of butter if chicken broth is not rich with fat. Bake in 350-degree oven until firm and brown on top.

Sylte or Head Cheese

Cook 5 lbs. veal shank in small amount of water with

1 medium onion, sliced, a bay leaf, salt and pepper, and whole allspice. Cool and put meat through food chopper. Strain stock and add meat to make a soft mixture. Season to taste and bring to a boil. Pour into loaf pan and weight with plate or saucer. Set in cold place. Cut into slices for serving.

Juanita's Spanish Rice

4 T fat or suet
3¼ c tomatoes
¼ t pepper
2½ t salt
1 lb. hamburger
1 c brown rice
4 T chopped onion
1½ c boiling water

Melt suet in cast-iron skillet. Add meat and onions and brown. Add rice, tomatoes, salt, pepper, and boiling water. Cover and simmer over low heat about 1 hour or until rice is cooked. Serve immediately.

Mom's Instant Spanish Rice

4 slices bacon
2 T parsley
½ t salt
2 c tomatoes
4 T chopped onion
3 c cooked rice
¼ t paprika

Chop bacon and saute in frying pan with onions. Add rest and cook together for 10 minutes, mixing frequently with fork.

Dutch Scrapple

This one originated with Pennsylvania Dutch immigrants (from whom my mother was descended) and was called "ponhos."

2 lbs. liver
½ c wheat flour
4 lbs. pork cheek
cornmeal

Cook liver and pork in salted water until done, then

grind and return to broth. Thicken with wheat flour and cornmeal. Pour into loaf pan. When cool slice, roll in flour, and fry slowly on cast-iron griddle or dutch oven with lots of butter, lard, or suet.

Swede Omelet

4 eggs
¼ t salt
4 T flour
1 pt. milk

Beat eggs, add flour and milk, and beat again. In a very hot pan put 1 T butter or bacon fat. Add batter and bake about 30 minutes in a hot oven or until done.

Filled Supper Rolls

2 c cooked and diced ham
12 finger rolls
1 can mushroom soup
melted butter

Combine soup with evaporated milk to a thick creamy state, then add meat. Season well with salt and pepper and dash of nutmeg. Heat well. Slice rolls leaving halves attached on one side. Remove the soft centers and brush with melted butter. Brown in oven, then fill with hot meat mixture. Keep in oven until ready to serve.

Part Four

Wintertime

Winter lies too long in country towns; hangs on until it is stale and shabby, old and sullen.

Willa Cather, *My Antonia*

— 1 —

Winter Comes to the Prairie

When the harvesting was all done, the crops stored or sent to market, and our home banked around the foundation with tar paper and dirt or manure to insulate against the coming freezing weather, every living thing instinctively began to gird for five or six months of a sort of hibernation. This usually began around Halloween, when we often had a heavy snowfall — or at least the first of a long series of wintry storms out of the northwest. We could usually expect "freeze-up" about this time, too. The river and the creeks and ponds would sheet over with ice, and the stubble and summer-fallowed fields would become hard and lifeless. After the first freeze we would usually start our butchering to obtain a fresh supply of meat for the winter. Quarters of beef and hogs were hung in screened boxes on the north side of the house and, once frozen, stayed that way all winter or until eaten. When meat was needed for a meal it was simply sawed off the carcass and brought inside to thaw.

By Thanksgiving Day the land was encapsulated in winter's relentless bond. But the tempo of life picked up indoors, where it was always cozy and comfortable, warmed by great wood stoves and fireplaces or by coal furnaces in houses that had basements. Deep feather beds and comforters kept one snug as a bug during the nights when the fires died down. First one up in the morning always fired up the kitchen cookstove (which had been banked with hot coals for the night) and put on the big coffee pot. The water reservoir behind the cookstove usually stayed warm enough all night to keep the sourdough pot bubbling. Breakfast during those good years of plenty was a big meal, designed to get one through the labors and outside activities of the day until suppertime.

The winter days provided a lot of leisure, and it was spent outdoors in recreations like skiing and skating and tobogganing, or hunting and trapping. The five-mile-long trapline I ran each morning and evening up Downing's Creek provided me with a little extra income from pelts of mink, weasel, rabbit, fox, badger, muskrat, and beaver that I shipped to one of the big fur companies in St. Louis. Even in those days a mink was worth about $20, a prime white weasel (ermine) $2 to $3, a muskrat from 80 cents to $1,50, and beaver up to $50. As a kid I considered such activity not only a source of much-needed cash for clothes, school, and spending money, but also a normal boyhood pursuit. Years later, with a family of my own, I have been somewhat stunned when confronted with the social changes and basic civilized ethics — to say nothing of the new concepts of wildlife preservation and the fancy principles of the new ecology. When I told our young son — who was born and raised in the big city and brought up on a diet of Disney fantasies and TV dinners — about my boyhood trapline, he turned to me puzzled and asked, "Dad, how did you get the skins off those animals without killing them?

That was the last time I bragged about "the good old days" to my children.

November was always a busy month filled with duck and goose hunting, getting skates and skis ready for the season, plunging into new studies and school activities, and making new friends and alliances. The farm kids who attended the higher grades and high school in town generally arrived after harvestime to board with families for

A remote homestead in the Wallowa Mountains of Northeast Oregon, in winter.

the winter. There were get-acquainted parties and other social activities that were always exciting.

This month, too, preparations for the holiday season feasts began. Families with ethnic or old-country backgrounds were especially busy, for the Thanksgiving-Christmas period was one of the major feast and religious festival seasons. From early November through January life was a merry round of parties, feasting, school activities, church socials, and good fellowships. One of my lasting memories is of the 'Round-the-World-Parties that were held at least once during the winter. This was a community affair. Various families would volunteer to provide one "port o' call" for a total of perhaps ten or twelve. Each family would provide its ethnic specialty dishes — Spanish, Norwegian, Icelandic, German, "Roosian," Swedish, Danish, Irish, Dutch, Welsh, English — for North Dakota was a great melting pot of nationalities of recent immigration. During the party day we would make the rounds from house to house enjoying the rich and varied fare. The small charge which was collected went to local charity projects. Everyone had a good time, eating like no king was ever privileged, and the community was drawn closer together.

Too bad events like this are no longer popular.

Winter was a time when one could sample all the traditional old-country recipes that had been handed down through generations. This was especially true during the holidays, for many of these recipes originated in ancient customs, religions, or festivals. Lutefisk is an example; preparations traditionally began just after Thanksgiving and culminated at Christmas. My memory of lutefisk is associated with church suppers in the basement of the Lutheran Church, where I learned to love this creamy white, steaming hot dish, made the ancient way.

The two-week school holiday from Christmas through New Year's Day was always a welcome one, filled with outside activities like skating parties on the ice of the Mouse River — warming fires on the bank and lanterns swaying and flickering in the brittle cold north wind. Winter nights were frequently filled with spectacular displays of northern lights, or aurora borealis, an awesome phenomenon of nature that left one strongly feeling the insignificance of man.

January usually brought the most violent weather, with frequent blinding blizzards, heavy snowfall, and sub-zero temperatures made even worse by the wind-chill factor, to use a modern term. The days were spent mostly inside, with heavy concentration on school studies. Only the necessary chores were carried on outside. Harsh weather continued, with lessening effect, through the spring equinox in March. By then the novelty of winter activities had worn off, leaving only a sense of survival. Everyone began to feel the tension of anticipating the first signs of spring and the renewal of life and the earth.

— 2 —

The Smorgasbord Tradition

Smorgasbord — N. A meal featuring a varied number of dishes served buffet-style; Swedish for "open faced sandwich," bread and butter, SMOR *or butter from Old Norse;* BORD, Old Norse for table.

The smorgasbord tradition came to North Dakota and other northern tier states along with immigrants from Denmark, Sweden, Norway, Iceland, and Finland. Happily, it has been continued through many generations of farm folk and adopted by many big city restaurants, classy or otherwise, in something called a "buffet table." Too often this is a table loaded with day- and week-old leftovers, the actual condition concealed by dim lighting.

As a kid, the smorgasbord table was one of my favorites, because I was and am a snacker. During the spring plowing, through the summer, and into the autumn, while the days were filled with unrelenting hard outdoor labor, and the womenfolk were occupied with endless chores, the table was a convenient way to feed the crew and drop-in neighbors without going to the fuss of setting tables and cooking meals. In some cases the smorgasbord was a prelude to a big Sunday meal, but at other times it was a snacker's heaven. Smorgasbord, incidentally, means literally "open sandwich table."

The contents of a smorgasbord table were limited only by the enthusiasm of the gals and the ingredients available, usually every dish was carefully arranged and decorated with endive, parsley, olives, pickles, nuts, fruits, and other garnishes. Some typical dishes found on a smorgasbord table were:

anchovies
cold meats
smoked herring
stuffed eggs
lefse
cheeses
pickles
salads
head cheese
boiled ham
cucumbers
pickled stromming
creamed chicken
French bread
crackers
flank roll
smoked oysters
fried chicken
sliced sausage
cookies
caviar
pickled herring
Swedish omelet
smoked salmon
liver paste
pig's feet
tongue
radishes
sliced tomatoes
boiled potatoes
pickled beets
Swedish meatballs
veal patties
pumpernickel bread
dips
sardines
stuffed peppers
boiled eggs
green onions
bacon strips

Scandihoovian Spring Soup

3 small carrots, diced
3½ oz. fresh spinach
2 c water
salt to taste
1 egg yolk
1 c small green peas
6 to 8 small cauliflower florets
2¼ c skim milk
1 T flour
3 T fine chopped parsley

Cut spinach and cauliflower into small pieces and cook in salted water with peas and carrots. Heat 2 cups milk and vegetable broth in pan. Add flour, blended with some milk. Beat egg yolk and ¼ cup milk, add to hot liquid with vegetables and parsley. Bring to simmer, don't boil.

Cold Country Mustard Sauce

3 T mild mustard
⅓ c corn oil
fresh dill, chopped fine
1 T white vinegar
1 T sugar (for sweetener)
salt and pepper

Mix in a bowl, mustard, vinegar, sweetener, pinch of salt, and pepper. Add oil slowly, stirring with wooden spoon. Mix in dill before serving.

Marinated Salmon

3 lbs. raw salmon	**2 T salt**
2 t peppercorns, crushed	**2 t corn oil**
dill, whole	

Clean salmon and dry on towel. Cut lengthwise, removing backbone and rib bones (filleting first will take care of this). Rub with oil and salt and pepper. Place salmon, skin side down, in pan with thick layer of dill, and also sprinkle dill on top. Place other half of salmon skin side up, with thick end opposite narrow end of bottom piece. Sprinkle with more dill. Refrigerate 2 to 4 days, turning once or twice. Serve sliced very thin with a cold mustard sauce or garnished with lemon and fresh dill.

Old-Fashioned Swedish Meatballs

1 lb. lean ground beef	**1 small red onion**
salt	**1 t allspice**
1 egg yolk	**2 slices bread**
2 ozs. butter or margarine	

Soak bread in half a cup of water. Combine all ingredients except margarine, mix and blend smooth. Shape balls and fry in melted margarine on moderate heat, browning evenly.

Potato Delight

8 medium potatoes	**3 onions**
2 c diced cooked lamb	**3 T margarine**
½ t pepper	**salt to taste**

Dice peeled potatoes, peel and chop onions. Fry potatoes until brown, saute onions in margarine until golden brown, add meat to onions and brown. Mix with potatoes and add seasonings. Cook 5 minutes more over low heat.

Dilly Veal

2 lbs. veal
1 Spanish onion
1 leek
½ celery root
8 peppercorns
salt to taste
2 carrots
1 T dry dill

Cube meat, mix in casserole dish with salt, peppercorns, and water to cover, bring to boil. Dice vegetables, add dill, mix with meat. Cover and simmer 1 to 2 hours.

A Typical Smorgasbord Table

Main dish: Hot meatballs with escalloped potatoes

Cold meats
hard-boiled eggs
tongue
jellied veal
summer sausage
rullepölse
sylte

Cheeses
American cheese
cheddars
brick or Swiss
gjetost
primost

Salads
macaroni
mixed vegetables
bean
celery
carrot strips
radishes
pickled onions

Fish
smoked herring
pickled sardines
smoked salmon
smoked sturgeon
smoked shad
caviar

Breads
buttered dark
toasted white
flatbrød
lefse

Soup
fruit soup
Norsk bakkelse
Flötegröt

Coffee
Ice cream

— 3 —

Old Country Favorites

If America was a melting pot of ethnic origins, then the Dakotas in the early 1900s was a boiling stew of many different nationalities, mostly those that had immigrated from Northern Europe and the British Isles. The descendants of these nationalities are today somewhat sneeringly referred to as WASP — or white Anglo-Saxon Protestants — as though there were some sort of dishonor associated with such ethnic origins. In any case, the so-called WASPS of the Prairie Country included Catholics, Jews, Mohammedans, and atheists, as well as Protestants. They were not all of Anglo-Saxon origin, and they most certainly were not all white.

The various ethnic groups got along well together, mingled freely, and contributed much to the common good of the community. Not the least of these contributions was the wonderful cooking from traditional old recipes.

We have collected many of these over the years, the ones that were brought to the Dakotas. There are some variations, naturally, in the same recipes, since many of them were used in more than one country, i.e., Norway, Sweden, Denmark. In some cases we have included these variations to show the differences. Naturally, a preponderance of these old recipes has to do with baking and pastry goods, as winter was a time for baking and making goodies. Some, like those for head cheese or sausages which call for blood or parts of animals not readily available, have been included mostly for reader interest, although readers who live on the land and raise livestock may find them useful. In most cases proportions of ingredients have been "modernized," so to speak, for better understanding.

The spellings of some of the old names cannot be vouched for. Names were mostly handed down orally, and often with accents. The best we hope for is phonetic accuracy!

Julekake

1 yeast cake
⅓ c shortening
½ t salt
1 c milk
3½ to 4 c flour
¼ c finely cut citron
¼ c lukewarm water
¾ to 1 c sugar
½ t ground cardamon seed
1 egg
⅓ c raisins

Dissolve yeast in lukewarm water. Mix shortening, sugar, and salt with cardamon in large mixing bowl. Pour scalded milk over. Add dissolved yeast, unbeaten egg, and 1 c flour. Beat until mixture is smooth and full of bubbles. Add rest of flour and fruit which has been dusted with flour. Mix well, then cover dough and let rise until doubled. Stir down and let rise until double again. Turn dough onto a floured board and shape into 2 round loaves. Place loaves on greased baking sheets and brush with melted butter or milk. Cover and let rise until double. Bake in 350 degree oven for 45 to 50 minutes. Let cool and glaze with thin frosting made of powdered sugar and hot water, with 2 drops of vanilla.

Fattigman

Fattigmans are known as the poor man's cookies.

3 eggs
3 T sweet cream
⅛ t salt
3 T sugar
1 t vanilla

Beat eggs lightly, then add sugar and blend well, adding cream, salt, and vanilla. Use enough flour to make a stiff dough. Roll out and cut into diamond shapes, with slits in diamonds. Deep-fry like doughnuts in hot oil until lightly browned. Sugar or not, as desired.

Fattigman Bakkels

3 well-beaten eggs	**3 T sugar**
6 cardamon seed	**3 t cream**
2 T melted butter	**pinch salt**

Mix well, add flour to roll soft dough, cut into diamonds, deep-fry like donuts.

Knakkebrod

1 c lard	**¾ c sugar**
3 c sour milk	**1½ t soda**
1 c oatmeal	**1 c bran**
3 c graham flour	**2 t salt**
2 t baking powder	**some white flour**

Mix soda into milk, then add rest of ingredients. Roll thin with white flour. Bake in oven on cookie sheets; cut into desired shapes.

Swede Scones

1 cake yeast dissolved in 1 T warm milk with 1 t sugar

3 eggs beaten	**¼ c melted butter**
4 c flour	**⅓ c sugar**
1 c milk scalded	**1 t salt**

A package of dry yeast can be used instead of cake yeast, but keep milk warm, not cold or hot. Combine ingredients and add 2 c flour, stirring well. Add 2 more c flour. Cover and cool overnight. About 4 hours before baking, divide dough into 4 parts and roll each into a round, ½ inch thick. Brush with butter. Cut into triangles. Roll each up from wide end. Let rise 4 hours on greased sheets. Bake 15 to 20 minutes in a 350 degree oven.

Lefse

1 t salt
3 t butter or lard
5 large potatoes
flour to roll

Boil potatoes, then put through ricer. Add shortening and salt. Let cool. Add flour, then roll pieces of dough as a pie crust. Roll very thin. Bake on a pancake griddle until light brown, turning frequently. Use only moderate heat to prevent burning. When done, cover with clean cloth to prevent drying out. Sprinkle with powdered sugar if desired.

Swedish Rye Bread

7 c water
½ c molasses
1 T salt
16 c white flour
½ c melted lard
1 c brown sugar
8 c rye flour
2 cakes yeast or packages

Mix rye flour, half the white flour, water, lard, molasses, sugar, and salt. Dissolve yeast in ½ c warm water and add with a pinch of salt. Let rise, then add rest of white flour. Knead until hard. Let rise until dough increases in size by about one-third. Bake 15 minutes at 375 degrees, then 45 minutes at 350 degrees. Makes 8 loaves.

Roosian White Rye Bread

We had a lot of "Roosians" in our community in the olden days. They were actually immigrants of German extraction from the Ukraine. They were hard workers, somewhat clannish, and the women were marvelous cooks. They contributed much to the culinary legends of North Dakota.

2 c rye flour
3 c warm water
1 pkg. dried yeast
4 c white flour
1 t salt

Blend yeast, dissolved in warm water, with rye flour and set overnight. In the morning add 4 c white flour, mix well, and let rise. Punch down, shape into loaves, and put in pans. Let rise again. Bake at 400 degrees for about 1 hour.

Irish Farm Bread

We also had many Irish immigrants, and this was a popular bread from the old country.

4 c enriched flour
1 t salt
2 T caraway seeds
2 c raisins
1 egg
½ c sugar
1 t baking soda
½ c butter
1½ c buttermilk
1 t baking powder

Sift flour, sugar, salt; stir in caraway seeds. Blend in butter, adding raisins. Mix buttermilk, egg, soda, and baking powder. Blend into flour mixture. Turn out on floured board and knead. Shape and place in greased pan. Cross top with knife, and brush with beaten egg yolk or cream. Bake at 375 degrees for 1 hour or until done. Cool before cutting.

Fastnachts Kuchlie

1 medium potato, peeled and sliced
2 c salted water
¼ c shortening
¼ c warm water
1 t salt
½ c sugar
1 pkg. active dry yeast
6 c sifted flour
2 eggs well beaten

Cook potato in 2 c salted water until tender. Drain and save 1½ c potato water. Mash and measure ¼ c potato. Beat with sugar, add eggs, blend. Add salt and shortening, then gradually add hot potato water until smooth. Dissolve yeast in ¼ c warm water. Beat into mixture. Stir in rest of flour gradually. Knead well on floured board. Place in greased bowl and let rise in warm place until double. Turn onto floured board. Knead well and divide. Roll each half into a batter about ⅓ inch thick. Cut into 2-inch squares. Place on greased cookie sheet. Cover. Let rise until double. With both hands pick up each square and stretch until center is thin and there is a rim around outside. Deep-fry in hot fat, while spooning hot fat over center so it will puff up. When brown on bottom, turn over and repeat process. Drain on paper towel and roll in sugar.

Rullepölse

1 beef flank
½ lb. veal
salt, pepper
½ lb. lean pork
1 onion
saltpeter

Make layers of beef, cutting into small pieces. Remove all fat, gristle, and cartilage. Slice pork and veal into narrow strips. Chop onion. Spread pieces of beef on board, cover with strips of pork and veal and chopped onion. Sprinkle with salt, pepper, and saltpeter. Roll up pieces and sew firmly. Wind each roll with cord to keep from opening when cooking. Put rolls in a brine that has been brought to a boil and cooled. Make brine from water heavily salted. Leave in brine 3 to 5 days. Drain and rinse in cold fresh water. Cook until tender. Slice for lunch snacks or sandwiches.

Potetesklub

4 c grated potatoes
1 onion
6½ c flour
3 t salt
4 t baking powder
1 ham bone

Sift together flour, baking powder, and salt. Mix with potatoes. Drop into boiling salted water into which you have put ham bone and onion. Cook for 1 hour. Prevent sticking to bottom of pan. Serve with spareribs.

Søtsuppe

This is a sweet soup.

2 qts. water
1 c raisins
1 lemon
1 c sugar
1 glass grape juice
½ c sago
1 c prunes
2 sticks cinnamon
1 T vinegar
1 lemon

Wash sago, raisins, prunes. Cook in water for 1 hour. Add sugar, cinnamon, sliced lemon, and vinegar. Boil 30 minutes. Add grape juice after 15 minutes.

Pultost

This is a cheese.

Heat 2 qts. sour milk but do not boil. Pour into bag and let drain. When cool, rub until fine and put into scalded jar. Cover and set in warm place (not hot) to ferment. In about 3 days salt to taste and knead. Keep stored in covered jar in cool place.

Surmelksupper

You can almost figure this one out by pronouncing the Norwegian word aloud: "sour milk soup."

Mix 1 T flour and 1 T butter to each pint of sour milk. Make paste and heat, stirring constantly to prevent curdling. Season with sugar, salt, cinnamon. Very mild soup often used in sickroom and for people who are out of sorts and cannot take heavy meals. Standard dish for us kids when down with "la grippe."

Fløiels Fløtegrøt

Boil 3 qts. whipping cream in a cast-iron kettle, stirring constantly. Use wooden spoon. Sift in flour until butter forms. Keep stirring while cooking to prevent scorching. As butter forms, scoop it off and keep warm. After butter is all formed and removed, add boiling milk gradually (about 2½ qts.), letting it come to a boil between each cup of milk added. Then add ½ c sugar and salt to taste. Serve with hot butter drippings, sugar, and cinnamon. Serves 30. Also known as velvet cream mush.

Kleiner Fattigman

1 c sugar
2 eggs
1 t vanilla
flour
½ c butter
6 T cream
1 t baking powder

Roll mixture about ½ inch thick and cut into strips. Slit each and form a twist. Deep-fry until light brown.

Kringler

4 c flour
½ c sugar
¼ t salt
1 c butter
2 c sour cream
1 t soda

Sift flour, sugar, salt, and soda. Cut butter into the mixture. Add cream and flour to make a soft dough. Roll into strips ½ inch wide and 9 inches long. Form into a figure 8. Dip in beaten egg white and sprinkle with sugar. Bake at 400 degrees.

Flatbrød

1 c graham flour
1 t salt
2 c boiling water
2 c white flour
1 T shortening

Mix and let stand until cold. Add more flour and roll very thin. Bake in oven on cookie sheet or stone.

Norsk Rømmedbrød

1 c thick sour cream
1 T cornmeal
flour
½ c shortening
1 T sugar

Blend cream, sugar, cornmeal, and melted shortening. Add flour to make a cookie dough. Roll very thin. Sprinkle sugar on top of dough while rolling. Bake on top of stove on low heat.

Svensk Knackebrod

This is a hardtack, celebrated in stories of the sea.

1 c milk
2 cakes yeast
2 T sugar
¾ c lard
1 t salt
4 c flour

Bring to a boil the milk, sugar, salt, and shortening. Cool and add dissolved yeast and flour. Make dough and form into buns. Let rise 1 hour. Roll out with rolling pin. Bake in oven on cookie sheets at 450 degrees until light brown. Makes a dozen. Will keep for centuries (!).

Swedish Tea Ring

2 cakes yeast
1 c milk
½ c sugar
2 eggs beaten
¼ c lukewarm water
¼ c butter
1 t salt
5 c flour

Dissolve yeast in lukewarm water. Scald milk and add butter, sugar, and salt. Add flour to make a thick batter. Add yeast and eggs and beat well. Use enough flour to make a soft dough. Turn out onto a floured board and knead until shiny. Place in greased bowl, cover, and let rise until double. Punch down, shape into tea ring. Let rise until double. Bake at 375 degrees for 25 minutes.

Kottbollar

3 lb. ground beef	**1 pt. cream**
1 c bread crumbs	**2 t salt**
¼ t pepper	**¼ t allspice**

Grind beef fine, add cream, and beat well. Then add seasonings and crumbs. Mix well and form into small balls. Saute in butter and make gravy from drippings. Simmer meatballs in the gravy.

Blodpölse

2 qt. pork or beef blood	**½ c pearl barley**
½ lb. fresh side pork	**½ t ginger**
1 T salt	**flour**
2 t baking powder	

Cook barley in boiling salted water 15 minutes. Drain and cool. Add everything except pork and stir well. Pour batter into wet cloth bags and add diced pork while filling. Tie up when ¾ full and cook in boiling water for 1½ hours. Serve hot with butter. Keeps well when cooled.

Faar I Kaal

3 lbs. leg of lamb	**1 cabbage**
1 t salt	**¼ t pepper**

Cut meat into small chunks. In a kettle place a layer of meat then a layer of cabbage, seasoned between layers. Cover with water and cook 2 hours.

Lutefisk

Remove head and tail of fish and cut into 4-inch

lengths. Soak in salted water overnight. Rinse in cold water 5 hours. Drain. Put in cheesecloth bags about half full. Drop bags into boiling salted water and cook for 5 minutes. Remove and drain. Skin and bone fish with a spoon. Serve warm with melted butter.

Sursild

4 large salt herring
1 c water
½ t sugar
6 bay leaves
1 c vinegar
1 T peppercorns
2 onions
1 c water

Wash herring, skin and remove bones, cut into chunks. Mix water, vinegar, and sugar. Add herring, sliced onion, peppercorns, and bay leaves. Let stand overnight in cool place.

Frau Monsen's Kake

½ c butter
3 eggs
1 t extract flavor
½ c sugar
1 c sifted cake flour
shredded almonds

Cream sugar and butter, add well-beaten egg yolks and flavoring. Fold in flour and beaten egg whites. Spread in buttered pan about 8 by 10 inches. Sprinkle top with sugar and shredded almonds. Bake at 350 degrees for 30 minutes. Remove and cut into small diamond-shaped pieces. Return to oven and dry at 250 degrees.

Sprit

1 c brown sugar
1 egg
½ t cream of tartar
1 t ginger
½ c butter
1 t soda
2 c flour
1 t lemon extract

Cream butter, add well-beaten egg and sugar. Stir

in soda, dissolved in warm water. Sift together flour, cream of tartar, and ginger and add to dough. Add flavoring. Form in cookie press and bake.

Sandbakkelse

1 c butter | **1 c sugar**
2 c flour | **1 egg**
½ c chopped blanched almonds

Cream butter and sugar, adding flour gradually, then egg and almonds. Press into tins and bake at 350 degrees.

Sprutbakkelse

½ c butter
½ c shortening
1 c sugar
1 beaten egg
½ t salt
2 c flour
1 t vanilla

Cream shortening, add sugar slowly with beaten egg and vanilla; add flour and salt, mixed. Form in cookie press and bake in different designs.

Norway Kringle

1 c sugar
1 c sweet cream
1 c buttermilk
1 t baking powder
1 t soda
6 c flour
nutmeg and salt to taste

Mix ingredients, adding nutmeg and salt to taste. Roll small chunks to strips about size of finger. Form into figure eights. Bake in moderate oven until crisp.

Scotch Scones

2 c flour
3 t baking powder
1 t salt
2 T sugar
3 T shortening
2 eggs
⅓ c milk

Blend dry ingredients, add shortening. Beat eggs and add to milk, then blend into dry ingredients. Roll out about ½ inch thick and cut into 2-inch squares. Brush with milk and fold corner to corner. Dust with sugar. Bake on ungreased cookie sheet about 25 minutes at 400 degrees.

Krum Kage

1 c sugar
3 eggs
1 t vanilla
1 c shortening
1 small can milk
1½ c flour

Beat eggs, add sugar, and beat some more. Add rest of ingredients, alternately with milk and flour. Heat the Krum Kage iron, don't grease. Drop dough on iron and brown. Roll while hot.

Swedish Mandelstränger

1 c sugar
2 eggs
½ c chopped almonds
1 c shortening
2½ c flour
1 t vanilla

Blend and roll small pieces of dough into rolls about 1 inch in diameter, as long as the cookie sheet. Press down with fork. Bake until golden brown and cut into bars. Walnuts may be used instead of almonds, but almonds are the traditional Swedish nut meat.

Berliner Krantzer

¾ c powdered sugar
2 c butter
4 egg yolks
4 c flour
½ t almond flavoring
1 c sugar
½ t vanilla

Cream butter, add sugar and blend. Add the egg yolks, beaten into a creamy blend. Add flavoring and gradually stir in the flour, a little at a time. Break off small pieces of dough, roll, and shape into wreaths. Brush tops with beaten egg whites. Sprinkle lightly with powdered sugar. Bake 8 minutes at 400 degrees.

Immigrant Slaw

Shred finely some cabbage and crisp in cold water. Beat yolks of 3 eggs with 2 T cold water. Add 1 T butter, ¼ c vinegar, salt and pepper to taste. Cook over hot water until thick. Pour over drained cabbage and heat. Serve piping hot.

Moussaka

What would any country cookbook be without one of the famous Greek moussaka recipes?

2 lb. ground lean beef
3 cloves garlic, chopped
3 T butter
1 t mint leaves
salt, pepper, oregano, nutmeg
2 medium onions chopped
1 can tomato sauce
2 T parsley chopped
½ c water
1 large eggplant, sliced

Combine in a buttered casserole or baking dish, top with a white sauce, and bake at 350 degrees until bubbling.

White Sauce:

½ cube butter
2 c milk
3 T flour

Blend and bring to a boil, pour over above mixture in casserole.

Traditional Lutefisk

Use any white-fleshed fish. Cut in sections, put in a cloth bag or cheesecloth. Place in kettle of salted water. Bring to a gradual boil, but do not cook fish.

Drain and serve with drawn butter or milk gravy in a separate dish.

Stockholm Fish Pudding

1¼ T butter
½ c milk
2 c finely minced boiled fish
¼ c flour
5 eggs
salt, pepper, and sugar to taste

Blend butter and flour in pan over heat. Add milk and cook until it does not stick to pan. Season to taste. Add fish. Cool and add egg yolks. Mix, and then add egg whites which have been stiffly beaten. Place in soufflé dish. Set in pan of water in 350 degree oven for 45 minutes. Goes well with lutefisk.

Rota-Mos

These are Swedish spareribs. You need about 2 lbs., along with a large rutabaga and 6 potatoes. Boil the spareribs in salted water until half done, or about 45 minutes. Add rutabaga that has been pared into thin slices. Cook for 15 minutes. Drop in potatoes and cook until tender. Remove the meat when it is done and brown lightly in frying pan or oven. Mash the potatoes and mix with 3 T butter, ½ t salt, and dash of pepper. Serve on platter with ribs around vegetables.

Swedish Links

⅔ lb. ground meat
6 medium potatoes, ground
salt, pepper, allspice
⅓ lb. ground pork
2 onions
sausage casings

Mix well together, fill casings, boil in water for 20 to 30 minutes.

Swiss Sour Cream Country Steak

Use round steak, pounded and cut into serving

pieces. Flour and brown on both sides. Slice 2 medium onions and place on top. Grate 2 T cheese and spread on top. Add 1 c water and 1 c thick sour cream. Cover and simmer ½ to ¾ hour. If necessary to thicken gravy, sprinkle on a little flour and mix.

Aurora, Oregon, is a little town along U.S. 99E between Portland and Salem. It was founded in 1856 by a Dr. William Keil as a communal society. Today the town has a population of about 500, mostly descendants of the original settlers, and has not changed much in 130 years. Neither has the tradition of good, wholesome meals and old-country cooking.

The colony was disbanded in 1878, following the death of Dr. Keil, and the property was divided among the members. Many of the old buildings have been restored. Aurora is today widely known as an authenic remnant of nineteenth century living and is visited by thousands of people each year — especially during the Aurora Colony Historical Society annual sausage dinner, usually held in April. The dinner menu on these occasions includes old-colony-style sausage, mashed potatoes and country gravy, green beans, cole slaw, rolls and butter, homemade jam, applesauce, and krumble cake with whipped cream — an old colony recipe.

Aurora Colony Krumble Cake

2 c flour
1 c white sugar
1 t soda
½ t salt
whipped cream
1 c brown sugar
⅔ c shortening or butter
1 t cinnamon
1 c sour milk or buttermilk

Blend flour, brown sugar, white sugar, and shortening. Save ½ c of this mixture for topping. To the rest add soda, cinnamon, salt, and sour milk. Beat well.

Spread batter in a greased 7-by-11 pan and sprinkle reserve mixture over the top. Bake at 350 degrees for 30 to 35 minutes. Serve with whipped cream.

North Dakota Kuga

A favorite of the old "Roosian" (German) communities in North Dakota was *Kuga*. This is a sort of coffee cake, very sweet and delicious.

1 pkg. dry active yeast
1 c milk
½ c shortening
1 egg beaten
1 t cinnamon
¼ c warm water
½ c water
1 t salt
½ c sugar
flour to make dough

To make the dough, dissolve yeast in ¼ c warm water and set aside. Blend milk, ½ c water, shortening, and salt and bring to a rolling boil. Let cool and add beaten egg, sugar, and cinnamon. Then add yeast and enough flour to make a bread dough. Let rise and punch down. Let rise again and knead. Roll dough very thin and place in greased pie pans. Bake as per pie shells.

Custard filling:

2 c cream or 1 can evaporated milk
2 eggs well beaten
1 t vanilla
¾ c sugar
1½ T flour

Mix cream or milk, eggs, sugar, vanilla, and flour. Bring to a slow boil, stirring to avoid scorching. Cook 5 minutes, remove from heat. Fill the baked pie shells with canned or cooked fruit. This can be crushed pineapple, cooked rhubarb, or cut prunes. Cover the fruit with custard filling. This filling recipe is enough for two pie pans.

Farmyard Pork Cake

1 c finely chopped pork
1 c sugar
½ lb. raisins
½ t salt
1 t cloves
1 t soda
1 c boiling water
1 c molasses
4½ c flour
1 t cinnamon
1 t nutmeg

Pour boiling water over chopped pork. Add sugar, molasses, salt, condiments, and the soda. Beat into the flour. Bake slowly in a loaf tin until a toothpick comes out dry from center of cake. Keeps well and improves with age. A popular wintertime delight on some prairie farms in the old days.

Iceland Vinetarte

1½ c sugar
½ t salt
1 t vanilla
3 t baking powder
3 eggs
1½ c sweet cream
5 c flour

Mix well. Divide dough into 5 equal parts and roll out as for cookies. Grease cookie sheets. Cover dough with wax paper until ready to cook. Bake in hot oven until tan.

Filling:

2 lbs. prunes
¼ c white sugar
½ c prune juice
¼ t cloves

Cook and pit prunes and run through chopper. Mix pulp, juice, sugar, and cloves and cook 5 minutes; cool and have ready. Turn first cookie sheet upside down and spread filling evenly. Place the next sheet on top, spread with filling, and so on for the rest. Cut in narrow slices. Let stand a day or so. Will keep 2 weeks. Ideal for weddings and holiday parties.

The Farm Kitchen Becomes a Wondrous Bakery

Winter was also the time for wondrous uninhibited exercise of kitchen baking skills. Flour and sugar were purchased in the fall in 50-pound bags and barrels in anticipation of the delightful treats that would brighten up the long, dark days indoors.

The reader will note that many of the recipes call for ingredients not readily available to the city dweller, who is dependent upon the supermarket for supplies instead of being able to get them direct from the producer. Also, modern food processing, for better or for worse, has resulted in some "technical" changes, at least in nomenclature.

Butttermilk is an example. This was plentiful in the old days, because it was a by-product of the butter-making process. If you can't find it at the store (at least the fresh kind), you can make a reasonable facsimile by mixing a tablespoon of vinegar to a cup of fresh milk.

Baking powder can be made by blending a tablespoon of baking soda with a half teaspoon of cream of tartar. Confectioner's sugar can be simulated by blending a cup of regular granulated sugar and 2 tablespoons of cornstarch. Heavy cream can be made from a cup of milk blended with a tablespoon or so of butter.

For most recipes, a bread flour with a high gluten content is preferred, especially for baking bread — rather than so-called all-purpose or refined flour. Most specialty stores and some supermarkets carry high gluten or bread flour in stock. You can also grind your own flour with grains obtained from health food stores and similar outlets. Don't use grains direct from an elevator or grain and seed dealer, for it may be contaminated with herbicides or insecticides. Your own ground flour, though, is by far the most nutritious and delicious when used in home-baked goods.

Sourdough and You

A great deal of legend, if not fantasy, has evolved around the use of sourdough — started, no doubt, by the romantic stories of gold rush days and the North Country, and kept alive by tales of families who inherited a sourdough pot from a prospector ancestor and who have kept alive the starter for lo these 100 years or more.

First of all, there is no mystery about sourdough. It is nothing more than "a dough in which both alcoholic and lactic fermentation is active — so-called from the use for making bread when camping . . ." according to *Webster's Third International Dictionary.*

The leavening or rising of dough is produced by the bubbling of the active elements — alcohol and lactic acid. The starter or sponge or whatever you want to call it, is the embryo, if you will, or the "yeast factory" that works when it is active. It will continue to work just as long as the temperature is ideal (lukewarm is the rule of thumb) and is replenished with flour and water. From time to time part of the active starter or sponge is removed and used in recipes for baked goods. The amount used must be replaced by an equal amount of fresh flour and water in order to keep the starter going. Theoretically, it is possible to keep the starter working for centuries, if not forever, under the proper conditions. This is where the old legends depart from fact.

Second of all, you don't have to inherit a sourdough starter from an old grizzled "sourdough" prospector. You can make a sourdough starter in less than five minutes. Here's how:

The fixin's for making a sourdough starter or sponge. Ingredients include only water and flour. The dry yeast can be used to accelerate the process. Room temperature should be not lower than 68 nor higher than 80 degrees. Getting a starter going is a simple, uncomplicated process, despite the folklore surrounding it.

Sourdough Starter

Put 2 cups of flour into a crock or plastic container (use no metal) that is at least room temperature. Add 2½ cups of lukewarm water and set the batch in a warm *but not hot* place. You can cover it with porous cheesecloth or something to keep the bugs and dirt out, but it must have fresh air to breath so the spores can live and multiply.

That's all there is to it. You have just made your own personal yeast factory — and maybe even started your own family tradition.

In about four or five days the pot will be bubbling merrily, like one of those Yellowstone Park springs, and the whole house will be filled with the heavenly aroma that has been called the "heady fragrance from the wine of the gods."*

There are short cuts, of course. You can help the whole process along by adding part of a package of yeast to the pot, folding in gently. (Don't stir or beat sourdough.) You can also use the water from boiled potatoes. This should cut the working time down about half or better.

Once a starter is made, you can keep it in the fridge for several weeks and even freeze it for later use, *but it must always be brought back to a lukewarm temperature* before it is used for baking. In the gold rush days of the Far North, prospectors and others who traveled the trails in summer or winter, on foot or with dog teams, carried the sponge or starter buried in the flour sack. In camp, the sponge was warmed by the fire and part of it used for baking flapjacks, quick bread, or ban-

*For more fascinating details about sourdough, its history and uses, see *The Complete Sourdough Cookbook* by Don and Myrtle Holm (Caxton).

nock. What was left was moistened well and placed back in the flour sack for the next leg of the trek.

Third of all, it is *not* necessary to keep a starter for a hundred years to be good. A starter can be used as soon as it is working or bubbling. If you lose a starter by removing too much for baking or by not using it regularly and replenishing it, you can easily make another as described above. Starters will "spoil" if not used and replenished regularly. You can tell by the color — a starter that is spoiling turns a sickly yellow or orange. Throw it out and start over if this occurs.

Some tips:

Sourdough starter expands greatly as it works; use a container that will contain it!

Don't be alarmed if a liquid forms on top. This is the product of the fermentation process. Gently, gently work it back into the dough, before using for baking.

So much for the hocus pocus and the legends. You have just graduated into the delightful world of sourdough baking.

The San Francisco Sourdough Story

As readers of our book, *The Complete Sourdough Cookbook,* know, cooking the sourdough way is an ancient and honorable pastime, going back as far as recorded history. It become a staple of the western frontier although it was commonly used in most rural households the world over and even gave its name to the grizzled stereotyped prospector of the desert, mountains, and frozen north country — who is now known in literature as a sourdough.

In the middle 1800s San Francisco became the bustling cosmopolitan Paris of the Pacific, fueled by an influx of gold seekers, fellow travelers, camp followers from all over the world. From the beginning, good food and good living were actively pursued in what is now known as "Baghdad by the Bay." This tradition continues to the present. Among the first establishments in San Francisco were small bakeries. By necessity they used local grain flour and leavening made from a sourdough starter. Over the past 150 years many of these starters, which originated back in the gold rush days, were continued by being renewed as each day's bread is made. A little of the starter or sponge was put back in the pot to continue "cooking."

San Francisco's sourdough bread, especially the sourdough French bread, has become world famous over the years for its crusty, wholesome tastiness. Today it is shipped, either already baked or as dough to be baked locally, to outlets throughout the West, and by air to the East Coast. Indeed, sourdough baking has become one of San Francisco's leading industries.

It was long thought that the superb quality of San Francisco sourdough bread was due to the climate or to some secret baking process. In 1973, a major scientific study was made of San Francisco sourdough bread by the Oregon State University Department of Microbiology under a grant from the U.S. Department of Agriculture. Although I made fun of this grant at the time — I considered it somewhat frivolous — the study was thoroughly scientific and resulted in some startling findings.

According to W. E. Sandine, professor of microbiology and leader in the research project, the unique San Francisco sourdough bread was unique *not* because of any process or climatic influence but because of the type of flour and the way it is handled.

"These two factors," according to Professor Sandine, "have resulted in the selection of a rod-shaped lactic acid bacterium called *Lactobacillus sanfrancisco* (a heretofore unkown bacteria) and a yeast called *Saccharomyces exiduus*, which work together in a fascinating way during fermentation."

The development of these two principal, and previously unknown, elements in bread making over the past 150 years of virtually unbroken local technique, undoubtedly resulted in this unique strain of sourdough starter.

The fermentation process, as scientifically broken down, is as follows:

1. Natural flour enzymes release a sugar called maltose, which the bacteria require to grow.

2. The bacteria produce acetic acid and lactic acid from this maltose to sour the bread; sourdough bread is *10 times** more acid than conventional bread.

3. The yeast uses products, including glucose, pro-

*Emphasis added to bring this fact to the reader's attention.

duced by the lactic acid bacteria to grow and produce carbon dioxide gas which is responsible for the leavening or rising of the dough.

4. Finally the leavened dough is baked 45 to 55 minutes at 370 to 390 degrees in a very "wet" oven.

The whole process used in San Francisco (in other words, the "secret") can be summerized as follows:

Starter sponge

100 parts sponge (from the last batch of bread dough
100 parts flour
50 parts water
Work 8 hours at 80 degrees F.; pH 3.8*

Bread Mixture

20 parts sponge
100 parts flour
60 parts water
8 hours set at 86 degrees F.; pH 3.9

Baking procedure

Make cuts in upper surface of dough.
Place directly into hearth oven.
Bake 45 to 55 minutes at 375-390 degrees F.
Use live, low-pressure steam until crust browns.
Package in open, nonplastic bag.

There you have the secret of San Francisco's famous sourdough bread. I am indebted to Professor Sandine, who personally supplied the scientific information (too technical to repeat here), and a layman's explanation of the findings of the OSU research project.

---

*pH is the measure of acidity in relation to alkalinity — p(otential) of H(ydrogen). There is a simple device for measuring this.

San Francisco sourdough *is* unique and superb. It is not due to any secret process or to the water or climatic conditions. It is due to the development — mutation, if you will — of a locally produced starter over a period of a century and a half.

Thus, there is some merit, which I long scoffed at, to the practice of keeping a sourdough starter going for years, even generation to generation, handed down to one's heirs — *but only* if this is done in one location, using a local grain flour.

It is also important that *the sourdough starter or sponge be replaced or replenished at least once every eight hours, as is done in a commercial bakery.*

Dr. Sandine also stated that further research is going on to develop ways to eliminate the starter sponge step. This will make the process easier to carry out in smaller bakeries and in the home, will create more outlets for the flour, and will make the bread more generally available.

Other findings of the research project to date:

• Sourdough bacterium is truly unique to the cooking process.

• As for nutrition, it is an important source of elements such as manganese, among other things.

• The organism is not pathogenic — that is, capable of causing disease.

• The sourdough bacterium has an "unusual type of carbohydrate metabolism."

It might be added that the research found some of the ingredients of other home sourdough starters "interesting," but none of them so far had *Lactobacillus sanfrancisco* in them, according to Sandine:

"The San Francisco starter, which uses water for liquid, apparently evolved from years of use, producing a distinctive yeast and bacterium in a successful fermentation partnership."

U.S. Department of Agriculture scientists found that two things are important in sourdough starters: something to cause souring and something to cause leavening or rising of the dough.

The newly discovered lactic acid bacteria cause the souring. These are produced by fermentation of the carbohydrates in the flour and provides the sour flavor. The acetic acid primarily keeps spoilage and disease-producing bacteria from growing in the dough.

Yeast cells do the leavening. Carbon dioxide gas is produced by yeast during the fermentation of the carbohydrates in flour. Ethyl alcohol, also produced by the yeast cells, evaporates during the cooking. The carbon dioxide provides the light, fluffy texture of flapjacks, biscuits, bread, and other sourdough bakery goods.

It has long been known that using beer or some carbonated drink such as 7-Up in baking and cooking performs the same functions as the gas produced in sourdough fermentation. This is used in many recipes, such as batter for breaded shrimp and fish and chips, and even in biscuits. It causes a fluffier batter, and the heating evaporates all the gas. Missing , of course, are the distinctive sour aroma of real sourdough batter and the leavening properties of sourdough starter.

A final tip for sourdough enthusiasts: Note that the San Francisco commercial bakeries do not usually accelerate the starter with yeast concentrate. They rely on the continuing fermentation of the sponge to carry on the process as new flour and water are added to make up for the sponge used in the baking batter; also they replenish the starter within eight hours of use so that there is an unbroken "line of descent" from one "generation" of sponge to the next.

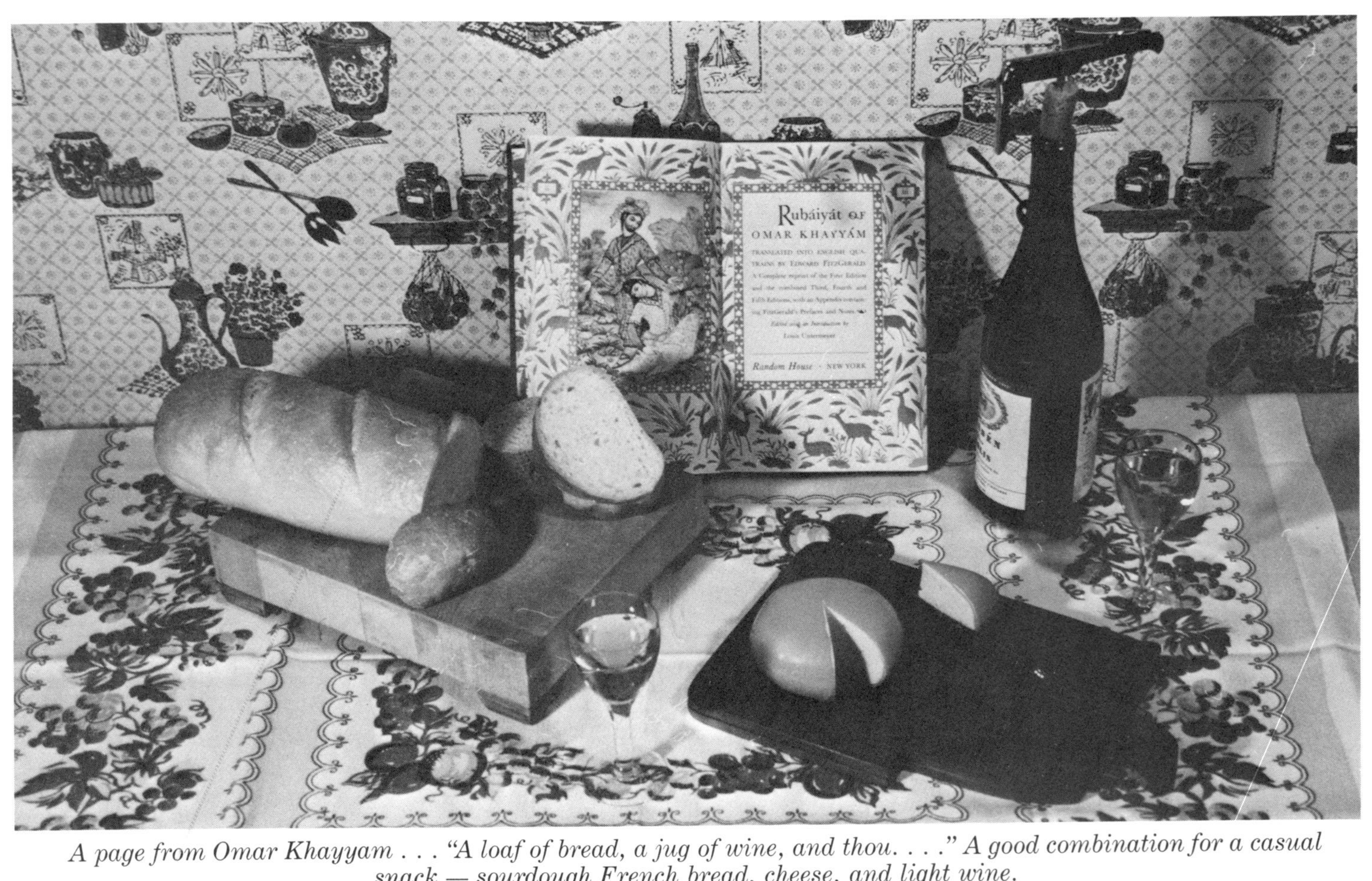

A page from Omar Khayyam . . . "A loaf of bread, a jug of wine, and thou. . . ." A good combination for a casual snack — sourdough French bread, cheese, and light wine.

North Country Flapjacks

Mix 1 c sourdough starter, 1 c flour, 1 egg, 2 T cooking oil, ¼ c instant or evaporated milk. Blend in 1 t salt, 1 t soda, 2 T sugar. Let mixture bubble and foam a minute, then drop spoonfuls onto hot griddle.

Prairie Flapjacks

Mix 1 c buttermilk pancake mix, ½ c sourdough starter, ½ c milk, 1 egg, 1 T cooking oil, ½ t baking powder. Let stand a few moments, then drop onto griddle. Berries can be added to any flapjack recipe.

Canuck Flapjacks

Beat 3 eggs. Add 1 c sweet milk and 2 c sourdough starter. Sift 1¾ c all-purpose flour with 1 t soda, 2 t baking powder, 1½ t salt, ¼ c sugar. Combine. Drop or spoon dough onto a lightly greased griddle. If an ungreased griddle is used, add ¼ c melted fat or butter to batter. Test griddle for proper temp by flicking a drop of water onto it. If it bounces, it's ready.

Old-Timer Flapjacks

This is the authentic pancake that was cooked over an open fire in a cast-iron skillet. It makes thin, Swedish-type cakes with a delicious nutty flavor and aroma. It uses a wheat flour starter, or part wheat flour (which can be added to any flapjack recipe for good results).

Make a good flapjack batter the night before, using a cup of starter, a couple of cups of flour, and warm water. Set in a warm place until morning. When you get up, stir up the batter a little. (Don't beat!) While the griddle is heating, add:

¼ c dry skim milk
2 t salt
2 t sugar
⅓ c melted shortening
2 eggs, beaten
1 t baking soda dissolved in lukewarm water and added just before spooning the batter onto griddle

Don's Favorite Waffles

Beat 2 eggs well, mix with ¼ c cooking oil, ½ c milk, 1 c buttermilk pancake and waffle mix, ½ t baking powder, ½ c sourdough starter.

Spoon the mixed batter in the usual way into the waffle iron, which has been preheated, and close lid. When it quits steaming, it's done. Serve the waffle with maple syrup, berries and whipped cream or warm applesauce — or use as the base for creamed seafood or chipped beef. This batch makes about a dozen waffles. Any not eaten can be frozen for later use. Take them from the freezer and pop them into a toaster.

Warning: Close the waffle iron lid tightly, for these waffles are so light they may float away behind your back.

Mary Rogers' Waffle Treat

Mary Rogers was the sourdough cooking champion of Mexico, Missouri. This is her favorite, which she sent to me:

½ c sourdough starter
1 c milk
1¼ c flour
1 egg, separated
4 T melted margarine
¾ t baking soda, dissolved
½ t salt
¼ t cream of tartar
1 T sugar

At bedtime make a batter of sourdough starter, milk and flour; cover and let set overnight. When batter is very light stir in remaining ingredients, except the cream of tartar and egg whites. Add tartar to egg white, beat stiff, and fold in last. Let set 30 minutes. Bake on hot waffle iron 5 to 6 minutes. Also makes good flapjacks.

Sourdough French Bread

Dissolve a package of dry yeast in 1½ c lukewarm water. Mix with 1 c sourdough starter in a large bowl, adding 4 c flour, 2 T sugar, and 2 t salt. Cover with cloth and let rise in a warm place until doubled in size.

Next, mix 1 c flour and ½ t baking soda. Stir this into the dough, adding enough flour to make a stiff dough. Knead on a flour-dusted board or marble slab until smooth and shiny. This kneading is the secret of good bread-making.

Shape dough into half-loaf sizes, place on greased paper or sheet sprinkled with cornmeal, and leave in warm place until again doubled in size. Brush the top lightly with cold water. Make a sharp slash about ¼ inch deep on top of loaf and bake in a 400-degree oven. Place a shallow pan with a little hot water on the oven bottom. Bake until dark almond brown. Brush with melted butter and hot water, and then crisp in oven for 3 to 5 minutes.

Glaze, if desired, with a mixture of egg yolk and canned milk or fresh cream.

Alaskan Sourdough Bread

1 c sourdough starter
2½ c warm water
4 T melted lard
½ c sugar
1 t baking soda
1 T salt
8 c flour

Combine ingredients, adding flour gradually, and knead until dough is smooth. Place in greased bowl in warm place and let rise. When double, knead down again and once more let rise. Shape into loaves and bake in moderate oven (about 375 degrees) for about an hour or until done.

Sheepherder Bread

This comes from the high, dry sagebrush plateaus of the West, with a tangy open-range aroma and taste.

1½ c sourdough starter
2 T sugar
1 t salt
1½ c lukewarm water
4 c flour
2 T melted shortening
¼ t baking soda

Sift the dry ingredients into a large bowl, blend in water and shortening. Dig a well in the center of the sourdough starter and blend the dry mix into it from the edges, with enough flour to knead until smooth and shiny. Place in greased pan and let rise. Shape into two loaves and place in greased pan. Bake at 375 degrees until done.

Mouse River Homestead Bread

Here's a bread the nester gals used to trap the farm boys — who fell for it like bees around a hive of wild clover honey.

2 c sourdough starter
2 T melted butter
½ c milk
1 t baking soda
3½ c whole wheat, rye, or white flour
2 t salt
1 T sugar or honey

Melt butter or margarine in saucepan. Add milk and honey or sugar. Turn into mixing bowl. Add starter, stirring in flour, salt, and baking soda. Turn out onto a floured board and knead lightly until smooth and shiny. Let rise double. (Put in warm oven with pan of water for faster rise time.) Punch down, and divide into two loaves. Let the loaves rise again until double. Bake in moderate oven, 350 degrees, for about an hour or until loaf pulls away from pan or sounds hollow when tapped.

Sourdough Biscuits

Here is a sourdough biscuit that alone makes it worth keeping a starter going. They are good even when cold, and the dough can also be used for cinnamon rolls. Use cooking oil or bacon fat for shortening. The bacon grease adds flavor, but oil is easier to use.

Mix ½ c starter, 2 T shortening , 1 c milk, and 1 c unsifted flour and let stand in a warm place for 4 to 8 hours. Then add:

1 c unsifted flour
¾ t salt
½ t baking soda
1 t baking powder
1 T sugar
½ pkg. active dry yeast

Mix together and turn out onto floured board. Knead lightly 8 to 10 times. Roll out dough to about ¾ inch thickness. Cut into biscuits and dip each in salad oil or bacon grease. Place in pan. Cover and let rise about 30 minutes. Bake in a 375-degree oven for 30 minutes.

Aunt Cora's Biscuits

Aunt Cora, a pioneer gal in Fossil, Oregon, gave me this one:

1½ c sifted flour
1 t salt
¼ c melted shortening
3 t baking powder
2 T sugar
1½ c sourdough starter
1½ t baking soda (more if starter is very sour)

Place flour in bowl, add starter in a well, then add melted shortening and the dry ingredients. Turn out onto lightly floured board and knead until consistency of bread dough, or of a satiny finish. Pat or roll out dough to ½ inch thickness, cut, and put on greased pan. Coat all sides with oil. Let rise over boiling water for ½ hour. Bake at 425 degrees for 15 to 20 minutes.

Wild Irish Rose Sourdough Prune Cake

½ c sourdough starter
1½ c sugar
2 c sifted flour
1 t cinnamon
1 c buttermilk
½ c chopped walnuts
½ c shortening
2 eggs
1½ t baking soda
½ t salt
1 c cooked prunes, drained and chopped

Be sure the starter is warm and very active. Cream the shortening and sugar. Add eggs one at a time, beating well. Add starter and buttermilk — be nice and gentle with the sourdough. Sift and add dry ingredients, prunes, and nuts. Bake at 350 degrees for about 40 minutes in a well-greased and floured cake tin about 9 by 13 inches. Test with finger-pressing method. If it springs back, it's ready. This batch will also make 2½ dozen cupcakes, but bake them only 25 minutes. If desired, top with an icing of your choice. Myrtle uses orange cream cheese icing on this one.

You'll be delighted at the smoothness of this batter as the starter begins working — to say nothing of the praise you'll find heaped upon you for thinking of it in the first place.

Mendenhall Sourdough Gingerbread

I first tasted this dessert in Juneau, at a little hole-in-the-wall cafe on the road to the Mendenhall Glacier. I don't remember the name of the cafe, but I do remember the dessert, and it deserves its majestic name.

1 c sourdough starter
½ c molasses
1 t baking soda
1 egg
1 t ginger
½ c shortening
½ c hot water
½ t salt
½ c brown sugar
1½ c flour
1 t cinnamon

Cream brown sugar and shortening. Add molasses and egg, beating continuously. Sift dry ingredients and blend into hot water, then beat into creamy mixture. Finally, add the sourdough starter slowly, mixing carefully to maintain a bubbly batter. Bake in pan at 375 degrees for about 30 minutes or until done. Serve hot, with whipped cream or ice cream.

Sourdough Lightbread

The universal quick bread of prairie farm life was sourdough lightbread, which had a pungent aroma that filled the house in the morning and guaranteed that the hired man would be out of bed on time. Unless the cook had a sourdough pot bubbling behind the stove, the modus operandi the night before was as follows: Several potatoes were boiled and mashed. The water was saved, and while it was still warm, but not hot, a couple of hard yeast cakes were crumbled into it. (Today a couple of packages of yeast powder can be used the same way.) In a warm place the yeast and water soon began to "work," bubbling merrily. The last thing you did before retiring was to stir the mixture, but not too much. You shouldn't beat it.

On arising, check the mixture to make sure it is still bubbling, then work in enough flour to make a stiff dough and knead for 15 to 20 minutes. Let rise and knead down twice more, then shape into loaves and bake at 325 degrees for 30 minutes. Bake 10 minutes more at 350 degrees or until delicous golden brown.

The dough can also be used for making doughnuts, breakfast rolls, coffee cake, and other goodies.

A little experimenting goes a long way. Bread making is especially susceptible to different conditions in the kitchen — air temperature, variations in ovens and thermometers, and especially in the type and kind of flour used. In the olden days we ground our own flour, always from hard spring wheat and other hardy grains. Today you may have to go to a health food store or a specialty flour mill that does batch-grinding the wholesome, old-fashioned way. Some large farmer's markets such as Corno's on Union Avenue in Portland, Oregon, also handle gluten and high-gluten flour that is milled for commercial bakers.

Don't despair if the first batch fails. Keep trying and you'll develop a technique especially your own.

Can You Bake a Cherry Pie . . . ?

Old-Time Religion Pumpkin Pie

Grandmother Smith was a woman wise,
And this is how she make pumpkin pies:
Wash a pumpkin and cut it small.
Put into and cook in a kettle tall,
So that the bubbles will not pop out
To splatter the stove around about.
Let the bubbles boil and stew,
All day long 'til brown all through.
Stir it often and when it's done,
Make it through a collander run.
Take of molasses, half a cup,
And with 3 of pumpkin, mix it up —
Cup and one-half of sugar white
And of salt one-half of a teaspoon quite.
Mix these well, stirring does no harm —
Then ginger, cinnamon, butter warm,
A teaspoon each of all the above
To season the pies of the Yankee love.
Then four fresh eggs and a quart of milk,
Beat well and stir 'til fine as silk;
Line three rough tins with pastry white,
Pour in your filling and bake them quite
A full half hour, 'til they're well done,
Then let them cook, and sire and son
And husband and preacher and family friend
Will praise your pumpkin pies no end.

*Champion's Cherry Pie**

2½ c drained sour cherries
2½ T tapioca
⅛ t salt
⅓ c cherry juice
1 c sugar
1 T butter

Drain cherries. Mix sugar, salt, tapioca, and juice. Let stand while mixing pastry. Add drained cherries to juice mixture and pour into crust. Dot with butter. Put on top crust and bake at 450 degrees for 10 minutes, then 350 degrees for 25 minutes.

Pastry:

1½ c flour
½ c lard or shortening
1 t salt
4 to 5 T cold water

Old-Fashioned Pumpkin Halloween Pie

2 c stewed and strained pumpkin
1 c brown sugar
1 t salt
2 t cinnamon
2 c cream
2 eggs
½ t ginger
½ t allspice

Mix pumpkin with sugar, milk, beaten eggs, salt, and condiments. Beat for 2 or 3 minutes. Pour into pie tin which has been lined with pastry shell. Bake in hot oven, 45 minutes or until firm.

A Good Piecrust

1 qt. flour
2 t baking powder
1 pt. sweet cream
2 t salt

Mix flour, salt, and baking powder and add cream a little at a time. Mix until you have a stiff dough. *Tip:* Use richest cream obtainable — preferably farm fresh. This batch makes 4 pies.

Real Brown Betty

Slice 5 apples and place in a deep, buttered layer cake

pan. Sprinkle with cinnamon. Spread over apples a mixture of 1 c brown sugar with 1 c butter and ¾ c flour. Cool and serve with whipped cream.

Grannie Barnes' Pumpkin Pie

1 c brown sugar
¼ t salt
1 c milk
¼ t nutmeg
1 c pumpkin
½ t cinnamon
2 eggs
½ t ginger

Mix eggs, sugar, salt, and spices. Add pumpkin and milk. Use 1 crust and bake in moderate oven until it bubbles in center. Cool and serve with whipped cream.

County Fair Plum Pie

4 c purple plums
3 T flour
1 T lemon juice
2-crust pastry shell
1 c sugar
1 t cinnamon
2 T butter

Wash and cut plums in half. Cut each lengthwise again. With about 4 cups measured, place half in pie tin on bottom pastry shell. Sprinkle with half of the sugar, flour, and seasonings. Add rest of plums and press down firmly with a plate. Dust over with rest of dry ingredients. Dot with butter and lemon juice. Press on the top crust. Split and bake in a preheated oven at 425 degrees 35 to 40 minutes. Serve hot with ice cream, whipped cream, or sliced cheese.

*Garden Pumpkin Pie**

1½ c pumpkin
1 t cinnamon
½ t ginger
1½ c milk
⅔ c brown sugar
½ t salt
2 eggs
½ c cream

Combine pumpkin with sugar and seasonings. Add

beaten eggs, milk, and cream. Mix well and pour into unbaked pie shell. Bake 10 minutes at 450 degrees. Reduce heat to 325 degrees and continue baking for 30 minutes or until firm. Makes one 9-inch pie.

*Banana Cream Pie**

1 8-inch pie shell, baked and cooled

¾ c sugar	**¼ t salt**
7 T flour	**2 egg yolks**
2 c milk	**1 t vanilla**
1 c sliced bananas (2)	**whipped cream**

Mix sugar, salt, and flour in top of double boiler. Beat egg yolks slightly, add milk, and stir slowly into flour mixture. Cook over boiling water until very thick, about 25 minutes, stirring occasionally. Blend in vanilla. Cool thoroughly. Shortly before serving, fold sliced bananas into cooled custard. Pour into pie shell. Let stand a few minutes. Top with whipped cream.

Rummy Apple Cream Pie

1-⅓ c rolled oats	**½ c melted butter or margarine**
½ c brown sugar	**2 c water**
1 c sugar	**2 T lemon juice**
2 apples (Delicious)	**3 T cornstarch**
¼ c sugar	**pinch salt**
1 c half-and-half	**2 T rum**
1 c raisins	**whipped cream, (sweetened)**

Press into a 9-inch pie tin, sides and bottom, a mixture of oats, butter, and brown sugar. Bake at 350 degrees for 10 minutes. Let cool.

Blend 1 c sugar and lemon juice, with water; bring to a boil. Add apples, which have been peeled, cored, and sliced. Poach gently until tender. Drain, holding back 1 c syrup. Combine cornstarch, ¼ c sugar and salt. Blend in syrup and half-and-half. Cook over medium heat, stirring in rum and raisins. Remove from heat. Pour half of cream mixture into pie shell. Arrange sliced apples over cream mixture, saving a few for garnish. Top with rest of cream mixture. Arrange remaining apple slices over top. Chill and serve with whipped cream.

*Charlie Russell Meringue Pie**

1-⅓ c or 1 can sweetened condensed milk
grated rind of 1 lemon **½ c lemon juice**
2 eggs **2 T sugar**
8-inch baked pie shell

Blend together the milk, lemon juice, grated lemon rind, and egg yolks. Pour into pie shell. Cover with meringue made by beating egg whites until stiff and adding sugar. Bake until brown in a moderate oven, 350 degrees. Chill.

*Graham Cracker Crust**

1 c or 12 graham crackers
¼ c butter
1 T sugar

Roll crackers to make crumbs. Cream butter. Mix both thoroughly with sugar. With hand, press into bottom and sides of a 7-inch pie plate. Put in moderate oven, 375 degrees for 5 to 7 minutes.

*Fluffy Pumpkin Pie**

Combine ½ c sugar, 1 t cinnamon, ½ t nutmeg, ¼ t cloves, ginger, and salt. Add 1 c pumpkin, 1 c milk. Add 2 eggs and 1 egg yolk, beaten. Fold in 1 egg white, beaten stiff. Pour into unbaked pie shell. Bake in hot oven, 425 degrees for 45 minutes.

*County Fair Coconut Caramel Pie**

¾ c sugar
2 c milk
½ c sugar, caramelized
½ t vanilla
1 baked 9-inch pie shell
½ c coconut
5 T flour
¼ t salt
3 egg yolks, slightly beaten
1 T butter
½ c sweetened whipped cream

Combine sugar, flour, and salt in top of a double boiler; add milk and egg yolks, mixing thoroughly. Cook over rapidly boiling water 10 minutes, stirring constantly. Remove from fire but leave over hot water.

Caramelize the sugar by placing ½ c in iron skillet over medium flame and stirring constantly until melted and straw-colored. Add at once to thickened mixture, stirring until blended. Add butter and vanilla. Cool, then turn into a pie shell. Garnish with a ring of whipped cream and sprinkle with coconut.

*Auntie's Lemon Pie**

1-⅓ c sugar
½ t salt
3 egg whites
2 t lemon rind
4 T cornstarch
2 c boiling water
3 egg yolks
½ c lemon juice

Blend sugar, cornstarch, salt. Stir into boiling water. Cook and stir until thick and clear. Stir in beaten egg yolks. Cook 2 minutes longer. Remove from stove. Add lemon juice and rind. Pour into baked pie shell. Cover with meringue and brown in slow oven, 325 degrees.

*Myrtle's Apple Pie**

4 to 6 apples, sliced thin
1 t cinnamon
¾ c sugar
1 T butter

Combine ingredients and bring to a boil. Fill crust

and cover with top crust. Bake at 425 degrees for 45 minutes or until done.

Piecrust:

1 c flour
¼ t salt
¼ c cold shortening
3 to 4 T cold water

Sift dry ingredients. Cut in shortening with knives. Add a little ice water at a time until dough forms ball.

*Red Cherry Pie**

2½ t tapioca
1 c sugar
1 c cherry juice
2 c cherries, drained
⅛ t salt
1 T melted butter

Combine ingredients, let stand about 15 minutes. Fill pie pastry, moisten edge with cold water, and cover with top crust. Bake 450 degrees for 15 minutes, then 350 degrees for 30 minutes.

Cakes That Trapped Many a Suitor

One time Myrtle baked a chocolate cake for a friend to take to an office party. The friend later reported that the boss was so enchanted with the cake that he exclaimed ecstatically, "I don't care who she is, I'll marry her!"

It's one of Myrtle's oldest and most treasured recipes. If you're thinking of trapping a bridegroom (or bride), this is the one to use.

*Matrimonial Chocolate Cake**

1½ c sugar
3 eggs
½ c milk
1 t soda
1 t vanilla
1 c sour cream
1-¾ c sifted cake flour
2 square chocolate
1 t salt

Boil milk and chocolate. Sift salt and soda into flour. *Whip the cream.* Separate eggs, and beat yolks, and add to cream, whipping together. Add sugar, beat, then combine with flour. Add chocolate, vanilla, and finally the beaten egg whites. Bake in a moderate oven, 340 degrees

*International Boundary Chocolate Cake**

This chocolate cake for more advanced young cooks is a real mouth-waterer for the special company that comes to call. It was a favorite with the Border Patrol and customs agents at Portal.

Sift together 1 cup flour and 1 c sugar. Add 1 t baking powder, 2 squares melted chocolate, and 1 T melted butter. Break in 2 eggs and enough milk to make a fluffy dough. Beat briskly and flavor with ½ t vanilla extract. Bake in 3 layers in moderate oven.

For the filling, mix 1 c each of grated chocolate and powdered sugar. Melt with strong coffee and spread between the layers and on top of the cake.

With a little practice you can whip up one of these masterpieces in no time — and it's guaranteed to cement goodwill across the borders, or across the back fence.

*Farmhouse Quick Cake**

When the McCormick Deering man or the county agent dropped by the farm unexpectedly on purpose for an afternoon snack of cold milk and cake, often there was nothing immediately available in the pantry. The emergency could be met with this one — even if the caller was the new young minister from St. Paul:

2 c flour
1 c sugar
2 eggs unbeaten
½ c milk
2 t baking powder
½ t salt
soft butter to fill ½ c
½ t vanilla

Bake in layers at 325 degrees for 25 minutes. By that time the minister or McCormick Deering man or county ag agent would have run out of small talk and be ready for a delicious man-sized chunk of cake hot out of the oven.

*Old Never-Fail Cake**

"Old Never-Fail" was a favorite of Myrtle's when she was a kid trying to keep out from underfoot in the farm kitchen while the womenfolk were busy with the fall canning. It had been handed down from family to family for generations; where it originated, she never knew. It's a good one for youngsters in the house to learn with.

1 c sugar
1 egg
4 T cocoa
flour
egg-size gob of butter
¼ c sour milk to which add 1 tsp. soda
½ c boiling water

Dissolve cocoa in boiling water and add enough flour to make a stiff batter. Blend in remaining ingredients. Bake in moderate oven.

*Tate's Fudge Cake**

Chocolate Fudge Cake was — and is — the all-time favorite with farm gals (to say nothing of farm boys). Here's how it was done in the Tate farm kitchen back in the 1920s and 1930s:

2 c sifted flour
½ t salt
1 c sugar
1 egg, well beaten
¾ c milk
2 t baking powder
½ c butter
2 squares milk chocolate, melted
1 t vanilla

Sift flour, baking powder, and salt three times. Cream butter thoroughly, through and through; gradually add sugar, eggs, chocolate, and vanilla. *Tip:* Add flour alternately with milk, blending into chocolate, until light and fluffy. Bake at 325 degrees for 1 hour.

Use care in mixing the ingredients, and you'll be rewarded immediately, not in the Hereafter.

Iceland Fruit Cake

¼ lb. citron
¼ lb. candied orange peel
½ lb. candied pineapple
½ lb. dates
½ lb. raisins
½ lb. sugar or 1 c
½ lb. flour or 2 c
½ t cloves
1 t salt
¼ lb. candied lemon peel
½ lb. candied cherries
½ lb. nuts
½ lb. coconut
½ lb. butter
5 eggs, well-beaten
1 t nutmeg
1 t baking powder
½ c fruit juice

Shred peel, cut cherries in half, chop up dates and nuts. Cut pineapple in small pieces, grate coconut finely. Coat the fruit with ¼ c flour or so. Sift remaining flour with dry ingredients. Cream butter and sugar, then add eggs. Blend with dry ingredients, fruit, and fruit juice, mixing thoroughly. Place in loaf tins well-lined with wax paper, filling only half full. Place the tins in a pan of shallow water in the oven and bake 2 to 3 hours at 250 degrees. The cakes can be decorated with pieces of fruit before placing in oven.

*Myrtle's White Fruit Cake**

Here's one you don't see anymore:

½ c butter
2 t grated orange rind
2 c cake flour
½ t salt
½ c chopped raisins
½ c chopped nuts
1 c sugar
½ c milk
2 t baking powder
4 egg whites, beaten stiff
½ c sliced citron

All-purpose flour well sifted can be used instead of cake flour. Blend all ingredients and bake 45 to 60 minutes in moderate oven. Simple, no?

Johnnycake, Gingerbread, and Old-Fashioned Biscuits

What is a johnnycake?

Call it Johnny Cake, Journey-cake, jonnycake, Jonny Cake — however you spell it, this traditional and throughly American product is enjoying a big comeback in antiquarian cookery circles. There is even an organization in Rhode Island for the promotion and preservation of johnnycake — the Society for the Propagation of the Johnnycake Tradition in Rhode Island (SPJTRI).

Jonnycake probably originated with the Narragansett Indians, who ground native corn between stones and mixed it with water to form a batter which was baked on hot stones in the ashes of campfires. The Pilgrims learned how to make it from the Indians and adopted it into their kitchen repertoire, also improving it. They scalded the cornmeal, added salt, milk, and molasses, and cooked the cakes — about ½ inch by 3 inches in size — on a skillet or board on the hearth.

Gradually the making of johnnycakes passed into colonial history. The method varied from one community to another. In one version the settlers used just milk and salt and made the cakes 5 inches in diameter. They were eaten with butter and molasses (later maple syrup) or sprinkled with sugar. Some ate them with bacon, eggs, ham, sausage, applesauce, or fried apple rings. Especially in New England, they were used with creamed chipped beef, pot roast gravy, or creamed codfish.

It may be virtually impossible to make a good authentic johnnycake today because the corn now available is different. Instead of Indian maize, today's product includes sweet corn, popcorn, dent corn, and flour corn, none of which is considered proper for real johnnycakes. You may have to grow your own maize or buy the flour from a health food store, made the old-fashioned way.

The essential ingredient seems to be stoneground white flint corn, in strains developed from the original Indian corn. Flint corn is hard to come by because farmers don't raise much of it. It is not disease-resistant, and it has a low yield. It also requires a lot of hot sun and plenty of moisture. It cannot be planted within a quarter mile of other varieties of corn, or wind-blown pollen will pollute it. Johnnycake *aficionados* who want to experiment with the real McCoy or the Pure Quill can obtain the original johnnycake flint corn seeds from the University of Rhode Island Extension Service, or possibly through one of the large seed catalogs.

Anyone interested in pursuing this fascinating subject further can write to SPJTRI, P.O. Box 4733, Rumford, RI 02916 for recipes, sources of flour and seed, and even addresses of restaurants that serve the authentic product.

Old-Fashioned Johnny Cake

1 c buttermilk
¼ c sugar
1 egg
⅔ c flour
½ c sweet milk
1½ c cornmeal
1 t soda
2 T shortening

Mix well together. Bake 25 minutes in a moderate oven. 1½ c sour milk may be substituted for the buttermilk and sweet milk.

Authentic Old Country Gingerbread

1 c molasses
½ c brown sugar
1 t cinnamon
pinch salt
1 t soda
½ c shortening
1 c boiling water
1 t ginger
2 c flour
2 well-beaten eggs

Add boiling water to molasses, shortening, sugar, and soda. Stir in eggs and dry ingredients. Bake in moderate oven.

Threshing Crew Buns

Dissolve 1 cake yeast or 1 pkg. quick yeast in lukewarm water, add to 4 c warm water, ¾ c melted butter or shortening, 1 c sugar, and 1 t salt. Mix with enough flour to make a stiff dough but not sticky and not too stiff. If yeast cake is used, let set and rise all day in warm place. Shape into buns in the evening, let rise until morning, and bake for about 20 minutes. While still hot, glaze the buns with a small cloth dipped in sugar that has been melted in hot water. You can bake the same day with packaged yeast — kneading and letting rise first, of course. This batch makes 50 buns.

Backyard Butterhorns

¾ c shortening
½ c sugar
1 cake yeast
2 eggs, beaten
4 c flour
½ t salt
1 c milk, scalded and cooled

Soak yeast in milk. Cut shortening into flour, sugar, and salt. Add eggs and liquids and mix well. Set in cool place overnight. In morning divide dough into 4 parts. Roll out each part, cut into fourths, and the fourths into halves. Roll each wedge, beginning with the wide side. Let rise. Bake for 20 minutes at 375 degrees. You can use package yeast and bake the same day, preparing dough this same way.

Cheese Delights

½ c butter
1 c flour
dash cayenne
3 oz. cream cheese
¼ t salt
some American cheese

Blend cream cheese and butter, gradually adding flour with salt and cayenne. Chill, then roll very thin and cut 2-inch rounds. Fold over like Parker House rolls, with a piece of American cheese inside. Chill before baking. Bake at 450 degrees for 8 to 10 minutes. Makes 3 dozen.

Sunday Morning Rolls

Late Friday evening dissolve ½ yeast cake in ½ c warm water. Add enough flour to make a light sponge. The following morning add 2 c cold water, 1 c sugar, ½ c melted lard or shortening, and a pinch of salt. Mix and knead and let rise. In the afternoon, knead again and let rise in a cool place. Saturday evening form dough into egg-size buns. Space out on a greased cookie tin. Let rise overnight. On Sunday morning bake in moderate oven until done. Serve hot with butter and jam.

*Baking Powder Biscuits**

2 c sifted flour
½ t salt
⅔ c milk
2 t baking powder
4 T butter
shortening

Sift flour, baking powder, and salt. Cut in shortening. Add milk gradually until soft dough is formed. Roll ½ inch thick on slightly floured board. Bake in hot oven at 450 degrees 12 to 15 minutes. Makes 12.

*Cream Puffs**

1 c boiling water
1 c flour
3 eggs
½ c shortening
½ t salt
2 t baking powder

Heat water and shortening in saucepan until it boils well. Add, all at once, flour sifted with salt. Stir vigorously till it leaves sides of pan. Take from fire as soon as mixed. Cool and mix in unbeaten eggs one at a time. Add baking powder and mix well. Bake in well-buttered tins for 30 minutes. When cool, cut a slit and fill with whipped cream.

Good Old-Fashioned Cookshack Biscuits

2 c flour
½ t soda
4 t baking powder
½ c lard or shortening
¾ c buttermilk
1 t salt

Work the baking soda thoroughly into the flour. Add the baking powder, then the salt, and finally the lard. Slowly work in the buttermilk (use more if necessary to make a good dough).

On a breadboard sprinkle some flour and work the dough over some more by hand, rolling out to about an inch thick, using a rolling pin. Cut with regular cutter, or break off pieces by hand. Bake in a moderately hot oven until deep golden brown, about 15 to 20 minutes. (Preheat the oven to 450 degrees if it has a thermometer. Old-time farm cooks tested an oven simply by opening the door and thrusting a hand inside to feel the heat.) The biscuits should be baked on an ungreased, or maybe slightly greased, pan or sheet.

Always serve hot with lots of butter, honey, homemade jam or jelly, or berry syrup.

You can make a whole meal of these. Leftover biscuits, if any, are excellent for snacks. As a kid I ate them sliced and filled with chokecherry or blueberry jam.

Cold leftover biscuits can also be rejuvenated by heating in a brown paper bag in the oven at low heat for a few minutes. Sprinkle them with water before putting into sack. Frozen biscuits can be handled the same way, although in the old days the only time we had frozen biscuits was: (a) when the fire in the cookstove went out on a cold winter night when the temperature dropped to 40 below or (b) when somebody forgot a plate full of them on the back stoop.

With gravy, buttermilk biscuits make about as good a lunch as you can find — and a lot cheaper than you'd have to pay at McDavid's.

Biscuits were also used for making chicken or turkey dressing, the chunks mixed with diced onions, seasoned with salt, pepper, sage, or poultry seasoning, a teaspoon of baking powder, and the basting juices from the bird. Bouillon, soup stock, or margarine can also be used with the juices, as well as the giblets.

Dressing is not the same as stuffing, the latter being cooked with the bird. Dressing is baked separately in a deep, well-greased dish or baking pan for 20 or 30 minutes.

Another use for the ubiquitous and versatile buttermilk biscuit is the "cake" part of strawberry shortcake. Split the biscuits, butter them, and heat on a cookie sheet in oven. When lightly browned remove and serve immediately, with sliced and sweetened strawberries topped with whipped cream.

*Ladies Aid Luncheon Rolls**

6 c sifted flour
2 c milk, scalded and cooled
4 T melted shortening
2½ t salt
1 T sugar
1 egg
1 yeast cake dissolved in
¼ c lukewarm water

Mix milk, shortening, sugar, and salt. Beat in egg. Add flour, then fold in dissolved yeast. Let rise. Form into twist rolls and bake about 20 minutes at 400 degrees. Dust with powdered sugar if desired.

*Simple Gingerbread**

3 T shortening or lard
½ c molasses
½ t soda
½ to 1 t ginger
¼ c boiling water
1⅛ c flour
½ t salt
½ t cinnamon

Put shortening in mixing bowl and add water and molasses. Sift flour with soda, salt, ginger, and cinnamon. Mix well and bake in moderate oven for 15 minutes. Serve with a cheese cream.

Cheese cream:

Work 1 to 1½ pkgs. of soft cheese until creamy. Fold carefully into 1 c cream, beaten until stiff.

*Hot Bran Muffins**

1 c bran
1 c milk, scant
1 egg
2 t baking powder
1 c graham flour
1 t melted butter
1 t sugar

Mix well and drop into muffin tin. Bake 20 minutes in hot oven.

Parker House Rolls

2 c milk
2 T sugar
¼ c butter
¼ c lukewarm water
1 t salt
6½ c flour
1 cake compressed yeast

Mix yeast in lukewarm water. Scald milk, add the dissolved yeast, and flour to make a drop batter. Beat well and let rise until double, adding flour to make a stiff dough. Let rise again until double. Roll out to about ½ inch or less thickness and cut with cookie cutter. Spread with melted butter and crease the middle with knife handle. Fold double, place in pan close together, and let rise until double. Brush with milk or beaten egg and bake in hot oven for 10 to 15 minutes.

Strawberry Patch Rolls

2 c flour	**1 t salt**
¼ c butter	**2 t baking powder**
1 egg	**3 T milk**

Sift flour, salt, and baking powder. Cut in the butter. Add milk to well-beaten egg, and add the flour to make a soft dough. Roll out on floured board to thin square.

Filling:

2 T butter	**1 egg yolk**
1½ c strawberries	**½ c sugar**
1 T milk	**1 t sugar**

Spread dough with softened butter and spread the berries, which have been cut in half, over the dough. Sprinkle with sugar and roll like a jelly roll. Cut into 6 slices about 2 inches thick. Add milk to beaten egg yolk and pour over rolls. Sprinkle sugar over top. Bake in moderate oven 30 minutes, cool, and serve with whipped cream. Yum!

Our Daily Bread

Sandy Baker is an English gal, married to Bruce Baker, Portland's retired police chief. They now spend most of their time aboard their forty-three foot ketch *Coeur de Lion*, cruising the North Pacific. Here's a recipe she gave me for an unusual French bread.

"While planning a six-week cruise this summer to Berkeley Sound, I realized we would not always be able to buy bread. After making several batches that resulted in total failure, I decided to seek some expert advice. The experts told me not to use general purpose flour. Commercial bread is made with a hard wheat flour that is high in gluten. You can make gluten; however it is time-consuming and messy. You can purchase high gluten flour from Corno's Market, 711 S.E. Union Ave., Portland, Oregon. It is called Power Flour, and is sold in bulk for 25 cents a pound. Moore's Flour Mill, 4001 S.E. Roethe Rd., Milwaukie, Oregon, sells a high protein unbleached white flour which is high in gluten and recommended for bread baking.

"Bread made with Power Flour has a good crust and a nice sponge texture inside. The flavor is excellent. You can add a cup of roman meal, whole wheat, or rye to add flavor. Power Flour is recommended for breads and rolls baked on a flat surface. The unbleached flour from Moore's Flour Mill may be quite similar to Power Flour, but I have not had a chance to test it."

Sandy's French Bread

1 pkg. dry yeast — **2 c water**
1 T butter — **1 T salt**
2 t sugar — **5¼ c unbleached flour**

Dissolve yeast in ½ c warm water. Combine 1 c hot water, butter, salt, and sugar. Add ½ cup cold water and yeast. Beat in 2¾ cups flour until smooth. Mix in remaining 2½ cups flour until blended. Knead 5 minutes. Place in greased bowl and cover. Let rise in warm place until doubled (about 1½ hours). Shape into 2 long loaves. Place on greased baking sheet sprinkled with corn meal. Let rise until light and doubled. Brush with slightly beaten egg white. With sharp knife make 3 diagonal cuts across top of loaf. Bake at 400 degrees for 15 minutes. Reduce to 350 degrees and bake an additional 30 minutes.

Boston Man Bread

The Pacific Northwest Indians called all Americans "Boston Men," from the fact that the first explorers and adventurer-traders to the Northwest Coast were Yankees from Down East. It is said that the staple of the New England Colonies was Boston brown bread. After it worked its way West, here is how it was made:

⅔ c sugar
2 c sweet milk
2 t salt
4 c graham flour
2 t soda
1 c brown syrup
2 eggs
1 c raisins, floured

Mix well, fold into a greased 3-pound coffee can and bake about 90 minutes in a moderate oven.

Camp Hot Bread

2 c flour
1 c milk
1 beaten egg
pinch of salt
4 t baking powder
¼ c butter
1 T sugar

Mix baking powder well with flour, then add other ingredients. Mix lightly, bake in pan or on slab at 350 degrees for about 15 minutes. Serve hot.

A loaf of newly baked sourdough bread.

Flathead Potato Bread

One of our favorite parts of the world is the Flathead Lake country of northwestern Montana. In the lee of the dark purple Mission Range there is a certain quality to the sky, the mountains, and the water that fills us with peace and tranquil thoughts. A favorite in this valley is a hidden spot on the east side of the lake, at the head of a little cove called Yellow Bay. Farther up the lake there used to be an old rustic cafe run by a flatland furriner from the Midwest, who brought this recipe for potato bread west with him:

5 to 6 new spuds	**2½ c flour**
1 pkg. active dry yeast	**1 T salt**
1 t baking soda	**1 c sourdough starter**

Boil the potatoes and mash them well, saving the water in which they were boiled. Pour this over the mashed potatoes (holding back a small amount), and then add another quart of cold water. Stir in the flour. Add a package of yeast which has been dissolved in the reserved potato water — or use 1 c sourdough starter. Let mixture rise overnight. In the morning strain the mixture and add a little more flour, stirring it in until you have a stiff batter. Add 1 t baking soda and let rise again. Next add 1 T salt and knead some more flour into it. Knead dough 100 times. Mold into loaves, let rise again, then bake about an hour at 375 degrees.

Alaska Sourdough French Bread

The night before, stir 1½ c flour into about 1 c of sourdough starter with enough lukewarm water to get the batter working overnight, keeping it in a warm place.

When ready to start, mix 1 c lukewarm water with ½ c warmed milk and 2 T melted butter. Blend in easily

1½ c sourdough. In a mixing bowl sift 5 c flour with 2 t salt and 2 t sugar. Bury the sponge in a hollow made in the flour. Knead until well mixed and then cover with damp cloth and let rise in a warm place until doubled. Turn out onto a floured board, divide into two loaves, roll each out to about 1 inch thick, then fold up edges like a jelly roll. Sprinkle cornmeal on a lightly greased sheet. Place loaves on this, well spaced. Slash the tops with a knife and brush with butter. Cover and let rise until double. Bake in a preheated 350 degree oven for 10 minutes. Reduce oven to 325 degrees and bake for 30 to 40 minutes longer. Remove and brush tops with butter while still hot. Cool on racks.

Puddings, Custards, and Yummy Desserts

There's no denying that the sweet tooth was all too common among past generations. No meal was complete without a proper dessert, and it was in this area that kitchen artists let down their inhibitions and experimented with mucho gusto.

After a big meal in those days it was thought that topping it all off with something sweet and tasty was good for digestion — or at least eased the distress of absorbing all that heavy food. Nobody in those days, when eating at somebody else's table, *ever* pushed away dishes or declined another helping. It was an insult to the cook and was considered a rejection of love and affection!

Argonaut Plum Duff

For more than a hundred years the favorite dinner and supper treat on the frontier, in the lonely cavalry outposts in Indian country, on the homesteads, and on the sailing ships that made the six-month trips from New York or New England to San Francisco, was plum duff.

Plum duff was sort of a pudding, usually served hot, and almost never made with plums. Fruit duff would be more accurate, because the basic ingredient was raisins, dried currants or apricots, canned peaches, any fresh fruit that was available, wild or otherwise, berries of all kinds, and vegetables like rhubarb. It could even be made with only a fruit flavoring. Whatever was in it, duff was much in demand and eagerly anticipated. The cookie who skimped on this made no friends in the camps, with the harvest crews, or on board the whalers and clippers.

On the voyage of the bark *Orion* to the gold fields of California from New England in 1849–50, it was apparently the favorite dessert among crew and passengers; the log records the captain ordering the stewards to "give us plently of duff."

Fortunately, one of the passengers leaves us a description of it on board the *Orion:* "Duff is composed of flour, lard, raisins, saleratus [baking soda], and water, with eggs mixed in when they can be had. When well mixed it is put into a canvas bag, wide at the top and very narrow at the bottom, boiled two hours, and then turned out into a platter and served with wine sauce when it can be had, or else with vinegar, butter, sugar, and water, boiled well together and thickened with flour and flavored with nutmeg."*

Plum duff was a staple aboard the clipper ships that made nonstop runs to China and back for tea and spices, and it was the U.S. Cavalry's secret weapon in the Indian Wars during the middle and late 1880s on the Great Plains.

My Great Uncle Ezra served with the Seventh Cavalry. From his rocking chair after retirement at Fort Snelling, he recalled his active duty days and said the Sunday dinner by tradition featured plum duff for dessert. Woe to the cook who neglected this! He would have to answer to the top kick. On patrol, through the heat and dust, the alkaline water and hard tack, fearing Indian ambush, it was the thought of getting back to the post and a special treat of plum duff that kept the troopers going.

**A Gold Rush Voyage on the Bark Orion*, Robert W. Wienpahl (ed); The Arthur Clark Co., Glendale (1978).

From the log of the bark *Orion*, comes another example of seagoin' plum duff. The sailors called it "dandyfunk." It was made of hard bread boiled with molasses, raisins, and cinnamon. "The hard bread or navy biscuit was soaked in water, mashed with a pestle, mixed with fat from the kettles in which meat was boiled, sweetened with molasses, and flavored with allspice, then put into a pan and baked in the oven," according to one passenger. "it isn't a very high-toned dish, but in the absence of something better, it is very palatable to the sailor."

Cantonment Plum Pudding

1 c sugar
1 c suet
1 c raisins
1 t soda
½ t nutmeg
½ c nuts
1 t salt
½ c molasses
1 c sour milk or buttermilk
1 c dry bread crumbs
½ t cinnamon
½ t cloves
2½ c flour

Mix well and steam for 2 to 3 hours.

Bunkhouse Plum Pudding

1 c sugar
1 c sour milk
1 lb. raisins
2½ c flour
1 t nutmeg
1 t cinnamon
½ c molasses
1 c suet
1 c nuts
1 t soda
1 t salt
2 eggs

Chop nuts, grind suet and raisins. Mix all ingredients. Steam for 2 to 3 hours. Serves 15.

Old Country Christmas Plum Pudding

12 oz. currants
2 oz. lemon peel
8 oz. brown sugar
½ t nutmeg
½ t cloves
8 oz. suet
2 oz. almonds
12 oz. raisins
2 oz. orange marmalade
1 lb. bread crumbs
½ t cinnamon
1 apple
1 T flour
4 eggs

Chop almonds, grate apple, grind suet. Mix ingredients with beaten eggs and seasonings. Add a little more milk if needed to moisten. Grease a large crock bowl, fill with mixture, cover with wax paper, then cheesecloth, and bind down with string. Steam in boiling water for 6 or 7 hours, adding boiling water as needed to keep level within an inch of top of crock. Pudding will keep indefinitely and improve with age. Before serving cold pudding, steam for a couple of hours.

*Peach Fluff**

Peel 4 peaches. Put the peaches through a fruit ricer. Whip ½ pt. cream. Sweeten cream with 2 rounded T powdered sugar. Stir in the riced peaches. Pile into sherbet glasses. Decorate with a cherry and chill. Serves 6.

*Apple Dumplin's**

2¼ c flour
¾ c shortening
6 medium apples
1½ t cinnamon
½ t salt
8 T ice water
½ c sugar

Make pastry and roll out dough about ⅛-inch thick, same as piecrust. Cut into 7-inch squares. Pare and core apples. Lay pastry squares in 8-by-12-inch baking pan and place an apple on each square, filling cavity of each apple with sugar. Then sprinkle with cinnamon and dot with butter. Wet edges of pastry and fold points or corners up over apples. Seal well. Set dumplings about 2 inches apart. Sprinkle with sugar. Chill in fridge.

Syrup:

1 c sugar
4 T butter
½ t cinnamon
2 c water

Boil 3 minutes. Pour hot syrup around chilled dumplings in a baking pan. Bake immediately for 40 minutes, starting at 500 degrees for 5 to 7 minutes and until crust is slightly brown; finish in a moderate oven or at 350 degrees.

*Orange Custard**

Bring 4 c milk to a boil. Mix 1½ c sugar and 1⅓ c flour and beat into the milk. Beat into this 2 egg yolks, 1 t vanilla, and a pinch of salt. Cut oranges into pieces and add to custard. Serve when cool.

*Dad's Special**

1½ c cooked apricots
½ c butter
¼ t cinnamon
1½ c fine bread crumbs
½ c chopped almonds
1 c sugar

Soak apricots and cook until tender. Sweeten slightly. Put butter, sugar, crumbs, and cinnamon into a saucepan. Heat until very hot, stirring constantly. When hot and only slightly brown, remove and pack tightly into a glass bowl. Cover with apricots and serve with plain cream.

*Cornstarch Pudding**

2 T sugar
1 c milk
2 T cornstarch

Boil until it thickens. Add a chunk of butter and beat well. Pour into dishes and add a dot of jelly to each.

*Apricot Pudding**

Stew and chop ¼ lb. evaporated or dried apricots. Beat the whites of 5 eggs until stiff. Add ½ c fine sugar, a little salt, and the fruit. Put in baking dish and bake 15 to 20 minutes. Serve cold with whipped cream.

*Pineapple Bavarian Cream**

½ box gelatine
½ c sugar
½ c water
1 pt. can pineapple
1 pt. cream

Cover the gelatine with water and soak ½ hour, then stand it over boiling water until dissolved. Add to it the sugar and fruit, crushed fine, and place in a dish. Place dish in a pan of cracked ice and stir constantly until it thickens. Then add whipped cream. Stir carefullyuntil thoroughly mixed. Pour into mold and stand in cool place to harden.

*Caramel Pudding**

½ c brown sugar
¼ c flour
¼ c additional milk
1½ c hot milk
2 eggs

Mix flour with beaten egg yolks and ¼ c milk. Add this to the sugar dissolved in 1½ c hot milk and stir until it boils. Boil until thick. take from fire, fold into stiffly beaten egg whites, and let cool.

*Mock Charlotte**

Moisten 2 T cornstarch with 4 T water. Add 1 c boiling water, ½ c sugar, juice of small lemon, plus grated rind. Stir and let cook until mixture boils, then pour over beaten whites of 3 eggs.

*Carrot Pudding**

1 c ground raw carrots
1 t soda stirred into potatoes
½ c shortening or butter
1½ c raisins
1 t cinnamon
½ t salt
1 c ground raw potatoes
1 c sugar
2 c flour
¼ t cloves
½ t nutmeg
1 t vanilla

Cream together butter and sugar. Mix in other ingredients. Steam 2½ to 3 hours.

*Chocolate Blanc Mange**

4 T cornstarch
¼ t salt
⅓ c cocoa
¾ c sugar
1 qt. milk
1 t vanilla

Mix cornstarch, sugar, and salt with cocoa and a little of the cold milk. Put remainder of milk on to scald. Add cornstarch mixture and cook until thick and smooth, stirring constantly. Add flavoring. Chill and serve with whipped cream.

Bread Pudding Bedtime Snack

2 c milk
½ c sugar
pinch salt
2 c bread cubes
3 T butter
2 eggs (beaten with milk)
1 T vanilla

Mix well, all but bread, and beat. Butter a baking dish and place the bread in it. Cover with the mixture. Bake at 350 degrees in a pan of water in oven for about 1 hour. Serve hot with cream or a sauce.

The "Table Cakes" Potpourri

Not all meals in those days threatened to collapse the dining table from sheer quantity and variety. Paradoxically, especially in the cold months, many a meal was built around a stack of hotcakes or waffles, or even creamed toast. Invariably these meals of "table cakes" were intimate family affairs — never served when company was there.

But such meals were easy to fix, inexpensive, and very tasty and filling.

*Dairy Waffles**

2¼ c sifted flour
½ t salt
2 T melted butter
1½ c milk
2¼ t baking powder
1 T sugar
2 eggs

Beat egg yolks separately. Sift dry ingredients together twice. Mix liquid ingredients and combine. Fold in beaten egg whites. Bake on hot, well-greased waffle iron. Serve with butter and maple syrup.

*Standard Waffles**

2 c flour
½ t salt
1 c milk
3 egg whites beaten until stiff
3 t baking powder
3 egg yolks beaten lightly
4 T melted butter

Sift dry ingredients twice, add egg yolks mixed with milk, then melted butter. Fold in egg whites. Bake on well-greased waffle iron. Serve with butter, honey, maple syrup, or jam.

Sourdough makes fine pastries of all kinds, including scrumptious waffles in modern waffle irons.

Cookstove Sour Milk Waffles

3 eggs, beaten separately
1 t soda
2 T sugar
½ t vanilla
¼ c melted shortening
1½ c sour milk or buttermilk
¼ t salt
2 t baking powder
3 c sifted flour

Dissolve soda with vanilla. Add to milk and beaten egg yolks. Sift dry ingredients into this and beat in the melted shortening. Let stand for a while so soda and baking powder can rise. Fold in egg whites and bake in hot waffle iron.

Immigrant Griddle Cakes

2 eggs
1 t baking powder
2 T butter
½ c flour
2 c buttermilk
1 t soda
1 t salt
2 c cornmeal

Sift together cornmeal, flour, baking powder, salt, and baking soda. Beat eggs, add buttermilk, then blend in dry ingredients and beat some more until smooth. On a hot griddle, lightly rubbed, bake like flapjacks. Serve with hot syrup or jam.

(Note: A "rubbed" griddle is a hot griddle that has been lightly brushed with a cloth [we used to use a piece of gunnysack] saturated with oil or melted lard. Do not overgrease the griddle; this would ruin the cakes. The griddle should be hot, not smoking; moist, not dry.)

Prairie Potato Pancakes

1 c milk
2 eggs
2 t baking powder ***or*** **½ c sourdough starter**
1 c mashed potatoes
½ c flour

Mix egg yolks with potatoes. Add milk, flour, and

baking powder (or sourdough starter). Blend in beaten egg white. Bake on hot, rubbed griddle. Serve hot.

Farm Fritters

2 T flour
2 c grated corn kernels
1 t salt
2 eggs

To beaten egg yolks add salt and flour. Blend in the corn and beaten egg whites, season with pepper and paprika. Bake on lightly greased griddle, moderate heat.

Slightly Simple Pancakes

2 eggs, beaten slighty
1½ c milk
½ t salt
2 T melted butter
2 T sugar
2½ t baking powder
2 c flour

Mix flour and baking powder, then add rest of ingredients. Cook on wide griddle that has been heated almost, but not quite, smoking hot, with no grease.

Another Flapjack

3 eggs, beaten
3 c sweet milk
3 c flour
¾ t soda
1½ c sour cream
4 T sugar
3 t baking powder
1 t salt

Mix well and cook on open griddle without grease.

Cinnamon Toast

Toast bread; butter while hot; then sprinkle with a mix of 1 part cinnamon to 4 parts sugar. Warm in oven until served. Have a shaker filled with sugar-cinnamon mix ready to sprinkle.

Melba Toast

Slice bread 1/8 inch thick, trimming crusts. Place in slow oven until toast curls and turns golden brown.

French Toast

Dip bread slices in mixture of 1/2 c milk, 3 beaten eggs, 1/4 t salt. Fry until golden brown in greased griddle pan. Serve with butter, syrup, jam, or jelly. French bread is best.

Milk Toast

Toast slices of bread and while hot cover with hot milk. Add butter and a pinch of salt.

A Repertoire of Cookie Cooking

It was a poorly run home that did not have a pantry loaded with jars of cookies, usually of many different kinds. Cookies were the all-day snacks, the lunch pail staple, and table decorations for parties and holidays.

There must be ten thousand different recipes for cookies, but here are a few old favorites from our family trees.

*Sade's Holiday Fruit Drops**

1 c shortening
½ c white sugar
1 t vanilla
¼ t soda
1 t salt
1 c brown sugar
1 egg or 2 yolks
4 c sifted flour
2 t baking powder
½ c milk

Blend shortening, sugar, eggs, and vanilla until light. Sift dry ingredients and add alternately with milk. Divide into two parts. To Part II add enough flour to roll, about 1 cup.

Part I, drop dough

Fruit drops: Chop ½ cup dates, ½ c figs, ¼ c nuts, ¼ candied cherries. Add to half of drop batter. Stir in 1 t almond extract. Drop by spoonfuls. Bake at 375 degrees.

Merlingue tops: Spread dough in pan ¼ inch thick, cover with meringue made of 1 egg white and 1 c brown sugar. Sprinkle top with ⅓ c chopped nuts. Bake in slow oven (325 degrees) 25 minutes. Cut in diamonds while warm.

Part II, roll dough

To half of the roll dough, add ⅛ t cloves, ¼ t cinnamon, and 1 c chopped gumdrops. Roll to a sheet ¼ inch thick. Bake at 375 degrees for 15 minutes. Cut while warm into sticks or stars. Roll in powdered sugar.

Date pinwheels: Cook to a paste 1 c chopped dates, ¼ c sugar, ¼ c water. Cool. Roll dough ⅛ inch thick and spread with date filling. Roll up like jelly roll. Wrap in waxed paper and chill, then slice crosswise. Bake at 375 degrees for 15 minutes.

*Mother Seabold's Kitchen Cookies**

1 c white sugar
1 c shortening
1 t soda
1 c raisins or dates
2 c flour
1 c salted peanuts
1 c brown sugar
2 eggs
3 t hot water
2 c oatmeal
1 c cornflakes

Drop from spoon and flatten. Bake in moderate oven until brown and crisp.

*Myrtle's Marshmallow Fudge Cookies**

Combine marshmallow and fudge in the same cookie and you've got . . . well, try this old recipe, long forgotten, and see for yourself.

2 squares chocolate, shaved
¼ t salt
2 c sugar
1 t vanilla
1 c chopped walnuts
1 c evaporated milk
1 T butter
24 marshmallows, cut into small pieces
3 c graham cracker crumbs

Combine chocolate and milk, heat over low flame until chocolate is melted. Add sugar and salt; stir until dissolved. Cook until mixture reaches the soft-ball stage. Remove from heat and add butter. Cool slightly, then add marshmallows, vanilla, graham cracker crumbs, and walnuts. Mix well. Press onto greased pans. Chill 8 to 12 hours or overnight. Cut into squares.

*Dolly's Date Delights**

1 c shortening
1 t vanilla
2 eggs, beaten
¾ t soda
2 c dates, cut
1 t salt
1½ c sugar
3½ c sifted flour
5 t milk
¾ c nuts, chopped

Blend shortening, salt, and vanilla. Add sugar gradually and cream well. Add eggs and mix thoroughly. Sift flour with soda and add to dough alternately with milk. Add dates and nuts last and blend well.

Drop from spoon on greased baking sheets. Let stand for a while, and then flatten drops with a glass covered with a damp cloth. Sprinkle with sugar. Bake at 375 degrees 12 to 15 minutes. Makes 72 cookies.

*Matrimonial Date and Pineapple Bars**

1 c brown sugar
2 egg yolks or 1 whole egg
1¾ c oatmeal
¾ c shortening
1 t soda
1½ c flour

Cream shortening and sugar. Add eggs and soda dissolved in hot water. Add flour and oatmeal. Divide dough into two portions. Press one-half to bottom of a greased pan and cover with the following filling:

½ lb. dates, chopped
½ c brown or white sugar
1 small can crushed pineapple
2 T water

Boil until thick. Pour onto first half of dough. Cover with the remaining dough and bake 20 minutes in a quick oven.

Then you'll find out why these are called "Matrimonial" bars.

*Butterscotch Goodies**

½ c butter
2 c brown sugar
2 eggs
½ t vanilla
½ t cream of tartar
½ t soda
3½ c flour

Mix ingredients and pack in greased pan. Let stand overnight. In the morning, slice and bake in moderate oven.

*Hermits**

An old homesteader, who lived in a sod house, often dropped by the Tate's place on his way into town. He was especially fond of these delights, always found in the pantry.

6 T shortening
1 c brown sugar
1 egg
½ c milk
1½ c flour
2 t baking powder
¼ t salt
1 t each, cloves, allspice, cinnamon
1 c seeded raisins
2 T citron

Mix well, roll out, bake in moderate oven. You'll be back for more.

*Original Icebox Cookies**

One of my old favorites was Icebox Cookies. The only trouble was I always ate so many they spoiled my dinner.

2 c sugar
1 c lard and butter mixed
2 eggs
1 c chopped nuts and dates
1 t soda dissolved in hot water
2 t vanilla
½ t nutmeg
4 c flour

Mix well and shape into rolls. Let stand in a cold place overnight. Slice and bake in moderate oven. Takes time to make, but worth every minute of it.

*Grandmother's Cookies**

This is how Grandma used to make cookies, and the recipe is as old as Old Glory — maybe older.

1 cup shortening or lard
⅔ c sour milk or cream
½ t nutmeg
1 qt. flour
3 eggs
1 t soda
2 c sugar

Mix lard or shortening with flour and soda. Add cream and sugar, eggs and milk for a soft dough. Bake in moderate oven until brown.

*Soldier Boy Cookies**

Here's an old favorite that the troopers with the Seventh Cavalry in Custer's outfit at Fort Lincoln fought for.

3 c sugar
1 c butter
1 t ginger
flour to mix smooth
2 c thick sour cream
3 eggs
2 t soda

Roll thin and spread with sugar. Cut and bake in moderate oven until brown.

*Small Fry Gingersnaps**

A longtime, all-time favorite with small fry is the gingersnap.

1 c molasses
3¼ c flour
1 T ginger
½ c shortening
½ t soda
1½ t salt

Heat molasses to boiling and pour over shortening; add dry ingredients, mixed and sifted well; chill thoroughly. Roll as thin as possible. Cut and bake in moderate oven until brown and crisp. When cold cover with powdered sugar icing. Makes 50 to 60 cookies.

Dorothy's Oatmeal Delights

Oatmeal cookies are an All-American favorite, and there are dozens of variations. One of the best comes from a long-time friend and co-worker, Dorothy Jones of Portland, Oregon.

1 c shortening
1 c granulated sugar
1 t vanilla
1 t salt
3 c Quick oatmeal
1 c brown sugar
2 well-beaten eggs
1½ c flour
1 t soda
½ c finely chopped nuts

Cream shortening and sugar. Add eggs and vanilla and beat well. Add sifted dry ingredients, then oatmeal and nuts, mixing well. Shape into rolls, wrap in wax paper and chill thoroughly overnight or at least 3 hours in fridge. Slice ¼ inch thick and bake on ungreased cookie sheet in moderate oven (350 degrees) for 10 to 15 minutes or until lightly browned. makes about 100 cookies.

*Toffee Nut Bar Treats**

Here's a honey that doesn't need honey — just some hungry kids to please.

For bottom layer:

½ c butter
1 c Gold Medal Flour
½ c brown sugar

Cream butter, add brown sugar gradually. Sift flour once before measuring. Add flour to creamed mixture and work it into a dough with your hands. Pat into the bottom of an ungreased baking pan and bake for 10 minutes in a moderate (350 degree) oven. Use a 9-inch pan.

For top layer:

2 eggs
1 c brown sugar
1 t vanilla
2 T flour
1 t baking powder
½ t salt
1 c shredded coconut
1 c chopped nuts

Beat eggs until light. Stir in brown sugar thoroughly. Add vanilla. Sift flour before measuring. Sift flour, baking powder, and salt together and stir into sugar mixture. Beat until smooth. Blend in coconut and nuts. Spread over a slightly cool bottom layer and bake 25 minutes in a moderate oven. Makes 27 bars, 1 by 3 inch.

*Country Graham Crackers**

Everybody likes graham crackers, and they're good for you, too, but how many cooks have ever made them at home? Once you've done it, you'll never buy another box of the store variety.

1 c sugar
½ c sour cream
graham flour
4 T butter
¼ t soda

Mix stiff with graham flour with the baking soda sifted in. Roll thin, cut into squares and bake in a moderate oven until crisp. Store in a dry place.

*Portal Peanut Crunchies**

½ c butter
½ c white sugar
1 egg
¾ t soda
¼ t salt
½ c peanut crunch
½ c brown sugar
1¼ c flour
½ t baking powder

Beat egg well. Cream butter and peanut crunch together. Add sugar and gradually blend. Add beaten egg. Sift flour once, add baking powder, soda, and salt and sift again. Mix all ingredients. Chill dough well and form into balls about walnut size. Flatten with fork and bake on greased sheet 10 to 12 minutes at 375 degrees. Makes 4 dozen.

*Wholesome Yummy Brownies**

Melt 3 squares unsweetened chocolate in double boiler. Add 1½ c condensed milk and stir until thickened. Add 2 c vanilla wafer crumbs and 1 c broken walnuts. Spread in buttered shallow pan. Bake in moderate oven.

*Elsie's Date Nut Rocks**

This one comes from a school chum:

3 c sifted flour
2 t baking powder
1 t soda
1 t salt
1 c shortening
1½ c brown sugar
3 eggs
½ c nut meats
¾ c chopped dates
coconut or raisins may also be added

Sift flour, baking powder, soda, and salt together. Cream shortening and sugar, add slightly beaten eggs, and beat thoroughly. Mix fruit and nuts with dry ingredients, add to creamed mixture. Drop by spoonfuls onto greased baking sheet and bake in moderate oven until brown.

*Peanut Macaroons**

Quick and easy:

Beat 2 egg whites until stiff and dry. Gradually add 1 c confectioners sugar, ¼ c pastry flour, and ¼ t salt. Fold in 1 c coarsely chopped peanuts. Drop from the end of a teaspoon onto a greased baking sheet about 2 inches apart and bake in a 400-degree oven for 10 minutes.

*Pineapple Drop Cookies**

⅔ c shortening | **1½ c sugar**
2 eggs | **4 T pineapple juice**
1 t lemon extract | **¼ t salt**
3 c sifted flour | **½ t soda**
diced or cubed pineapple for topping

Cream shortening and sugar, add unbeaten eggs and pineapple juice, whip for 3 minutes. Add soda dissolved in 1 T hot water and whip well. Stir in the flour and flavoring; beat until smooth. Drop by teaspoonfuls onto buttered pans, pressing a tiny bit of pineapple into each cookie. Bake 12 minutes in a medium oven.

*Chocolate Drop Cookies**

Melt together 4 T cocoa and ½ c butter. When smooth, add 1 c brown sugar, ½ c milk, 1 egg, scant cupful of flour, 1 t baking powder, and 1 t vanilla. Drop on greased baking sheet and bake in moderate oven. Cover with icing when cooling.

*Pecan Nut Yums**

Pecan is one of my favorite nuts. Unfortunately, pecans don't grow well north of the Mason-Dixon Line. Fortunately, you can now buy them in almost any food store. This is Myrtle's yummiest formula:

½ c butter | **1 c brown sugar**
1 egg | **½ t vanilla**
½ t cinnamon | **½ t cloves**
1¼ c flour | **½ t soda**
¼ t salt | **½ c pecans**

Shape into rolls. Let stand overnight. Slice thin and bake in hot oven 12 to 15 minutes.

A gallery of sourdough cookies — four kinds of scrumptious cookies made from the same batter. Every old-time pantry was well-stocked with these and other favorities for good munching when the kids got home from school, and on weekends and holidays.

*Unbeatable Date Fills**

The date-filled cookie was always a favorite around my house, and my mother used them to bribe me into doing extra chores. From Myrtle's old recipe notebook comes an equally delicious version.

2 c brown sugar
1 c lard or shortening
1 t soda
3 c flour
2 eggs
4 t warm water
1 t cream of tartar

(Note: In recipes calling for lard, one can always substitute shortening. In the old days on the farm, lard was a staple commodity, shortening unheard of.)

Dissolve soda in warm water. Combine dry ingredients. Cream sugar and shortening. Add eggs and mix all ingredients. Beat well. Roll out, cut, place filling in center and cover with another cookie. Bake in moderate oven until brown.

Filling: Pit and chop one pkg. dates. Combine with ½ c white sugar and water to cover. Boil and stir until thick. Cool.

*Peanut Butter Goodies**

1 c butter
2 eggs
3 c flour
1 t soda
1 c brown sugar
1 c white sugar
1 c peanut butter

Cream butter and sugars. Beat in eggs, peanut butter and soda. Add flour. Roll pieces of dough into small balls, place on greased cookie tin, and press flat with a fork. Bake at 375 degrees for 10 minutes.

*All-Time Oatmeal Cookies**

Another old favorite with country kitchen cooks,

then and now, is oatmeal cookies. Here is the best and simplest recipe I have yet come across:

1 c sugar
6 t cold water
½ c raisins
2 t baking powder
1 t vanilla
½ c butter
2 c oatmeal
2 c flour
2 eggs

Blend and drop on a greased and floured pan in walnut-sized gobs. Bake in moderate oven. Oatmeal cookies are famous for their keeping qualities — except when hungry snackers raid the pantry late at night.

North Country Florentines

½ c butter
2 eggs, beaten
½ t salt
1 t baking powder
1 c sugar
½ t vanilla
2 c cake flour

Cream butter and sugar, adding eggs and vanilla. Sift flour before measuring and then sift with salt and baking powder. Add to creamed mix. Beat lightly and spread mixture ¼ inch thick in three greased 8-by-8 pans. Add topping.

Topping:

½ c chopped nuts
1 egg white, beaten stiff
½ c brown sugar

Sprinkle nuts over cookie dough in pans. Beat sugar into egg white and spread thinly over dough. Bake in 375 degree oven for 30 minutes. Cool and cut into strips while still in pan.

Candy Kept the Family Together

Candy making was a favorite indoor activity on cold winter nights on the farm or prairie homestead before TV or radio — and even before we had a telephone in our home. I inherited a sweet tooth and learned early how to satisfy it with homemade fudge, originally taught me by my mother but over the years gradually refined into what I call "Don's Quick Fudge."

The key to success in fudge making (take it from an old sweet tooth) is, *first*, using the right proportion of sugar and cocoa; *second*, heating to just the right temperature; and, *third*, beating until it begins to harden before pouring on buttered plate.

Mix sugar and cocoa until the color of dark clay. To tell the right temperature, simmer the mixture until a drop in cold water turns firm quickly. Remove from heat immediately. Start beating when quick-chilled. Don't add extract or nuts until the very last.

Don's Quick Fudge

2 c white sugar	**milk**
cocoa (about 3 T)	**vanilla extract**
nuts if desired	**1 T butter**

Mix sugar and cocoa to a light brown color, and add enough milk to make a thick mixture. Cook on a slow fire in pan (or double boiler if available) until the mixture bubbles and simmers. Test frequently with drops in cold water. Have buttered plate or pie tin ready. When drops test firm, and just before turning hard, remove from heat and let simmering and bubbling subside. Place pan outside on the snow if necessary for a few minutes. Than add a walnut-sized chunk of butter, a few drops of extract, and beat until so thick it offers resistance. Add nuts if desired, and spoon out onto plate. When hard, cut into squares about 1 inch thick. *Note:* If not properly beaten, it will not harden. Also, *never* beat when mixture is cooking, as it will then turn to sugar. For a variation of this receipe brown sugar can be substituted for white.

*Peanut Butter Fudge**

2 c brown sugar
2 squares chocolate
½ c peanut butter
5 T cream
1 T butter

Cook all ingredients except peanut butter until it forms a soft ball when tested. Add peanut butter, beat, and pour out onto greased pan.

*Divinity Prairie Style**

3 c sugar
1 c hot water
1 t vanilla
pinch of salt
¾ c light corn syrup
3 egg whites
⅔ c nuts

Add salt to egg whites and beat stiff. Cook sugar, syrup, and water until a drop forms a ball in cold water. Pour slowly over egg whites, beating continually until quite stiff. Add nuts and vanilla, beat until stiff enough to hold a point. Drop from spoon onto buttered plate.

Country Caramels

2 c white sugar
½ c butter
1 tall can evaporated milk
½ c chopped nuts
2 c white corn syrup
⅛ t salt
1 t vanilla

In a 2-quart saucepan boil the sugar and corn syrup,

then add the butter and salt. Still boiling, slowly add a can of evaporated milk, stirring constantly. Cook to 242 degrees F. on a candy thermometer.

Add the vanilla and chopped nuts. Pour into well-greased square tin. Allow to cool 3 hours. Turn out onto board and cut with heavy knife. Wrap in wax paper. Makes about 3 pounds.

*Maple Ice Cream Candy**

Mix 2 c sugar, 1 c water, and ½ c vinegar. Boil without stirring until it spins a thread. Stir in ½ t maple extract. Pull until creamy.

*Cinnamon Taffy**

1½ c sugar
10 T water
1 t cinnamon flavoring
4 T vinegar
1 t butter
pinch salt

Mix sugar, vinegar, water, salt, and butter. Stir, then boil without stirring to hard-ball stage. Add flavoring. Pour into greased dish. When cool, pull until white and porous.

Winter Mints

2 c sugar
¼ c white corn syrup
½ c hot water
vegetable coloring
extract: wintergreen, spearmint, peppermint, maple, vanilla

Combine sugar, water, and syrup in a pan and cook over a slow fire, stirring constantly, until soft ball forms in cold water. Pour into bowl, cool slightly, and add color and flavor. Place bowl in pan of hot water to keep it soft, and beat until creamy. If mixture gets hard too fast, add a little hot water and beat some more. Make patties by dropping mixture onto wax paper while warm. Mints can be colored green, pink, yellow, orange, or white. May be topped with nuts or fruits.

Cream Pulls

2 c sugar	**2 c white corn syrup**
1 c cream	**1 c nuts**
1 t vanilla	**butter**

Boil sugar, cream, and corn syrup over a slow fire until a ball hardens in cold water. Add vanilla, nuts, and small chunk of butter. Pour out into large buttered pan. Pull until light-colored and stiff. Cut off pieces with shears and arrange on buttered dish.

Apple Caramel Dip

6 apples	**2 c brown sugar**
¼ c water	**¼ c corn syrup**
¼ t salt	**2 T butter**
2 T vinegar	**1 t vanilla**

Cook mixture to hard-ball stage. Add 1 t vanilla and dip in apples on a stick. Set on wax paper to harden.

Pullin' Taffy

2 c sugar	**2 c Karo syrup or molasses**
¼ c vinegar	**2 t vanilla**
1 T butter	**½ t soda**

Boil syrup and sugar until thick. Add vinegar. Boil until a drop hardens in cold water. Add soda and butter. Remove, add vanilla, and beat hard. When you can't beat it anymore, pull and pull until it's cold.

Marshmallows

2 c sugar	**½ c water**
1½ t vanilla	**¾ c light corn syrup**
4 t gelatine	

Boil sugar, syrup, and water until stringy. Dissolve 4 t gelatine in 8 t water while boiling other mixture. Pour sugar mix over gelatine and beat for at least 30 minutes. Add vanilla. Line an 8 x 12 pan with powdered sugar and pour in mixture. After it is thoroughly cool, remove from pan and cut into bite-size pieces.

Canned Cow Candy

1 can sweetened milk
2 pkgs. chocolate chips

Melt together in top of double boiler. Add pinch of salt and a cup of nuts after beating, if desired. Pour out into pan and chill thoroughly.

Cracker Jacks

popcorn
2 c sugar
1 c molasses
½ t soda
1 T butter
2 T vinegar
shelled peanuts (optional)

Pop corn and place in large bowl. Boil remaining ingredients, except soda, until drop hardens instantly in cold water. Add soda and pour over popcorn. Can also add shelled peanuts. So good you don't need to look for prizes.

Country Divinity

Combine 3 c sugar, 1 c corn syrup, and ½ c water and boil until stringy. Beat 3 egg whites with 1 t baking powder and ¼ t salt until stiff. Pour hot syrup slowly over egg whites, beating constantly. After the syrup has been added, put in 1 c nuts, if desired, and vanilla. Continue beating until candy holds its shape, then drop onto wax paper with a spoon.

*The "Holey" Donut and Sundry Legends**

Doughboy: A flour dumpling; a piece of bread dough fried in deep fat and served as hot bread; so called from the large round brass buttons on the U.S. infantry uniform in the Civil War.
Doughnut: A small cake fried in deep fat; a typical ring-shaped one made of rich dough leavened usually with baking powder; one shaped like a ring or a ball and made of yeast-leavened dough — called also raised doughnut.

Webster's Third International Dictionary

The "sinker," or "Salvation Army Angel Food," or "Holeycake," otherwise known as the doughnut, is probably one of man's (and woman's) oldest culinary inventions. All it took to originate the doughnut was to accidentally drop some leavened dough into a pot of hot grease. Anyway, many legends persist. One has it that the donut was invented by thrifty Down East ship captains. To believe this, you must start with the hole, and how it originated.

As the legend goes, a stingy New England captain of a whaling ship, leaving for the far-off Bering Sea, packed in the ship's stores several barrels of small round "cakes" baked by his wife. As a treat for the men, who might be away from family and loved ones for three or four years, she inserted a walnut or almond in the center of each. The little cakes were an immediate sensation with the crew, but the miserly captain fretted over the cost of the expensive nuts. He came up with an idea that would avoid a mutiny and also eliminate the costly nuts.

*The reader will notice that the word is spelled either "doughnut" or "donut" rather interchangeably in this book. The both mean the same thing, but "donut" usually implies a recipe of newer origin.

He had his wife bake the little cakes without the nuts, leaving only a hole where they had been.*

According to *Americana Magazine*,** doughnuts did not originate in America, but Americans have taken credit for them. The author says that a Camden, Maine, sea captain named Hanson Gregory could not stomach his mother's little cakes because they were so soft and doughy in the middle. He politely suggested to her that she cut a hole in the center. His mother did, and the sinker was born.

The Dutch probably were the first to bring the doughnut to America. They were called *olykoeks* and were round, raisin-filled cakes common in New Amsterdam in the early seventeenth century. During the Civil War one writer reported in 1867 that some ladies in Augusta, Maine, distributed more than fifty barrels of doughnuts to the Third Volunteer Regiment. During World War I the doughnut became a distinctive American treat when a Salvation Army volunteer was publicized making a big batch for enthusiastic soldiers on a troop train.

In the 1920s and 1930s there was even a trade journal called the *Doughnut Mazazine*. It was published by the Donut Machine of New York, which operated a 900-seat Donut Palace and Casino at the 1939 World's Fair. The same company had operated a fancy donut casino at the 1933 Chicago World's Fair, which I visited with another young Velva boy, Paul McDonnell. He and I hitch-hiked to the Windy City from north central North Dakota. I was 13; Paul was 16.

---

*Readers who want to delve further into this fasinating legend should read the chapter on donuts in *The Complete Sourdough Cookbook* by Don and Myrtle Holm (Caxton Printers, Ltd.).

**"Not All Have Holes" by Florence Fabricant, *Americana Magazine*, Jan./Feb. 1980.

The *Doughnut Magazine*, long out of print, used to enhance the image of the doughnut by printing favorite recipes of famous people. One was reputed to be from Olivia DeHaviland. It featured split doughnut halves topped with canned peaches, whipped cream, and a maraschino cherry — a sort of doughnut shortcake.

"Doughnut Shops" (or "Shacks") have been a feature of the American roadside scene for at least as long as the automobile has been in use. Some bakeries specialize in doughnuts and offer sometimes unbelievable varieties of flavors, mixtures, and concoctions. There is at least one large chain of doughnut shops which has thousands of outlets in the United States, Canada, and even Japan, with sales reaching about half a billion dollars a year.

The Oxford Universal Dictionary lists "doughnut" as originating about 1809 in America. "Doughboy," the nickname of the American soldier in World War I, comes from association with the Salvation Army donut, which was formerly called a "doughbory." It was also known as a "boiled flour dumpling." "Doughboy" seems to have originated in 1685. Incidentally, the soldier in the Civil War was also called a "doughboy."

It seems likely that the doughnut was a universal spontaneous creation of many ethnic origins — probably most often with religious connotations. The *fastnachts* of Germanic sects were usually square cakes of yeast and potato. They were later made triangular so they were easier to dunk — a term that comes from Dunkards, a religious sect.

In Spanish or Mexican the doughnut is a *brunuelo*. Italians call them *zeppole*. Greeks have a honey-dipped *loukoumades*. The famous Mardis Gras "Fat Tuesday" is a term that comes from the little, deep-fried cakes that were traditionally hawked on the streets on the day preceeding Ash Wednesday.

Sourdough doughnuts cooking in hot oil. Sourdough doughnuts characteristically do not absorb cooking oil and thus are not greasy.

The first recorded use of the word "doughnut" seems to have been by American author Washington Irving in the early nineteenth century.

No one yet has come up with a satisfactory word for the hole in the doughnut. Some call it a "doughnut ball," but this is singularly prosaic. There is at least one large specialty bakery in the country, however, that produces *only* doughnut holes — mass produces them with a special machine. It's the "holiest" business in town.

The doughnut was the inspiration for our book, *The Complete Sourdough Cookbook*. It was the many years of experimentation with the old sourdough ways of cooking that led to the "invention" of what I call Sourdough Sams.

Sourdough Sams are not only the lightest doughnuts I have ever tasted but are distinctively nutty in flavor — and greaseless. My bride, who is a born-and-bred Wholesome Country cook, raised on a farm and taught by experts, at first did not believe my claims. She had never heard of such a thing. I prevailed upon her to try them, and she became an immediate convert. For years she regularly whipped up a batch — freezing for later enjoyment what we could not eat right away. Thawed, not only are they as good as fresh, but the freezing seems to improve the taste.

Here's how to make 'em:

Don's Sourdough Sams

½ c sourdough batter
2 T shortening
1 t baking powder
½ t nutmeg
½ t baking soda
⅓ c sour milk or buttermilk
½ c sugar
2 c flour
2 egg yolks or 1 whole egg
¼ t cinnamon
½ t salt

Sift dry ingredients, stir in liquid, roll out and cut. Heat some cooking oil to 390 degrees F. and deep-fry one or two at a time. This makes 17 doughnuts and holes. Dust with granulated sugar or a mixture of sugar and cinnamon in a shake bag, if desired.

(Note: Sourdough batter is started the night before, using sourdough starter with added flour and enough lukewarm water to get the batter working overnight. Keep it in a warm place.)

Myrtle's Applesauce Doughnuts

We call plain doughnuts "cake doughnuts" and others by whatever flavor or glazing they have.

This is one of Myrtle's specials:

2⅔ c flour | **1½ t baking powder**
½ t baking soda | **1 t salt**
½ t nutmeg | **½ t cinnamon**
½ c sourdough starter | **2 T shortening**
½ c sugar | **2 egg yolks**
½ t vanilla | **½ c applesauce**
¼ c buttermilk (can substitute 1 T sour cream for part)

Knead well. Roll out and cut. Let stand to chill. Deep-fry in 390 degree oil. Takes longer than usual. Makes 2 dozen.

Sourdough Banana Doughnuts

Sift 2⅔ c flour with 1½ t baking powder, ½ t baking soda, 1 t salt, and ¼ t nutmeg. Cream ½ c sugar with 2½ T shortening. Add 1 whole egg or 2 egg yolks. Mix well, stir in 1 t vanilla, ¼ c buttermilk, ⅔ c sourdough starter, and ½ c mashed ripe bananas. Mix with dry ingredients, thoroughly sifted. Turn out onto floured board and knead. Add just enough flour so dough handles well. Roll out, cut into shapes, and place on aluminum foil. Heat cooking oil to 390 degrees and deep-fry. Drain on double paper towels. Sugar if desired. These freeze well; put in double plastic bag, seal, and place in freezer. Take out just enough to eat at one time and bring to room temperature for about 30 minutes, or warm in oven.

Back Stoop Doughnuts

1 c sugar
2 eggs, beaten
flour to roll out
¼ t salt
½ t nutmeg
2 T butter
1 c sour milk
½ c sweet cream
1 t soda

Mix and fry in hot fat, as usual.

(Note: The secret of good doughnuts is the deep-fry oil or lard. It must be hot enough to smoke. Adding cold dough tends to cool the oil, so don't put too many in to fry at the same time. Also, a good doughnut will *not* be soggy with grease. You should have just as much cooking oil left when you finish a batch as you had in the beginning.)

Puffy Doughnuts

Blend and let rise:

1 c scalded milk
½ c sugar
1 cake yeast
1 c riced potatoes
1 c potato water
⅓ c butter
2½ c flour
1 t salt

Add:

2 eggs, beaten
5 c flour (approximate)
1 T grated lemon rind
1 t mace

Cover and let rise again. Roll dough to ½ inch thick, cut, cover with cloth, and let rise once more. Deep fry. Can be sugared or glazed.

Coffee, Tea, Cocoa, and Other Winter Breaks

Old-Fashioned Cocoa

It is surprising how many people don't know how to make good, old-fashioned cocoa nowadays, preferring to buy expensive, instant-mix powders. Here's a simple and inexpensive way that tastes much more wholesome:

2 sq. chocolate
dash of salt
3 c milk
2 to 4 T sugar
1 c cold water

In a double boiler place chocolate, sugar, and salt, adding water to boil. Stir until chocolate is melted. Add milk, but don't boil. Beat well until light and foamy. Serve at once, while still frothy.

Punch and Judy Cocoa

2 T malted milk powder
1 T sugar
1 T cocoa
¾ c milk

Mix dry ingredients, add milk, and beat thoroughly.

Easy Egg Nog

1 egg
⅔ c canned milk
nutmeg
2 T fruit juice
⅔ c ice water

Beat egg yolk, add fruit juice, and blend in milk and icewater. Pour into tall glass. Top with beaten egg white, and sprinkle with nutmeg.

A coffee grinder for home-ground coffee beans, and a delicious sourdough prune cake prepared by Myrtle Holm.

Homesteader Tea

Use only an earthenware teapot, rinsed with boiling water. Toss in a spoonful of tea leaves for each cup plus 1 for the pot. Pour boiling water over this and let steep for 3 or 4 minutes. Serve in china cups with sugar, cream, or lemon to taste.

Swede Coffee

The Scandahoovians never put sugar in tea or coffee. Instead, they put a cube of sugar in the mouth and then sip through it.

For a good coffee, use a medium grind, about 4 t with 2 T beaten egg. To this, add ¼ c cold water. Stir, and blend in 1¾ c boiling water. Put on stove and bring to a boil. As it begins to roil, stir down. When it finally comes to a full boil, remove from heat and let set for 3 or 4 minutes. Pour into mugs at once without straining. A crushed egg shell is often placed in the boiling brew. This makes about 2 mugs of clear, heady coffee, the old country way.

Appendix

Abbreviations

t	Teaspoon
T	Tablespoon
c	Cup
pt.	Pint
qt.	Quart
pk.	Peck
bu.	Bushel
oz.	Ounce
lb.	Pound

Equivalents

2 c butter	1 pound
4 T flour	1 ounce
2 T butter	1 ounce
4 c flour unsifted	1 pound
2 c sugar	1 pound
2 c lard	1 pound
2 c rice	1 pound
2½ c navy beans	1 pound

Size of Cans

Picnic	1 cup	8 ounces
No. 1	1½ cups	
No. 1 tall	2 cups	
No. 2	2½ cups	
No. 2½	3½ cups	
No. 3	4 cups	
No. 5	7 cups	
No. 10	13 cups	

Liquid Measure

16 fluid ounces	4 gills
4 gills	1 pint
2 pints	1 quart
4 quarts	1 gallon

5 quarts	1 imperial gallon
31½ gallons	1 barrel
63 gallons	1 hogshead

Cooking Measure

1 t	1/16 ounce
1 T	½ ounce
16 oz.	1 pt.
2 pt.	1 qt.
4 qts.	1 gal.
1 firkin	9 gal.

Units of Measure

3 t	1 T
4 T	¼ c
8 T	½ c
12 T	¾ c
16 T	1 c
2 T	1 oz.
1 c	1 pt.
⅓ c	5⅓ T
2 T fat	1 oz.
½ c fat	¼ lb.
1 c fat	½ lb.
2 c butter	1 lb.
2½ c granulated sugar	1 lb.
3½ c confectioners sugar	1 lb.
2¼ c brown sugar	1 lb.
4 c sifted flour	1 lb.
5 c grated cheese	1 lb.
3½ T cocoa and ½ T butter	1 oz. chocolate
16 marshmallows	¼ lb.
9 graham crackers	1 c
2 T vinegar and sweet milk	1 c sour milk
1 lemon	3 to 4 T
8 to 10 egg whites	1 c
12 to 14 egg yolks	1 c
8 large eggs	1 lb.
1 c uncooked rice	4 c cooked rice
3 lb. dressed chicken	1½ cooked or diced
1 T cornstarch	2 T flour

What It Means

• *Steep:* Let it stand in hot liquid, i.e., tea leaves.

• *Scald:* As milk; in a pan over low heat until beads form around the edges.

• *Blanch:* Pour boiling water over, letting vegetables, fruit, or nuts stand until wrinkles appear. Drain and remove.

• *Knead:* Work dough vigorously with hands, folding outer parts over and inward, constantly, to thoroughly blend.

• *Grease:* Wiping pan or cooking utensil with lard, fat, butter, or margarine to prevent sticking.

• *Parboil:* Cook over low heat, such as rendering, usually in preparation for combining with other ingredients.

• *Rendering:* Simmering slowly, without cooking, to separate oil or tallow from fat or meat.

• *Puree:* Usually cooked food pressed through a sieve or blender.

• *Dredge:* To dip or roll in flour or dry ingredients so that it is completely coated.

• *Saute:* To brown quickly in a fry pan with small amount of grease or oil.

• *Blend:* To smoothly stir one ingredient into another or in combination.

• *Beat:* Whip, as in beating eggs or cream or candy, with beater, fork, or large spoon. "Whipping" is generally considered to beat until fluffy.

• *Measure:* Unless otherwise stated, all measures are level, not heaping. If less, "*Scant*" is sometimes used. When measuring molasses, honey, or syrup, a greased spoon or cup is helpful for accurate measuring.

• *Brown:* To cook quickly on outside, prior to further processing; to finish off a cooking step, with a quick hot period to provide a golden crust; to "brown flour," by heating flour in a pan in oven, stirring to prevent burning, and sifted while warm.

• *Clarify:* Heating in pan and skimming off froth as it appears; slowly pouring off liquid, leaving residue in pan.

Oven Temperatures

Slow	250 to 300 degrees F.
Slow moderate	350
Moderate	350
Quick moderate	375
Moderate hot	400
Hot	425
Very hot	475 to 500

Cooking Temperatures

Item	Boiled	Steamed	15-Lb. Pressure Cooker
Asparagus	10–25 min.		10 min.
Lima beans	20–30		15
String beans	15–25		15
Wax beans	15–30	50–60 min.	
Beets, small	30–45	45–60	10
Beets, large	50–60	50–90	30
Broccoli	10–20		10
Brussels sprouts	10–18		
Cabbage	5–20	15	10
Carrots, young	10–20	20–50	10
Carrots, mature	20–24		10
Cauliflower	8–30	10–25	
Celery	5–15		10
Corn, on cob	5–10	10	10
Eggplant	5–15	15	
Kohlrabi	25–30	30	15
Okra		20	
Onions, whole	30–45		5
Onions, sliced	15–20		10
Parsnips	20–40	30–45	10
Peas	10–20		10
Potatoes, whole	20–40	40	15
Sweet Potatoes	20–35		
Pumpkin			10
Rutabagas	20–35		15
Spinach	5–10	15–18	
Squash, summer	10–15	15–20	15
Squash, winter	15–25		5
Tomatoes	5–15		5
Turnips	15–40	20–25	10

Roasting Birds

Kind	Wt.	Oven	Minutes Per Lb.
Chicken	3½ lb.	350° F	40–45
	to 6	325–350	30–35
	6 plus	325	25–30
Duck	3½–6	325	25–30
Goose	10–12	325	30–40
Turkey	8–10	325	20–25
	10–14	325	18–20
	14–18	300	15–18

Roasting Meat

Kind	How Cooked	Internal Temp. °F.	Minutes Per Lb.
Beef	rare	140	18–20
	medium	160	22–25
	well done	170	27–30
Pork	fresh	185	30–35
	smoked	170	20–30
	tenderized	160	15–20
Lamb	medium	175	30–45
	well done	180	30–45
Veal		170	25–45

Broiling

Beef steak	Rare: 15–20 minutes	Medium: 20–45 minutes
Lamb chops	15–25 minutes	
Pork, smoked	20–30 minutes	
Bacon	4–5 minutes	

Testing Candies

Item	Temp. °F	Temp. °C	Viscosity	Characteristic
syrup	230–234	110–112	thread	2-inch thread drops from spoon
fondant fudge pancha	234–240	112–115	soft ball	drop in cold water forms soft flat glob
caramel	244–248	118–120	firm ball	drop cold water forms firm round ball
divinity marshmallow nougat popcorn balls saltwater taffy	250–265	121–130	hard ball	in cold water forms very hard ball, yet plastic

butterscotch taffy	270–290	132–143	soft crack	separates into threads, not brittle
brittle glace	300–310	149–154		separates into hard brittle threads
barley sugar	320	160	clear liquid	sugar melts
caramelized sugar	338	170	brown liquid	melted sugar turns brown

*Quantities for Chuckwagon or Harvest Crews (Serves 50)**

meat loaf or balls . . . . 10 lb.
ham (baked) 25
roast chicken 25
creamed chicken 20
pot roast 25
roast beef 25
roast pork 25
salad chicken 20
veal cutlets 15
pork chops 15
chipped beef 5
swiss steak 15
mashed potatoes . . . . 1¾ pk.
boiled potatoes . . . . 1½ pk.
scalloped potatoes . . . . 10 lb.
potato chips . . . . 2½ lb.
peas, beans, beets . . . . nine No. 2 cans
creamed carrots . . . . 10 lb.
sweet potatoes . . . . 12½ lb.
corn, cob . . . . 50 ears
lettuce . . . . 5 heads
new green peas . . . . 35 lb.
beans . . . . 12 lb.
spinach . . . . two No. 10 cans
bulk ice cream . . . . 7 qt.
brick ice cream . . . . 8 qt.
shortcakes . . . . 50 individual servings
strawberries (for shortcake) . . . . 10 qt.
whipped cream topping . . . . 1 qt.
pie . . . . nine 8-inch pies
layer cake . . . . four 8-inch cakes
sponge cake, tube center . . . . 4 large ones
coffee . . . . 3 lb.

---

*All of these ingredients are not needed, of course; only the amount of each item desired on the menu.

sugar	3 lb.
cream	2 qt.
salad dressing	1 qt.
rolls	8 doz.
bread	5 loaves
salted nuts	3 lb.
lettuce salad	13 heads
tomato jelly	12 qt.
mixed salad fruit	7 qt.
salad cabbage	8 qt.
pineapple	2 qt.
oysters, scalloped	2 gal.
stewed oysters	6 qts.
milk	6 qts.
salmon loaf	six 1-lb. cans
white sauce	3 qt.
cranberry jelly	4 qt. cranberries
sugar	6 c
water	1¼ qt.
celery	10 bunches
olives	2 qt.
chopped pickles	2 qt.
small pickles	2 qt.

Baking Secrets

- Bake fruit, molasses, and chocolate cakes at lower temperatures than white cake, for they burn quickly.
- Sponge cakes need a "slow" oven.
- Small and layer cakes want a hotter oven than a loaf cake.
- Large or loaf cakes need a moderate oven.
- If oven gets too hot, place a pan of cold water on the top grate.
- If cake is browning too fast, place a sheet of paper over it.
- Cake is done when it springs back when pressed gently with finger.
- Insert toothpick into center of loaf; if comes out clean, it is done.
- When done, cake shrinks from sides of pan.
- Never open oven door until cake has formed.
- For oven rising, place cake in center of lower grate first.

- For pies, chill all ingredients (some cooks say yes, others say no).
- Use least possible amount of moisture for pies.

• For light and crunchy crusts, use sour cream for half of water called for.

• Single crusts for shells should be baked over an inverted pie pan.

• Perforate crusts with fork before placing in oven to prevent air bubbles.

• Divide the dough for two-crust pies, using larger half for lower crust.

• Use soda with chocolate to get reddish brown color.
• Use 2 T baking powder to 1 c flour.
• Use ½ t soda with 1 c sour milk.
• 5 eggs equals 1 c.
• 8 egg whites equals 4 eggs.
• 4 c flour equals 1 lb.
• 4 c flour equals 1 qt.
• 16 T equals 1 c.

Troubleshooting Cake Baking

Too Coarse

Not enough liquid
Too much leavening
Shortening not creamed thoroughly
Oven too slow or low

Texture Too Heavy

Too much sugar
Too much shortening
Oven too low or slow
Too much beating

Crust Too Thick

Too much baking
Too hot oven
Too much flavor
Not enough sugar
Not enough shortening

Crust Too Moist and Sticky

Too much sugar

Cake Falls

Too much shortening
Too much sugar
Too much leavening

Oven too low or slow
Not baked long enough
Moved or jiggled during baking

Top Cracked

Too much flour
Too much sugar
Too much shortening
Oven too hot

Dry Cake

Too much flour
Too little sugar
Too little shortening
Too much leavening
Egg whites overbeaten
Baked too long at low temperatures

Soggy Layers

Ingredients not well mixed
Egg yolks not well mixed
Too much liquid

Cake Undersized

Oven too hot
Not enough shortening
Pan too small

What's the difference?

According to Webster's New International Dictionary:

Baking powder: a powder used as a leavening agent in bakery goods (as quick bread or cake) and consisting essentially of a carbonate (as baking soda) an acid substance (as cream of tartar) and starch or flour so that when the mixture is moistened the carbonate and acid react, liberating carbon dioxide which raises the dough.

Baking soda: (see sodium carbonate bicarbonate) a crystalline salt that is less soluble in water than normal sodium carbonate and gives a weakly alkaline reaction that evolves carbon dioxide when heated; that is found in nature and is also made by passing carbon dioxide into a solution of the normal carbonate or by purifying the intermediate product of the Solvay process, that is used chiefly in baking powders, in carbonated beverages and effervescent salts, in fire extinguishers and in medicine as antacids, and that with carbonic acid constitutes the principle inorganic buffer system of blood and other body fluids; sodium hydrogen carbonate — called baking soda.

Baking powder is most often called for in bakery recipes, while baking soda is found more frequently in dishes such as baked beans.

Systematic White Sauce

Viscosity	Flour	Shortening	Milk	Condiments
Runny	1 T	2 T	1 c	¼ t salt, ⅛ t pepper
Just right	2 T	1½ T	1 c	same
Thick	4 T	1 T	1 c	same

Take your pick. First melt the shortening, then add flour and seasonings, stirring thoroughly. Add lukewarm milk and stir in well. Bring to a boil and pour over whatever.

Frostings and Finishes

Many cakes and bakery goods do not call for frostings or toppings, or perhaps you want to try something else. Here are some tips for completing without using frosting:

Top the hot cake with sugar, cinnamon, and nut meats, corn syrup, or grated orange peel and honey.

Fill and top cake with berries or diced canned fruit like apricots or peaches.

Gingerbread can be topped with cream cheese.

Place a lace doily on top of cake, then sift confectioner's sugar over this. Carefully lift off doily, and you have a frosty design. *Voila!*

- Top chocolate cupcakes with marshmallows halves before baking.
- Sprinkle cake with finely chopped walnuts before baking for a crunchy top.

Caramel Icing

¾ c brown sugar **⅓ c butter**
¾ c white sugar **⅓ c milk**
vanilla

Boil all together 3 minutes; then add ½ t vanilla and cool. Beat until ready to spread.

Peanut Butter Topping

2 c powdered sugar **2 T melted butter**
3 T peanut butter

Cream sugar and butter. Add peanut butter, either smooth or crunchy, and beat well. Spread on chocolate, spice, or white cake.

Rocky Mountain Frosting

1 c white Karo syrup **2 egg whites**

Beat slowly and smoothly until very stiff. Flavor with ½ t vanilla or other extract.

Sour Cream Filling for White Cake

5 egg yolks, well-beaten **1 c sugar**
1 c sour cream **½ c nuts**

Heat until mixture is thick. Remove from heat and add nuts. Spread.

Frostings or icings often make the difference between good and delicious pastries. In the old days every competent country cook had a whole repertoire to fit every occasion. Here are some from Myrtle's old dog-eared notebook:

Brown Sugar Frosting. 1 c brown sugar, ½ c sweet cream, ½ t vanilla. Boil sugar and cream until thick.

Cooked Powdered Sugar Frosting. 1 c powdered sugar, ½ c sweet milk, butter size of walnut. Boil until thick, beat until cool.

Boiled Frosting. 2 c sugar, 1 c water, stiffly beaten whites of 2 eggs. Boil sugar and water until it threads, then gradually pour onto beaten eggs, beating rapidly until cool.

Fudge Frosting. 4 T cocoa, ⅔ c cold milk, 2 c sugar, dash of salt, 2 T corn syrup, 2 T butter, 1 t vanilla. Add melted cocoa to milk and heat gradually, beat for 1 minute adding sugar, salt, corn syrup. Stir until sugar is dissolved and mixture boils. Cook until it forms a soft ball in cold water. Remove from fire, add butter and vanilla. Cool to lukewarm and beat stiff.

Caramel Nut Frosting. 1 c brown sugar, 1 unbeaten egg white, 3 T water, 1 t baking powder, ½ t extract, ½ c chopped walnuts. Boil sugar, egg white, and water, and beat with egg beater for 10 minutes while on stove. Add other ingredients, cool, and spread on cake.

Sea Foam Icing. 1 c brown sugar, ⅓ c water, white of egg, 1 t baking powder. Boil water and sugar without stirring until syrup spins a thread. Add hot syrup slowly to beaten egg white, beating continually. Add baking powder, spread when icing foams.

Chocolate Boiled Frosting. 2½ c sugar, 1 t corn syrup, 1 c boiling water, 3 egg whites, stiffly beaten, 6 squares chocolate, melted and cooled. Combine sugar, corn syrup, water. Stir constantly until it boils, continue cooking until it spins a thread. Pour onto egg whites, beating constantly until stiff enough to spread. Fold in chocolate.

Divinity Frosting. 3 c sugar, 1 t corn syrup, 1⅓ c boiling water, 4 egg whites stiffly beaten, 1 t vanilla. Mix as in Chocolate Boiled Frosting but do not add chocolate.

Marshmallow Icing. 2½ c sugar, ½ c light corn syrup, ¼ t salt, ½ c water, 2 egg whites, 1 t vanilla, 8 marshmallows, cut. Place sugar, syrup, salt, and water in pan and cook to the firm-ball stage. Pour hot syrup slowly into well-beaten egg whites, beating constantly. Add vanilla extract and continue beating until frosting will hold its shape when tossed over back of spoon. Add marshmallows.

Eagle Brand Chocolate Icing. ½ cup sweetened condensed milk, 1 square chocolate, 1 t water. Melt chocolate in double boiler, stir in milk and cook over boiling water for 5 minutes until thickened. Remove from fire, add 1 t water and spread over cake.

Mocha Icing. 5 T butter, 2 T cocoa, 1½ c sifted powdered sugar, coffee. Cream butter, add cocoa and sugar, and pour in just enough strong coffee to make icing of right consistency. Spread on a cold cake.

Swiss Chocolate Frosting. 1 pkg. cream cheese, 4 t cream, dash of salt, 2 c powdered sugar, 1 oz. melted chocolate, ½ t vanilla. Soften cheese with milk or cream, add salt and sugar gradually, beating well. Add chocolate and beat until smooth, finally add vanilla.

Banana Filling. (For Black-Eyed Susan Cake.) 3 T flour, 3 T sugar, ½ c milk, ½ c mashed bananas, 2 t lemon juice, 3 T melted butter, salt. Mix flour and sugar, add milk gradually, stir over hot water until thick. Mash bananas, add lemon juice, and combine with first mixture. Cool, add butter and salt. Stir until smooth.

Coffee Frosting. 1 c sugar, ⅓ c strong coffee, 2 egg whites, ½ t vanilla, pinch salt, salted almonds. Cook sugar and coffee together to soft ball stage. Beat egg whites stiff. Add coffee syrup slowly, beating constantly. Add vanilla, salt, and almonds.

Coconut Frosting. 3 T butter, 2½ c powdered sugar, 2 T lemon juice, dash salt, grated rind of ¼ lemon or orange, 1½ c shredded coconut. Cream butter until soft, add sugar alternately with lemon juice. Add salt. Beat until smooth and light and add grated rind. Spread on cake and sprinkle thickly with coconut.

Nougat Frosting. 2 egg whites unbeaten, 1½ c sugar, 4 T water, 2 T light corn syrup, 2 T honey, ¼ t cream of tartar, ½ t vanilla, ¼ c blanched chopped almonds. Put egg whites, sugar, water, corn syrup, honey, and cream of tartar in top of double boiler and mix thoroughly. Place over rapidly boiling water and beat constantly with rotary eggbeater until mixture will hold a peak, about 7 minutes. Remove from fire, add vanilla, and beat until thick enough to spread. To ⅓ of frosting add almonds, spread between layers. Spread plain frosting on top and sides of cake. Melt 1 oz. chocolate with 1 t shortening; pour over frosted cake to decorate.

Marshmallow Meringue. ¼ lb. marshmallows, 1 T milk, ¼ t vanilla, 2 egg whites, ¼ t salt, ¼ c sugar. Place marshmallows and milk in saucepan. Cook over low heat, folding over and over until marshmallows are melted down to about half original size. Remove from heat. Add vanilla and continue folding until mixture is smooth, light, and fluffy. Beat egg whites until stiff. Add salt and sugar slowly, beating constantly. Carefully fold into slightly warm marshmallow mixture. Pile on pie, pudding, or cake. Brown slightly in oven.

Butterscotch Fudge Frosting. Add 2 c light brown sugar, firmly packed, to ½ c butter and cook over low flame, stirring constantly, until mixture darkens slightly, about 5 to 6 minutes. Remove from fire and add 1¼ c granulated sugar, ¾ c top milk or cream, ½ c water. Return to fire and cook until small amount of mixture forms a very soft ball in cold water. Remove from fire. Cool to lukewarm, then beat until ready to spread. Makes enough for top and sides of a 2-layer cake. If desired, add ½ c chopped pecan meats to part of frosting and use as filling. Spread remaining frosting on top and sides of cake and decorate top with pecan halves.

Burnt Sugar Cake Icing. 2 unbeaten egg whites, 1½ c sugar, 5 T water, 1½ t light corn syrup, 2 T burnt sugar syrup. Combine egg whites, sugar, water, and corn syrup in top of double boiler. Beat until thoroughly mixed. Place over rapidly boiling water. Beat constantly and cook 7 minutes or until frosting stands in peaks. Remove from boiling water, add burnt sugar syrup. Beat until thick enough to spread.

Father's Favorite Chocolate Frosting. Combine ¾ c light brown sugar, ⅓ c boiling water 4 squares chocolate, and dash of salt in top of double boiler. Place over rapidly boiling water and heat until chocolate is melted. Then beat with rotary beater until blended. Cook 6 minutes longer. Cool to lukewarm. Cream 4 T butter, add 1 c sifted confectioners' sugar gradually. Add 2 egg yolks, one at a time, beating well after each. Add ½ t vanilla; add chocolate mixture, small amount at a time, beating well. Continue beating until ready to spread. Makes enough for 2 average cakes.

Pineapple Parfait Frosting. 2 unbeaten egg whites, 1½ c sugar, 5 T canned pineapple juice, 1 t light corn syrup, ⅓ t grated lemon rind. Combine egg whites, sugar, pineapple juice, and corn syrup in top of double boiler and mix thoroughly. Place over rapidly boiling water and beat constantly with rotary beater until mixture holds up in peaks, about 7 minutes. Remove from fire, add lemon rind, and beat until cool and thick enough to spread.

Date Nut Filling. 1½ c dates, prunes, or apricots, ½ c sugar, ½ c water, 1 T butter, 1 T lemon juice, ½ c nuts, cut. Cook dates, sugar, and water over direct heat until thickened, stirring constantly. Remove from fire and add butter, lemon juice, and nuts. Cool.

Metric Conversions

Multiply	*By*	*To Get*
gallon	3785	cubic centimeters
gallon	0.1337	cubic feet
gallon	231	cubic inches
gallon	3.785	liters
imperial gallon	1.2009	U.S. gallons
grams	0.0353	ounces
grams	0.0022	pounds
liters	0.2642	gallons
liters	2.113	pints
liters	1.507	quarts
ounces (fluid)	0.0296	liters
kilograms	2.205	pounds
cubic centimeters	0.0010	liters
cubic centimeters	0.0011	quarts

Temperature

Celsius (C) times 9 divided by 5 plus 32 equals Fahrenheit (F)

Fahrenheit minus 32 times 5 divided by 9 equals (Centigrade) Celsius.

Sprouting Table

SPROUTING SEED VARIETY	ALFALFA	BLACK-EYED PEAS	CABBAGE	GARBANZOS	LENTILS	JUMBO MUNG BEANS (Bean Sprouts)
DRY SEED MEASURE	1½-2 T	1 cup	⅓ cup	¾ cup	½ cup	½ cup
SPROUT YIELD	1 quart	1 quart	1 quart	1 quart	1 quart	1 quart
SOAK TIME	4-6 hours	8-12 hours	8-12 hours	12-16 hours	8-12 hours	8-12 hours
SCREEN TOPS	Begin fine, change to medium	Coarse screen	Begin fine, change to medium	Coarse screen	Begin medium, change to coarse	Begin medium, change to coarse
RINSE HULLS AWAY	3rd or 4th day	No hulls	3rd or 4th day	No hulls	3rd or 4th day for seed skins	3rd or 4th day
GROWING TIME	4-5 days	3-4 days	4-5 days	3-5 days	3-4 days	3-4 days
HARVEST LENGTH	½-1½ inches	¼-¾ inch	½-¾ inch	½-1 inch	¼-½ inch	½-2 inches
SPROUTING TIPS	Place in indirect sunlight 1-2 days before harvest, to develop chlorophyll	Allow ample room for expansion during soak time	Allow time to develop chlorophyll, but sharp flavor if too old	Combine with Wheat for nutritious mixture	Tasty and crispy if grown longer, but less nutritious	Grow in dark, at warmer temperature; when rinsing soak one minute before draining
NUTRITIONAL HIGHLIGHTS	Tops list in content of minerals, protein, Vitamins A, B-complex, C, D, E, K	Protein, minerals, Vitamins A and C	Rich in minerals, Vitamins A and C	Complete protein, numerous minerals	Complete protein, B vitamins	Protein, Vitamins A, C, calcium phosphorus, iron
SERVING IDEAS	Enjoy raw in salads, sandwiches, or use The Tube™ sprouter to grow a Sprout Loaf	Tastes like fresh peas in a pod; delicious raw, in salads	Use alone, or combine with alfalfa for cole slaw Sprout Loaf in The Tube™ sprouter	Nutty flavor, good in salads, marinate them for delicious finger food	Delicious in soups, salads, dressings, or spreads	Omlettes, Oriental dishes, salads, soups

Sprouting Table

SPROUTING SEED VARIETY	RADISH	SOYBEANS	SUNFLOWER (Hulled)	WHEAT BERRIES	TRIPLE TREAT® SANDWICH SPROUTS	FAVORITE FIVE® SALAD SPROUTS
DRY SEED MEASURE	¼ cup	1 cup	2 cups	¾-1⅓ cups	3 T	⅓ cup
SPROUT YIELD	1 quart	1 quart	1 quart	1 quart	1 quart	1 quart
SOAK TIME	8-12 hours	12-16 hours	8-12 hours	8-12 hours	4-6 hours	About 8 hours
SCREEN TOPS	Begin fine, change to coarse	Coarse screen	Begin medium, change to coarse	Medium screen	Begin fine, change to medium	Begin fine, change to medium if desired
RINSE HULLS AWAY	3rd or 4th day	No hulls	3rd day for seed skins	No hulls	3rd or 4th day	3rd or 4th day
GROWING TIME	3-5 days	3-5 days	2-3 days	2-3 days or 4-7 days	3-4 days	3-4 days
HARVEST LENGTH	½-1½ inches	½-1 inch	Not more than ½ inch	¼-1 inch	½-1 inch	½- 1 inch
SPROUTING TIPS	Develop chlorophyll, snappy flavor, a touch of colorful red	Best sprouted alone, do not use soak water, extra rinsing desirable	Sprout will get bitter if allowed to develop green leaves	Length grown depends upon intended use	Shake firmly when rinsing first 2 days; develop chlorophyll	Develop chlorophyll last day; final cold rinse extends storage in refrigerator
NUTRITIONAL HIGHLIGHTS	Potassium, other minerals	Complete protein, vitamins A, B-complex, C, E	Minerals, proteins, unsaturated fatty acids, Vitamins D and E	Good protein, Vitamins B-complex, C, E, complete nutrition	Excellent source of minerals, most vitamins, and protein	Combination offers complete protein, numerous vitamins, minerals and useful enzymes
SERVING IDEAS	Salads, meat loaf, sandwiches, blend in dips	Base for cheese or yogurt, in casseroles, salads, or steam them	Delicious as is, in salads, or spreads, with fruit or desserts	Short: salads, soups, casseroles Long: dessert, breads, or juice	Crispy and delicious on all sandwiches. Use The Tube™ to grow a Sprout Loaf	Serve with sliced avocado, cheese, or hard-cooked eggs for a complete meal

Lunar Logic

January	The Winter Moon
February	The Trapper's Moon
March	The Fisherman's Moon
April	The Planter's Moon
May	The Spring Moon
June	The Cattleman's Moon
July	The Summer Moon
August	The Dog Days Moon
September	The Autumn Moon
October	The Harvest Moon
November	The Hunter's Moon
December	The Christmas Moon

*Sources and References**

Geo. W. Park Seed Co., Inc.
P.O. Box 31
Greenwood, S.C. 29646
Excellent source of seeds, plantings, garden equipment, herbs.

Henry Field Seed & Nursery Co.
Shenandoah, Iowa 51602
Seeds, cuttings, sets, vegetables, fruits, nuts, garden supplies; nice catalog.

Gurney Seed & Nursery Co.
Yankton, SD 57079
Old-time dependable supplier of all kinds of seeds, plantings, garden stuff.

Stokes Seeds
2192 Stokes Bldg.
Buffalo, N.Y. 14240

Thompson & Morgan, Inc.
P.O. Box 531
Pittston, PA 18640

J. E. Miller Nurseries
504 West Lake Rd.
Canandaigua, N.Y. 14424

Johnny's Selected Seed
Box 301
Albion, Maine 04901

Nichols Garden Nursery
Pacific North
Albany, Oregon 97321

Harris Seeds
310 Moreton Farm
3670 Buffalo Rd.
Rochester, N.Y. 14624

Kelly Bros. Nurseries, Inc.
312 Maple St.
Dansville, N.Y. 1 14437

W. Atlee Burpee Co.
2723 Burpee Bldg.
Warminster, PA 18974

The Country Kitchen Catalog
The Garden Way
Charlotte, VT 05445

*These are only a few of the seed companies, picked at random.

BIBLIOGRAPHY

Barlow, Max G. *From the Shepherd's Purse.* McCammon, Idaho: Spice West Co., 1979.

Consumer Guide. *The Food Preserver.* Skokie, Ill.: Publications International, Ltd., 1976.

Holm, Don. *The Old-Fashioned Dutch Oven Cookbook.* Caldwell: The Caxton Printers, Ltd., 1969.

Holm, Don and Myrtle. *The Complete Sourdough Cookbook.* Caldwell: The Caxton Printers, Ltd., 1972.

———. *Don Holm's Book of Food Drying, Pickling, and Smoke Curing.* Caldwell: The Caxton Printers, Ltd., 1978.

Fisher, Nancy (Mrs. Chester C.). *Botanical Chart-Catalog, 16th Ed.* Monmouth, Oregon: Herbs N' Honey Nursery, 1980-1985.

Girard, May Shipton. *The Cruel Cold Land.* Portland, Oregon: Metropolitan Press, 1980.

Kerr. *Home Canning & Freezing Book.* Sand Springs, Oklahoma: Kerr Glass Manufacturing Corp., n.d.

Nevada Landmark Society. *Carson City Historical Cook Book.* Carson City, Nevada, 1974.

Nickey, Louise K. *Cookery of the Prairie Homesteader.* Beaverton, Oregon: The Touchstone Press, 1976.

Sriranganathan, N., Seidler, Ramon J., Sandine, W. E., and Elliker, P. R. *Cytological and Deoxyribonucleic Acid-Deoxyribonucleic Acid Hybridization Studies on Lactobacillus Isolates from San Francisco Sourdough.* Corvallis, Oregon: Department of Microbiology, Oregon State University, 1972.

U.S. Department of Agriculture. *Complete Guide to Home Canning, Preserving, and Freezing.* New York: Dover Publications, Inc., 1973.

U.S. Department of Agriculture, Agriculture Handbook No. 8. *Composition of Foods — Raw, Processed, Prepared.* Washington, D.C.: U.S. Government Printing Office, 1963.

Watt, Bernice K., Merrill, Annabel L., and others. *Handbook of the Nutritional Contents of Foods*. New York: Dover Publications, Inc., 1975.

INDEX TO RECIPES